THOROUGHBRED BREEDING
PEDIGREE THEORIES AND THE SCIENCE OF GENETICS

THOROUGHBRED BREEDING

PEDIGREE THEORIES AND THE SCIENCE OF GENETICS

Dr Matthew Binns
and Tony Morris

J. A. ALLEN

© Tony Morris and Matthew Binns 2010

First published in Great Britain in 2010

ISBN 978 0 85131 935 3

J.A. Allen
Clerkenwell House
Clerkenwell Green
London EC1R 0HT

www.allenbooks.co.uk

J.A. Allen is an imprint of Robert Hale Limited

The right of Tony Morris and Matthew Binns to be identified as authors of this work has been asserted by them in accordance with the Copyright, Designs and Patents Act 1988

A catalogue record for this book is available from the British Library

Design by Judy Linard
Illustrations supplied by the authors
Edited by Martin Diggle

Printed in Thailand

CONTENTS

Preface   7

1. The Thoroughbred's Obscure Origins   9
2. The Beginnings of Pedigree   15
3. Steps Forward – and Back   21
4. The First General Stud-Book   29
5. The First Analysts Have Their Say   35
6. Widening the Debate   42
7. Fresh Ideas against a Background of Change   49
8. Modest Progress towards Enlightenment   56
9. Missed Evidence and a False Dawn   62
10. The Thoroughbred's Part in the Birth of Genetics   70
11. From Mumbo-jumbo to Common Sense   76
12. Enlightenment Remains Elusive   83
13. Why the Horseman Needs to Know Genetics   91
14. The Equine Genome   99
15. Coat Colour I – Grey, a Dominant Trait   105
16. Coat Colour II – Mendel and Beyond   114
17. Bruce Lowe Families and the Role of Mitochondria   124

18. Big Hearts, The X Factor and Tortoiseshell Cats	131
19. The Musculoskeletal System	142
20. Heritability of Athletic Performance	147
21. Genetic Drift and Inbreeding	153
22. Nicks and Broodmare Sires	160
23. Selective Breeding	167
24. The Genetic Health of the Thoroughbred and the Future of the Breed	176
Appendix	181
Bibliography	183

PREFACE

If, as it is often claimed, the Thoroughbred can be aptly described as 'man's noblest creation', no Englishman need feel diffident about alluding to its place of origin. The Thoroughbred was fashioned in England, developed initially by noblemen and gentry whose roots lay in Yorkshire and the Tees Valley, before their countrymen in the south followed their example, making their own significant contributions.

The identities of many of these creators are known; their crucial roles recognised and we know – to a certain extent – how they accomplished what they did, and why they did it. Essentially it was all about employing stallions imported from the Middle East on the native mare population, with the aim of producing bigger, tougher, stouter and faster racehorses. It was an experiment that yielded the desired results within a relatively short period of time.

But while we admire the enterprise of these pioneers, and applaud the outcome of their experiments, we must recognise that what they achieved was something of a happy accident. They had no idea that the crosses they effected would result in the rapid development of a different breed, a distinct new branch of the equine family so ideally suited to its purpose that within a few generations any further experimentation would prove futile.

All they set out to do was to produce better racehorses, and they accomplished that aim. It never occurred to them that they had created a new hybrid, with distinctive characteristics that set it apart from its ancestors; something that would require a new name to express its identity. When their successors recognised that need, they adopted the designation 'Thoroughbred', which the Arabs had applied to their superior stock, and it soon gained currency as the term that identified the 'enhanced English racehorse'.

The Thoroughbred was not exclusively an English racehorse for long. Within the lifetime of the last significant imported stallion, the Godolphin

Arabian (who died in 1753), specimens of the new breed were arriving in America; by the end of the eighteenth century, several other countries, including France, Germany and Russia, had acquired Thoroughbreds from England and were raising stock from the foundation material. What was to become a global industry was under way.

However, neither at home nor abroad was the Thoroughbred understood. The breed had been established in ignorance, and though it was generally recognised that pedigree was important, and increasing emphasis was placed on correct identification of individuals, the problem of how to interpret pedigree was universal. That was inevitable. There was no knowledge of how heredity worked, and there were limits as to what traditional horse-lore and observation could impart.

This book traces what might be termed the history of the mystery, and its partial unravelling over two and a half centuries. It shows how man came to express pedigree and to develop theories about it, and how practical breeders behaved in the light of their understanding. It explains why many theories – including some still widely granted credibility today – are fallacious, examines the very real progress in knowledge since the principles of genetics were discovered, and focuses on the exciting developments of the last few years, when eminent geneticists have applied their expertise to the subject of the Thoroughbred.

Complete understanding continues to elude us, and that will probably always remain the case, but many of Nature's jealously guarded secrets have now been exposed. Pioneering work on the equine genome has established facts that were formerly hidden, and scientific proofs have become available in areas where theories based on intuition and observation were all that the student of pedigree and the practical breeder had been previously able to employ.

After having developed man's noblest creation for some thirty to forty generations, we are at last able to comprehend, in many respects, just what it was that our forefathers created. Much of the new knowledge has not previously been published outside the specialist scientific media, where it was expressed in terms that only a highly trained geneticist could recognise. It has been our endeavour to present that information in a form that may be readily understood by anyone who shares our love for the Thoroughbred and our fascination with what makes the breed what it is.

TONY MORRIS AND MATTHEW BINNS   July, 2010.

CHAPTER 1
THE THOROUGHBRED'S OBSCURE ORIGINS

James Edwards, one of the foremost trainers of his day, earned respect and renown in the employment of noble patrons, saddling five Derby winners between 1811 and 1836. He also unwittingly acquired a final, if dubious, honour by dying at the age of 71 on 1 July 1837, the day on which an Act of Parliament came into force, making compulsory the registration of all births, marriages and deaths.

Filling out the first death certificate ever issued in Newmarket, the home of horse-racing, the town's official registrar, John Thomas, dutifully – and no doubt sorrowfully – recorded that the distinguished horseman had made an undignified exit, succumbing to a bout of *delirium tremens*.

The how, when and where of James Edwards' departure from this world are in the public domain. Not so his arrival, and it is unlikely that Edwards himself could have pinpointed the date with certainty. The gentry had their family bibles, in which it was customary to employ the endpapers for informal notes logging the dates of 'hatches, matches and despatches', but among the servant class, to which humble training grooms belonged, literacy was uncommon and family history, such as it was, tended to be passed down by word of mouth.

If Edwards had ever wanted to trace his family tree, he would have found the task very difficult. Assuming that he could read, which is by no means certain, he would have had to search parish registers which may or may not have been assiduously compiled and, if his family had moved around a lot, merely acquiring the knowledge of where to look for information would have presented problems.

However, it would have been no bother for a literate Edwards to learn about the antecedents of any of the horses he trained. Throughout his lifetime there were published records of racing, annual volumes containing results from around the country having appeared since 1727, and since 1791 there had been a companion work, providing the pedigrees of Thoroughbreds (so far as they were known) from the dawn of the breed. With the first publication of his *General Stud-Book*, James Weatherby did for the nation's horse population what Parliament finally did for its human citizens nearly half a century later. By 1836, when James Edwards won his final Derby with his greatest horse, Bay Middleton, the *General Stud Book* (the hyphenated form, *Stud-Book* was dropped after the first volume) had grown to four volumes, a massive resource giving identity to all the native-foaled members of a breed that had been created in England and was already establishing firm foundations in numerous other countries.

Even so, those records went only so far. In many respects, the origins of the Thoroughbred were extremely obscure, and they remain so. We can point to events and personalities that were influential late in the evolutionary process, and even cite names (without precise identities) of some of the important horses, but we know all too little about what constituted most of the raw material.

There had been horses in England for millennia. The Romans had them, and conducted races with them, during their occupation. In the Dark Ages, for all the relative lack of recorded history, we know there were horses. The Venerable Bede (died 735), in his *Ecclesiastical History of the English People*, referred to clergy riding mares; the Vikings are known to have brought horses on their raids, and are said to have conducted trotting races with them.

In mediæval times, horses featured extensively as man's partner in battle, in transport, in work, sport and leisure. While there was a general vagueness about what kind of horses they were, there were references in the fourteenth century to the hobby, in the fifteenth to the jennet, and Shakespeare has us believe that the Galloway had a presence in the reign of Henry IV (1399-1413). Any one of those three might have saved Richard III on Bosworth Field.

Unfortunately, the rare descriptions and depictions of the horses employed for racing purposes in those times give few clues as to how they were bred. The hobby would surely have featured in the races staged in conjunction with fairs around the country in Plantagenet and Tudor times; we know that the Galloway, a similarly small, strong and nimble horse, was a favourite breed for racing when accounts of the sport were first published in the seventeenth century. But there are also grounds for believing that warriors returning from the Crusades in earlier centuries had imported Eastern-bred horses, and these would have been crossed with native stock. The earliest documented evidence of a horse-breeding establishment we have concerns the royal studs at Malmesbury, in Wiltshire, and Tutbury, in Staffordshire in the reign of Henry VIII. In 1576 Henry commissioned the distinguished Italian horse-master, Prospero d'Osma, to inspect them and to report on their status, making recommendations as to their management and administration. That report has been preserved, and it throws some light on the composition of England's horse population of the period. Not the least interesting revelation is that importations were already common – long before they became a fashion statement in the late seventeenth century.

D'Osma's long lists of the stock in residence included brief physical descriptions of all, but none was identified either by name or pedigree; they were simply grouped under the definitions of coursers, small coursers and jennets. He advised that the three 'varieties', as he termed them, should not be inter-bred, and he named the jennet as the fastest of the trio.

All three had derived from foreign stock, the coursers and small coursers probably acquired from Italy, the jennets from Spain. The English word 'jennet', first spelt 'genet', came from the Spanish '*ginete*', but its root lay in the Arabic 'Zenata', providing a clear indication of the breed's earlier origins. It is known that both coursers and jennets were ridden in tournaments in earlier times, but, curiously, at no point in his 117-page document did D'Osma allude to the purpose for which they were bred by Henry VIII.

The theory that the so-called 'royal mares' who appear at the head of Thoroughbred families may have descended from the coursers and jennets of Henry's day remains unproven. Besides, we are aware of other importations into the royal studs during the reign of James I (1603-25), including jennets and Barbary horses, some from Spain and others from Savoy and Morocco. These arrivals all came at the instigation of the King's notorious court favourite, George Villiers (1592-1628), Master of the Horse from 1616, and virtual ruler of the country during James's last years and the early years of Charles I's reign.

Promoted rapidly from a knighthood (1615) to Viscount (1616), then Earl (1617), Marquess (1618) and finally to Duke of Buckingham (1623), Villiers was entrusted with the lengthy negotiations toward a projected marriage between Charles and the Infanta Maria. While those proceedings prospered, he accepted numerous gifts of horses from the Spanish Ambassador and the King of Spain on behalf of his sovereign, but the supply was inevitably cut off after the final collapse of negotiations. Buckingham, held responsible for the failure by the Spaniards, promptly persuaded James to declare war on Spain.

Widely unpopular by reason of his gross abuse of privilege and the ineptitude he displayed in public life as both soldier and politician, Buckingham was stabbed to death at Portsmouth by John Felton, a naval lieutenant who claimed to act for the people, but who also held a personal grudge against him. If posterity were to allow that Buckingham had earned his burial in Westminster Abbey, it would only be on account of the part he played, albeit unknowingly, in the importation of stock from which the Thoroughbred descended. However, we cannot say for certain that the acquisitions of his era were important.

One event of that time, perhaps also attributable to Buckingham's influence, was the arrival in James I's stud of the horse who came to be known as the Markham Arabian. A bay, described rather unflatteringly as 'little, and no rarity for shape', he was sold to the King by Gervase Markham (1568-1637), a minor poet in the shadow of Shakespeare, but a major and prolific author on the subject of horsemanship. Markham was a keen promoter of the Arab in his writings, allowing that Neapolitan coursers, Spanish jennets, Turks and Barbs could all make respectable stallions, but that the horse of Arabia was peerless, having the purity and virtue of all other horses. By reason of that authenticated sale to the King in 1616, Markham was for a long time credited as the importer of the first Arab stallion to have been used in the royal studs; however, verification of the story has proved impossible.

The fact of the horse's sale is beyond dispute, but the tale, as told over forty years later by William Cavendish, 1st Marquess (and later 1st Duke) of Newcastle, has led later researchers to assert that the horse was more likely to have been the son of an imported Arab, as he was reportedly trained for a race – and beaten by all of his opponents. Authorities believe that a pure-bred Arab, because of rearing methods of that time, would not have proved a suitable subject for racing. Whatever the truth of the matter, the so-called Markham Arabian's supposed distinction as the first oriental ancestor of the Thoroughbred is meaningless; he remains just a name, and no record of his contribution to the Thoroughbred exists.

James I was the monarch who first established Newmarket as a sporting centre, albeit one where hawking and hunting, rather than racing, were the principal pursuits. William Cavendish (1592-1676), first ennobled under James as Viscount Mansfield, and elevated to Earl and Marquess of Newcastle under his successor, Charles I, was raised to the Dukedom under Charles II, in the era when Newmarket became the nation's racing capital. A lifelong royalist, Cavendish was appointed Governor to the younger Charles (then Prince of Wales) in 1638, and was his first instructor in horsemanship. At the onset of the Civil War he was Commander-in-Chief of the Royalist Northern Army, and his departure for the Continent after the rout of the King's forces at Marston Moor in 1644 was evidently not held against him, because after the execution of Charles I he was appointed to the Privy Council of his exiled nominal sovereign. He spent the interregnum years in Germany, France, and finally Belgium, and it was in Antwerp that he founded a celebrated riding school and published his first work on horsemanship, *Méthode et Invention Nouvelle de Dresser les Chevaux*, a book eventually translated into English as *A General System of Horsemanship*.

During Parliamentary rule in the period following the Civil War, racing was banned in England, not because Cromwell disliked it – the contrary was true – but to discourage large gatherings. The Protector recognised the importance of horse-breeding, and even arranged for the purchase of a number of coursers and Arabians from Italy but, no less significantly, he ordered the dissolution of the royal stud at Tutbury. There were 140 horses in the King's possession at the time of his execution, and all were sold or otherwise disposed of within a year.

The inventory of the stock, many of whom were certainly bred for racing purposes, identified most by vague physical descriptions and their sources of acquisition rather than by parentage and, though some undoubtedly contributed to the evolution of the Thoroughbred, no definite links can be established. Some twenty individuals carried the designation 'Newcastle', indicating their origin in the stud of William Cavendish, so he was clearly well qualified to make observations on breeding for racing. In his book he strongly advocated the use of Barb stallions, which he recommended as better than native English horses as sires of racehorses, and cheaper alternatives to the Arabians, and his opinion must have carried weight with other breeders of the period.

Cavendish returned to England on the restoration of the monarchy, and would have welcomed the enthusiasm for racing that Charles II at once embraced. While we have no record of his joining in the revels at Newmarket, where the King rode in matches, won his share, and presided over the promotion of the sport among the nobility and gentry, we do know that the now-ageing Duke busied himself with horses and laid out his own racecourse at Welbeck.

It would be hard to overestimate the impetus given to racing by the royal imprimatur. Such was the Merry Monarch's passion for the sport that he removed the Court for months on end to Newmarket and endeavoured – not very satisfactorily, according to contemporary accounts – to rule the country from there. His self-indulgence proved infectious, and while Wren rebuilt the old royal palace in the town, and perhaps had a hand in the erection of the world's first racing stables nearby, the King's noble cronies acquired horses to provide him with competition.

The names of some of the riders and trainers employed in the King's service have been preserved, as have the results of some of the matches from the earliest days of Newmarket racing. But only some of the horses had names; none was identified by the briefest of pedigrees. The accounts suggest that this was pure sport, simply about the aristocracy at play, and the breeding of the human competitors was held to matter infinitely more than the breeding of their horses – at least, in the minds of those who recorded the results.

It must have been different for the participants. There were prizes for the winners, and there was wagering; the 'running-horse' must have had a commercial value above that of the common riding horse, and the fact that people such as Markham and Newcastle made observations about the best way to produce such horses surely indicates that breeding mattered to those involved.

Could it be that the lack of any documentary record of pedigree meant that such knowledge was the breeder's privileged information, intended to be kept a closely guarded secret? If that was so, it could hardly remain that way in perpetuity.

CHAPTER 2
THE BEGINNINGS OF PEDIGREE

On his return from exile in May 1660, Charles II wasted no time before directing his attention to horses; only nine days after his arrival in London, he appointed James D'arcy as Master of the Royal Stud. Of course, no such establishment had existed for a decade, but D'arcy was commanded to visit the old premises at Tutbury, inspect the land, and advise on the best way to restore its former glories. His report, some months later, contained good news and bad news.

D'arcy informed the King that the land had been ruined, and was no longer suitable for the raising of horses. However, he had an alternative proposition, and had good reason to suppose it would appeal. Instead of going to the expense of acquiring the necessary stallions and broodmares, Charles could have '12 extraordinary good' foals annually from D'arcy's own stud for a consideration of £800. That amount, he was at pains to point out, was substantially less than the maintenance of Tutbury had cost the King's late father.

This was an arrangement that was calculated to suit both parties. D'arcy's appointment would not just have been about rewarding a member of a staunch royalist family; he must have acquired a reputation as a breeder of good horses at Sedbury, the Yorkshire estate which had come to him by his marriage to Isabella, daughter of Sir Marmaduke Wyvill. The deal, soon confirmed after Charles had consulted his Lord High Treasurer, meant that the King could depend on a regular supply of quality stock at reasonable cost, while D'arcy could operate from home as before, flaunting a rather grand title, and was guaranteed ready income for some of his products.

The association of the D'arcy family with numerous 'royal mares' has long been established and, while the designation may have been acquired as a result of their relationship as breeder and buyer, it is commonly believed that a number of the mares in the Sedbury paddocks had been acquired in the dissolution of Charles I's stud. If that were the case, James D'arcy was effectively selling his King the products of mares which, in the normal course of events, would have been his own.

What is clear is that the relationship was not maintained on the original terms throughout Charles's reign, and D'arcy's expectations of a guaranteed lifetime income from the deal were not fully realised. By the time of D'arcy's death in 1673, the arrangement was for only five foals at an annual cost of £500, and the King had failed to make the payment for the last two years. D'arcy's son, another James, was only 23 at the time, and if he imagined that he would assume his father's role as Master of the Horse, he was disappointed.

Charles chose instead to install one Sutton Oglethorpe in the post at Hampton Court, while young James spent the next thirty years petitioning in vain from Yorkshire for the moneys due to his father; after Charles's death in 1685, James II, William III and Queen Anne, in turn, all ignored his pleas. The request to William even suggested payment in kind; he presumed to beg that as His Majesty's Fleet was then (1689) based in the Mediterranean, perhaps it might return with half a dozen good Barbary or Arabian stallions for the petitioner.

The request proved all too presumptuous. William, with his own stud to supply, would have felt no obligation to assist a competitor breeder who bemoaned the facts that he could find no good stallions in England that were not of the Sedbury breed, and could not afford to trade with merchants overseas for horses to serve the 'great number of breeding mares' in his possession.

Though ignored by the King, D'arcy's petition was to prove a fascinating document to historians; within a couple of sentences we learn of the size and significance of the Sedbury stud, and of a disinclination to employ close inbreeding, and we obtain confirmation of the fashion for stallions imported from the Mediterranean.

Certainly, there is ample evidence of a substantial increase in importations of horses from the East in the second half of the seventeenth century. They came in numbers, most described as Arabs, Barbs or Turks, with the odd Persian among them; their designations did not always denote their true origins, which in many cases could never be known. The areas where they were acquired served to 'identify' some, and no doubt there were instances of a false provenance, taken on trust by buyers from smooth-talking merchants.

All we can be sure of is that these were horses derived from stock developed over many generations by men from a largely Muslim background; from the Ottoman Empire, they spread with the Moors into Spain, and across North Africa as far west as Morocco. English agents did deals over a wide area of the Ottoman Empire, including Aleppo, a Syrian port at the eastern end of the Mediterranean, and Constantinople, on the Black Sea, while other horses arrived either as gifts to royalty or nobility, or as spoils of war. Among the last group, supposedly, were two destined to have a major impact on the development of the Thoroughbred. The Lister Turk, who features at several points in the pedigree of Eclipse, was captured at the Siege of Buda in 1686 and imported to England in the following year. Evidence for a similar provenance for the Byerley Turk is lacking, and in recent years some scholars have formed the view that he was probably born in England.

None of the imports came with a precise identity, and their breeding backgrounds were no doubt as diverse as they were obscure but, with few exceptions, they had one factor in common; they were male. The Arabs, from the time of the Prophet and probably before, had identified their horses by their female lineage, and prized them according to the purity of their descent on the distaff side. They believed that the continued excellence of their breeds depended on the maintenance of the mother-to-daughter chain, and for that reason, while they were prepared to bargain over colts, they could rarely be cajoled into parting with their fillies.

There are examples, in the *General Stud Book*, of females at the root of families who were reputedly pure Arabs. Some historians have even insisted that the foundation mares of the Thoroughbred were, like the founding sires, all, or nearly all, of pure Oriental origin. It could hardly be so. There is no evidence of large-scale importations of mares from the East, nor is it likely that mares would have been bought, or otherwise acquired, from such reluctant sellers.

The Thoroughbred is a hybrid, formed from the merging of breeds, and, frustrated though we may be over our inability to establish the identity of the native English mares whose crosses with the imported stallions created the new breed, speculation in the absence of evidence is futile. Arabs mated with Arabs produce Arabs; Arabs mated with nearly pure Arabs produce horses with predominantly Arab characteristics. The Thoroughbred is a distinct breed, and it was the difference from the Arab background that made it so.

The paucity of authenticated records of importations of Arab mares in the second half of the seventeenth century suggests that few actually took place, and the attributions of such origins, made decades afterwards, are in many cases hard to accépt as fact. The dam of Dodsworth (foaled around 1670) had a plausible provenance, as had Queen Anne's Moonah Barb mare (of a rather later date), and some credibility may be allowed in the instances of one or two others who allegedly arrived from North Africa, but at the Arabia/Asia Minor end of the Ottoman Empire a mare would hardly ever have become available. It seems likely that would-be purchasers of Arab stock recognised the futility of trying to bargain over mares there, and concentrated on the male of the species in consequence. Besides, the advocacy of the esteemed Duke of Newcastle, among others, of the Eastern horse – either Arab or Barb – as the preferred stallion for the production of racehorses in England would have persuaded many breeders to adopt that policy.

It is ironic that the man who directed the dissolution of the royal stud and banned racing in England might also, inadvertently, have helped to fuel the demand for stallions from the East. The 'might' is a necessary caveat as, in common with so much else that has been reported from this period, it is impossible to confirm the assertion as fact. We know that Oliver Cromwell took delivery of a stallion purchased for him in Aleppo in 1657, and that some years later his stud-master, Rowland Place, out of a job on the death of the Protector in 1658, was back at his home in Dinsdale, Yorkshire, standing a stallion who came to be known as Place's White Turk.

In spite of the absence of any concrete evidence, some historians jumped to the conclusion that Place had taken possession of his late master's horse. The theory seems less plausible if one or two early pedigrees in the *General Stud Book* (suggesting a later date for the horse) are to be accepted, but the flaws in that work, in relation to century-old events, are so numerous as to make almost any theory plausible. What is certain is that Place's White Turk acquired renown as a sire, thereby enhancing the reputation of the imported stallion.

Unfortunately, for those who tried to make sense of early pedigrees decades and centuries afterwards, Place's White Turk acquired more than renown; he acquired different names – at least two of them – and that phenomenon was widespread during the last part of the seventeenth and early part of the eighteenth centuries. A change of ownership frequently meant a change of name, which might not have been too confusing for the *cognoscenti* of the period, but it was to provide all too many problems for researchers of a later date who lacked written documentation. In the case of Place's White Turk, he became known as D'arcy's White Turk when he moved 10 miles up the road, and those who preferred to identify him by his new location called him the Sedbury Turk.

In the first (1791) edition of the *General Stud-Book*, attention was drawn to two stallions – the Stradling (or Lister) Turk and the Marshall (or Selaby) Turk – with dual identities among the seventeen foreign horses listed; subsequent editions expanded the inventory of importations, with the final (1891) version including just over 100, of whom fifteen had alternative names. However, researches did not stop there, and have never ceased. In the 1920s Charles Prior, in his *Early Records of the Thoroughbred Horse*, established that Place's White Turk and D'arcy's White Turk were the same horse; a decade later Lady Wentworth, in her monumental *Thoroughbred Racing Stock*, suggested, among other revisions, that the horse most familiarly known as the Alcock Arabian may have had as many as seven aliases. Since the turn of the twenty-first century other authorities have developed convincing arguments derived from previously neglected sources to combine many other 'split personalities', most notably that identifying Dodsworth with D'arcy's Yellow Turk.

The root cause of all these problems, with both males and females in the breeding population, was that few breeders kept accurate records of their production, or, if they did, those records did not survive until the period when pedigree became a matter of real concern to growing numbers of participants in a developing industry. Also, some breeders whose records *were* preserved employed terminology that became archaic and was easily misinterpreted by later generations.

The lack of published accounts of breeding activity persisted as the new breed evolved. Most of the pieces in what might be termed the Thoroughbred jigsaw were already in place before John Cheny issued his first annual compilation of racing results, covering the year 1727, but it was still not possible to give many of them real identity. In the Preface to the initial volume of his *Historical List of Horse-Matches Run*, Cheny admitted that 'two or three noblemen and very many gentlemen' had requested that the pedigrees of the horses mentioned should be included, but he had found that task impracticable. He did undertake, in future volumes, to supply the sire and the dam ('or the lineage of her') of runners in all Royal Plates, and in the Stakes at Newmarket and Wallasey, but it proved a rash promise, and the 1728 volume contained little of what he had led his readers to expect.

Already cognisant of the demand for breeding information while compiling his first annual, Cheny must have been made increasingly aware of this as he travelled the country to witness a sport that was growing in popularity, rapidly gaining both adherents and participants. However, he had enough on his plate to fulfil the original commitment he had made to his subscribers – merely to provide an account of race results – and though he picked up some knowledge of sires and dams on his travels, and was pleased to pass on such as he heard, it was quite beyond his powers to act as the nation's collator of stud records as well.

More than six decades were to pass before anyone took up that challenge, and meanwhile the Thoroughbred had become a distinct breed, its members racing, changing hands, and producing other generations, many of them never properly identified by their breeding background. Mistakes were inevitable, both accidental and deliberate, and it is no wonder that confusion reigned.

Nevertheless, Cheny's innovation was a major step forward, and few of his subscribers were going to complain about the inadequacies of a book which supplied data never previously made available. He launched it at a time when racing was conducted at a local level, and pretty much in secret so far as inhabitants of the next county were concerned. Who, in a largely static population, would even have realised that racing was a national pastime? Cheny recognised it, reported it to the best of his ability, and unquestionably aided its expansion by the publicity he provided.

Cheny effectively brought racing out of the Dark Ages, and while he could not immediately do the same for breeding, the success of his venture was a key factor in enabling that to happen in time. In his first volume, the printed list of his subscribers occupied ten pages; by the tenth volume twenty-four pages were required. The names included most of the nobility and gentry in the land, and in addition to the fully indexed annual, they received a fortnightly account of races past and advertisements of racing to come. Pedigrees were still in short supply, but within a few more years, Cheny had started to throw light on that area as well.

CHAPTER 3
STEPS FORWARD – AND BACK

John Cheny suffered pangs of conscience about the dearth of pedigree data in his annuals, which, despite the promise he had made in the first volume, provided only the occasional reference to sires and dams for the next fifteen years. In 1743, perhaps tired of receiving requests for such information and frustrated that nobody else had taken on the task, he attempted to atone for all his previous sins of omission. The edition for that year was by far the most important he had published, providing, in the index to runners, an extended pedigree of many of the more notable horses, along with detail on some of their ancestors.

While it is regrettable that nothing of this kind had seen the light of day before, it is hardly to be doubted that Cheny's old excuse about impracticability was genuine. In 1727 he was finding his way in a new field, at a time when little or no documentary evidence would have been available to him, and it would have taken years both to acquire the confidence of those with information and to learn which of his informants were to be trusted with what they vouchsafed to him. Even in 1743 he felt compelled, in several instances, to express doubts as to the veracity of the pedigrees he printed.

Nonetheless, the time had certainly come for the provision of such data, because the business of breeding was beginning to obtain a profile alongside the sport of racing. As early as the second decade of the eighteenth century, provincial newspapers had carried advertisements for stallions, often indicating that the horses would travel to seek custom, and stating where and when they would be available for covering. The practice of moving the stallion from place to place was common for a while but, by 1743, when Cheny's annual contained the first stallion advertisement in a specialist publication, it was made clear that the mares must visit the horse at his fixed base. That historic notice proclaimed that 'the noted horse called Blaze' would cover the next season at 'a guinea and a half a mare, and a shilling the servant'. Along with the details of his location in the Yorkshire town of Beverley and his racing achievements came a physical description: 'free from all natural blemishes, full 15 hands high, and well known to be a fine proportioned horse' – and the all-important pedigree background. That stated:

> Blaze was bred by Thomas Panton Esq., and got by the Devonshire Childers out of the Confederate Filly, which was got by Grey Grantham, son of the Brownlow Turk. Her dam was got by the late Duke of Rutland's Black Barb, out of a thorough bred mare called Bright's Roan.

The way the pedigree was expressed is fascinating. Blaze's promoters saw no need to give any more identity to his sire than his name, while elaborating on the distaff side to three generations. Of course, there was no more famous horse at the time than Devonshire Childers (more familiarly known later as Flying Childers), but the extension of the female line hints that English breeders were as concerned about that aspect of pedigree as their counterparts in the Arab world. The use of the term 'thorough bred' in relation to Bright's Roan would have conveyed to mid-eighteenth century readers no more than the information that, although her parentage could not be verified, she was deemed to come from a respectable background.

Ironically, Cheny's admirable efforts at substituting elucidation for confusion did not always succeed, and he supplied a slightly different version of Blaze's pedigree in his index, albeit with a caveat. He noted:

> I have been informed, but cannot say that I absolutely depend upon the truth of the whole, that the Confederate Filly was out of a mare called Young Bets and a Turk of the late Duke of Rutland, and that her dam, called Whirligig, was full sister to Leedes.

Cheny set himself a tremendous task in trying to gather accurate information on pedigrees past and present. With no written records to help him and the frequent name-changes to which horses were subjected among many factors calculated to hinder him, he was at the mercy of informants who might or might not be reliable. His pedigrees, as he set them out, tended to be long, convoluted, and sometimes difficult to understand, a notable example being that of Bucephalus, the very first in his 1743 index. That one stretched over three pages, and his plan was evidently to include every scrap of knowledge he had about all of the ancestors he could identify, detailing other relationships, racing and stud achievements, plus a smattering of anecdote here and there.

In his notes on the background of Bucephalus, Cheny remarked:

> I have been assured by a person of rank and honour that the horse called by sportsmen the Byerley Turk was in fact an Arabian. He was Capt. Byerley's charging horse in Ireland at the time of King William's wars, and proved afterward a very excellent stallion.

With reference to the grandsire of Badsworth, he commented that he was:

> Mr Darley's, of Buttercrumb, near York, a brother of which gentleman, being an agent in merchandise abroad, became there a member of a hunting club, and thereby acquired interest to procure this horse for a tolerable sum, which he sent over to England to his brother before mentioned. This account I received from a gentleman that was a near and intimate relation of these other two gentlemen, though I know it has been reported that the said horse was procured abroad by a clandestine method, and that the instrument thereof was never since heard of.

Cheny endeavoured to trace his pedigrees as far back as possible, giving equal weight to male and female sides, and where he could not be confident of the accuracy of his information, he said so. Having identified Windham's dam as 'a daughter of the Marshall or Selaby Turk, his granddam was got by Bustler, his great grand-dam by the White Turk that got Wormwood, his great great grand-dam by Dodsworth', he remarked, 'This is the pedigree as I have received it, but I am sensible there have been objections made to the reality of it, though I have never heard any plausible reasons for the said objections.'

There was dispute also over the pedigree of Bartlett's Childers, said by some not to be out of the same mare as Devonshire (Flying) Childers. Cheny answered that with the observation, 'Yet I have heard the contrary from so many gentlemen of worth and honour that I cannot but be of opinion that this stallion was full brother to the aforesaid Devonshire Childers.'

Even when he had good cause to believe his information, he was at pains to mention the doubts of others. In his remarks on Almanzor, Cheny commented:

> He was bred by the late Mr Brewster, and his dam was also the dam of Old Terror and Champion. This mare, as the said Mr Brewster assured me in his own house (looking in his book at the same time for the account thereof), was a mare that had been Sir Matthew Peirson's, and that she was got by Old Hautboy, yet others I have heard positively affirm that she was got by Old Merlin.

The references in connection with such as Windham, Bartlett's Childers and Almanzor made it clear that Cheny was deeply concerned about the accuracy of the information he imparted, and for that reason subsequent researchers have paid him the respect of trusting the material he presented in his 1743 and later volumes. Some flaws, inevitably, have emerged, and his terminology has in a number of cases been misinterpreted, but as the 'father of pedigree', the innovator who brought the identities of the earliest Thoroughbreds into the public domain, Cheny did sterling duty for both breeders and the breed.

The novel idea of stallion advertising pioneered in Cheny's 1743 volume soon caught on. In the following year Blaze no longer had the field to himself, being joined by six others at the back of the book, and their locations showed, just as the 1727 volume had in regard to racing, that breeding was now a national industry. The Thoroughbred had been, essentially, a North Country creation, evolving principally in the North Yorkshire/Tees Valley area, with a key contribution from Henry Curwen's stud in Cumberland. Newmarket, so important for racing, did not emerge as a breeding centre until much later, but by 1744 there were studs in numerous areas, and stallions advertised to cover the following spring in Warwickshire, Wiltshire, Suffolk and the heart of London, in Lincoln's Inn Fields. The best sire in the country, not advertised, was the Godolphin Arabian, based in Cambridgeshire.

Curiously, the Godolphin Arabian was never to achieve extensive recognition from Cheny, not even after the retirement to stud – and the advertisement of the fact – of his unbeaten son, Regulus. Over forty years later, the compiler of the *Introduction to a General Stud-Book* was to lament that 'of this stallion (strange as it will undoubtedly appear) scarce any records are extant'. That could only relate to the absence of information in Cheny, whose failure to remark on the influence of the horse who represented, to all intents and purposes, the last piece of the jigsaw in the development of the Thoroughbred, was decidedly odd. Perhaps Cheny and the Earl of Godolphin did not see eye to eye for some reason; no chronicler of the times could have failed to notice the impact of the peer's celebrated stallion, and it is hard to escape the impression that Cheny chose to ignore something that was obviously important.

It may well be that the records of the 2nd Earl of Godolphin's stud, made available to Charles Prior two centuries later, were not placed at Cheny's disposal, but is it conceivable that he would not have asked for information about the leading sire of his era, and, if he had, would he not have been favoured with a response? The Godolphin Arabian was the most important horse ever imported to England, and while that fact would not have been evident in Cheny's lifetime, his merits as a sire were certainly established and several of his sons were already at stud, patronised by leading breeders.

The 24th volume of the *Historical List of Horse-Matches Run* was the last to appear under Cheny's name, and it was prefaced by an apology for a delay in publication, 'occasioned by the confused situation Mr Cheny left his affairs in at the time of his death'. That situation was sufficiently confused to render the 1750 edition a product inferior to its immediate predecessors; no pedigrees were supplied, even for the winners of the Royal Plates.

Cheny's death resulted in a battle for the market in which he had held a monopoly. In 1751 Reginald Heber took over the Cheny title, while John Pond, an auctioneer with premises in Newmarket and London, launched a rival publication, the *Sporting Kalendar*. Heber's book was the more complete in terms of pedigrees, and he introduced a useful list of stallions who had covered that season; Pond countered by giving the rules of racing in force at Newmarket at that time, plus a resumé of all the matches run there from 1718 to 1750.

It is apparent from the lists of subscribers published in each work that most of the nobility and gentry preferred to support Pond, doubtless because of his Newmarket connection, but it was the more innovative Heber who emerged on top in the long run. The latter's keener appreciation of breeders' needs was surely a factor in that development. While Pond's volume remained essentially unchanged, Heber introduced a section listing winning horses under their sires in 1754, and two years later he included a page entitled A Pattern for a Stud Book, showing how a breeder might compile accurate records of his production. Pond had had enough of the competition, and after 1757 he withdrew to concentrate full-time on auctioneering again.

A PATTERN for a STUD BOOK.

Year 1759	Month and Day when the Mare was cover'd.	By what Stallion with the Pedigree thereof.	The Dam, with her Pedigree.	When Foaled.	Colt or Filly, with Marks and Colour.	To whom fold and what for.	Remarks.
	May 1.	Regulus, 20 Years old, was got by the Godolphin Arabian, his Dam was called Grey Robinson, which was got by the Bal'd Galloway, &c. &c.	A Bay Mare, rising 5 Years old 14 Hands 3 Inches high, got by Snip, her Dam by Crab, &c.	April 3.	Bay Colt with a Star or Snip, and the off Foot behind only white.	Tho. Stevens, Esq; 150 l.	Large, Strong and Bony, &c.
1760	April 13.	Tartar, 17 Years old, was bred by Ewd. Leeds, Esq; got by Partner; his Dam was Meliora, got by Fox, his Grand Dam was Whitty's Milkmaid, &c. &c.	A Grey Mare, 7 Years old, bred by the late Mr. Routh of Yorkshire, 15 Hands high; she was got by Devonshire Childers, her Dam by Bay Bolton, &c. &c.	March 20.	Black Colt, the 2 hind Feet white and the off fore Foot, with a Star only.	Mr. Wm. Trueman, 75 l.	Strong but not large.

Heber's Pattern for a Stud Book.

Heber was not, however, the originator of the stud-book plan. A number of prominent breeders, including the Duke of Ancaster and the Earl of Godolphin, had been compiling records in a similar fashion for years, and Heber was probably acquainted with them. However, we may be sure that Heber regarded orderliness in record-keeping as a rarity, and that he intended to encourage it; that page appeared in his annual for ten consecutive years, after which time he perhaps assumed that everyone had got the message.

If all breeders had taken Heber's hint, keeping records of their mares and produce in that manner, and retaining them safely for inspection, it would have made the compilation of the first *General Stud-Book* a less arduous task. His Pattern certainly had some effect. It is noticeable that the records from 1760 onwards are much more complete, indicating that many breeders did become more conscientious in that regard after Heber had shown them the way.

However, there were steps backward as well as forward with Heber's publication. Long before his final volume was published in 1768, he had dispensed with the extended pedigrees, and while he maintained his useful list of successful sires, and attached the sire's name to most of the runners in his index, there was no account of dams. The only part of his book where a dam was to be found was in the list of horses engaged in future races.

On Heber's death, another brief power struggle developed over the provision of racing information. Benjamin Walker tried for two years to keep the *Historical List* going, but found that he could not compete with a rival publication, *The Sporting Calendar*, by William Tuting and Thomas Fawconer, respectively Keeper of the Match-Book and Secretary to the Jockey Club. Two such eminently well-qualified individuals might have been expected to bring enhancements; in fact, they removed the names of sires from their index to runners, and dams' identities remained missing.

In Tuting and Fawconer's second volume, presumably after complaints from readers, the sires returned to the index, but dams continued to be ignored, and it was noticeable that the compilers were now described differently. Tuting had become Clerk of the Course at Newmarket, while Fawconer had moved to London. James Weatherby, formerly a solicitor in Newcastle, had been appointed to fill both of the roles previously held by the partners.

Weatherby soon revealed himself to be a ruthless businessman, quite without scruples. In 1772 he persuaded Tuting to desert Fawconer, then seized and concealed 1,600 copies of Fawconer's annual for that year shortly before the date of publication. Tuting conveniently died in 1773, when Weatherby launched his own *Racing Calendar*, inevitably acquiring the patronage of many who had been disappointed by the non-appearance of Fawconer's book in the previous year.

Thoroughly outmanoeuvred by his rival's devious tactics, the furious and embittered Fawconer was stubborn enough to maintain his challenge by issuing further volumes up to 1776, but it was always going to be a losing battle against the Jockey Club's official appointee. Fawconer died in 1777, whereupon Weatherby announced brazenly that he was able to supply copies of his late rival's 1772 volume, which had 'hitherto been distributed to but a few of the subscribers'.

Embroiled as they were in their battle for four years, neither Weatherby nor Fawconer did anything to improve his product, and in the monopoly situation that followed Weatherby did not feel motivated to introduce changes. Fortunately, his monopoly did not last long, and the first issue of William Pick's *Sportsman and Breeder's Vade Mecum* in 1786 gave him a jolt that was to have far-reaching implications.

Pick, based in York, recognised that breeders were being short-changed by Weatherby's publications, as they had been by some of their predecessors. The index to his annual showed pedigrees – not just the sire, but frequently the dam and broodmare sire as well, and occasionally more distant connections. The *Vade Mecum* followed hard on the heels of two other publications which revealed Pick's talents as a historian, a volume providing results of all the races run at York between 1709 and 1785, and, more significantly, his *Pedigrees and Performances of the Most Celebrated Racehorses*, which incorporated notes on the 'most favourite Arabians, Turks, Barbs, English Stallions and Broodmares'.

In that last-named work, Pick revived Heber's old plan of a stud book, with slight modifications which might have persuaded the uninitiated that it was his own invention. Many of his pedigrees he traced back several generations, an area neglected by other publishers for some twenty years. Weatherby had now encountered a doughty competitor, and if he did not take steps to meet that challenge, the supposed advantage of his Jockey Club appointment would count for nothing.

CHAPTER 4
THE FIRST GENERAL STUD-BOOK

James Weatherby was 40 years old when he became publisher of the *Racing Calendar*, combining that role with his duties as Keeper of the Match Book and Secretary to the Jockey Club. For a man in his prime, it was no problem both to serve an employer and run his own business, even when that meant frequent travelling between London and Newmarket. Inevitably, though, there came a time when the burden seemed too great, and at that point, Weatherby drafted in his nephew, another James, to help on the publishing side. The one-man band was suddenly a family business, and one that would become inextricably identified with racing and breeding down to the present day.

However, it is arguable that the man primarily responsible for the enduring power and influence of the Weatherby family in that connection was an outsider, one William Sidney Towers. It was Towers who conceived the idea of the *General Stud-Book* and who compiled the first few editions; his brainchild effectively established Weatherbys as the supreme authority in the field of breeding records, while also providing the model for countless emulations in other parts of the world.

We have no record of how Towers first became acquainted with the Weatherbys, but we do know that he was based in London and a subscriber to their *Racing Calendar* from 1781. We also know that he was an admirer of Pick's work, and that he initially began to compile pedigrees 'solely for his private amusement'. We may surmise that one of the Weatherbys, given a sight of Towers' researches, recognised both the worth of his efforts and the commercial opportunity they represented; while the thought of becoming official registrar of Thoroughbred births would not have occurred, the prospect of being able to supply hitherto unavailable information to an ever-increasing group of enthusiasts would have appealed.

Even so, the younger James Weatherby, who assumed responsibility for the publication, could not be sure of his market when he advertised its imminent appearance in the 1790 *Racing Calendar*. He made it seem attractive, offering 'the pedigree of every horse, mare, etc. of any note, that has appeared on the turf for the last 50 years, and many of an earlier date, arranged in a peculiar manner', but he did not invite subscriptions, which was usual at the time, instead depending on sufficient casual buyers at half a guinea to make the project viable. The fact that he entitled the work *An Introduction to a General Stud-Book* further suggested the speculative nature of the enterprise; he would want encouraging sales of the prototype before committing himself to an ongoing arrangement.

Fortunately, Weatherby received all the encouragement he needed, and within two years he had over a hundred subscribers for a more complete edition, called simply the *General Stud-Book*, and could confidently market that to non-subscribers at fifteen shillings a copy. The success of the venture was easily explained, and Towers' Preface to the *Introduction* provided one of the keys. Having noted that followers of the Turf had long been keen to 'rescue it from the increasing evil of false and inaccurate pedigrees', he provided examples of corrections he had been able to make to previously published data, and he gave his readers further confidence with his observation that 'nothing is here inserted for which there is not some authority, as little as possible is hazarded on uncertainty, and nothing upon conjecture'.

Scarcely less important than the editor's assurances of his conscientiousness was the reader-friendly way in which he set out his information. That ingeniously simple plan had an index to all the horses at the front, followed by broodmares arranged in alphabetical order, with their pedigrees and produce appended. If James Weatherby did not immediately recognise that he had a winner, William Towers surely suspected as much. He hoped 'at some future period to render his work more worthy of public attention', he promised to 'cheerfully labour in search of further information', and he assured his readers that 'any authentic intelligence left at the publisher's office would be thankfully received and attended to'. Those were the remarks of a man confident that he had found a job for life.

The *Introduction* represented a gigantic leap forward in the field of pedigrees. William Pick had made – and was continuing to make – important contributions, but where the Yorkshireman chose to be selective, Towers endeavoured to be comprehensive. It was no wonder that many of

the nation's leading breeders became eager subscribers to the first edition of the *General Stud-Book* in 1793, and it seems reasonable to suppose that they became reliable suppliers of information to Towers as he sought to 'render his work more worthy'.

As amateur researcher, Towers initially gleaned his data 'entirely from Racing Calendars and the less certain information of sale-papers', but there can be no doubt that once his diversion became a profession, the Weatherbys opened doors to intelligence for him by providing him with contacts. Nevertheless, he had set himself a monumental task, and his lament that he had never seen a (private) stud book from an earlier date than 1764 amounted to proof that Heber's encouragement to breeders to keep such records had been both necessary and, to some extent, heeded.

It is interesting to note that Towers made no reference to pedigrees obtained from newspaper advertisements for stallions in earlier years. Perhaps that kind of information was simply unavailable to him, in which case it seems ironic that twenty-first century researchers are currently discovering a mass of data on the subject from early newspapers, the contents of which now appears on the internet. However, as those new discoveries regularly provide conflicting versions of pedigrees, it may be that Towers was very much aware of what had been published in advertisements and was inclined to distrust much of it. Here, perhaps, was the very 'evil of false and inaccurate pedigrees' that he wanted to eradicate.

Towers must have been kept busy by the massive increase of information that flowed in, and required sorting and authentication, after the publication of the *Introduction*. Two years later, the index to the first *General Stud-Book* had doubled in size from twenty to forty pages, while the main body of the work had grown from 207 to 325 pages. The effort always promised to be worthwhile. That long subscription list allowed confidence, and there would have been further reassurance from the successful launch, in October 1792, of the *Sporting Magazine*, a compendium of news and features in which the Turf figured prominently.

The first issue of that monthly publication led with an article on 'The Origin and Progress of Horses and Horse-Racing in This Island', and included a portrait of Diomed, the first winner of the Derby. The third number carried details of the auction in which the Prince of Wales and the Duke of York disposed of their racing and breeding-stock with pedigrees – some in short form, others extended in the female line –

provided for all the horses. The first contemporary account of the running of a Derby appeared in the May 1793 edition.

The years 1792 and 1793 also brought the publication, in three volumes, of *The Jockey Club*, an anonymously authored work which scandalously lampooned most of the royalty, nobility and gentry active on the Turf. This was clearly a time when demand for information on all aspects of racing and breeding had reached an all-time high, and there was no shortage of publishers eager to satisfy it.

If it was understandable that the *Sporting Magazine* should refrain from mentioning *The Jockey Club*, which achieved immediate notoriety because of its scurrilous content, it is perhaps surprising that it should fail to remark on the appearance of the *General Stud-Book*, a work of reference that was bound to appeal to its readers. It did, after all, devote more than four pages to pre-publicity, in January 1794, for *The Turf Review*, a projected series of works set to feature 145 prints of famous horses by George Stubbs, together with pedigrees and anecdotes and, in a glowing puff for a venture that never materialised, it even included full details of subscription costs.

Perhaps there was no love lost between the publishers of the *Sporting Magazine* and the *General Stud-Book*; it is a fact that the death of the senior Weatherby rated no more than a single sentence mention in the August 1794 issue – a sentence in which he was described only as 'an eminent attorney at law, and Keeper of the Match-Book, Newmarket'. That curt send-off was in marked contrast to an obituary in nine instalments for Richard Tattersall, founder of the auctioneering firm and owner of Highflyer, the following year.

Could there really have been rivalry between the publisher of a monthly magazine that sought to entertain followers of all sports and the publisher of a one-off (as it then was) work of reference concerned only with providing information of an esoteric nature? It was possible. Pedigrees and performances of notable horses, sometimes accompanied by an engraving, soon became one of the most popular features of the *Sporting Magazine*. Details for that could easily be cribbed from the Weatherby publications, which had not been copyrighted, and many of the magazine's readers, with no need for facts about the breed as a whole, would have been content with data on the few horses who had achieved fame. In addition, each issue of the magazine carried the latest racing results, with lists of races to come, providing another reason why its readers might forgo purchase of the current Weatherby *Calendar*.

However, the damage that might be done to the Weatherby publishing business by the *Sporting Magazine* was inconsequential, compared with what William Pick might accomplish if he were allowed to steal a march. Towers' *Introduction* was rushed out in a form that both publisher and compiler recognised as far from complete, but they could reasonably hope that it would deter their possible rival from attempting something similar. Sure enough, while Weatherby and Pick remained competitors where their annuals were concerned, Pick elected to stick to his own successful formula in the pedigree field, concentrating on particular notable runners in a series he called *The Turf Register*, and allowing Weatherby free rein to chronicle the produce records of the breed as a whole.

Even so, simply by virtue of the fact that he was first into print with his pedigrees, it was Pick, rather than Towers, who was regarded as the premier authority in the early days; when a crib was required, the correspondents of the *Sporting Magazine* favoured the Yorkshireman's fuller detail over the Towers version, which was generally simple and succinct.

A typical example is that of Bay Bolton, referred to by Towers in 1793 as 'a good runner, and proved an excellent stallion, as will appear from the great number of his get mentioned in this list', with the brief pedigree: 'Grey Hautboy—Makeless—Brimmer—Diamond—Sister to the dam of Old Merlin.' (The first three long dashes signify 'out of a mare by', the last, simply 'out of'). By way of comparison, the Pick version of 1785 read:

> …was eminent both for his figure and running, and likewise as an excellent stallion: He was bred by Sir Matthew Pierson, Bart. of Yorkshire; his sire was a large grey horse, bred by Sir William Strickland, Bart. called Hautboy, son of Wilkes' Old Hautboy. Bay Bolton's dam was a black mare of Sir Matthew Peirson's, got by Makeless, son of the Oglethorp Arabian; out of a daughter of Brimmer,—Diamond, and out of a full sister to Old Merlin.

In 1795 the *Sporting Magazine*'s writer repeated the pedigree given by Pick in 1785 almost word for word, but added 'got by the Darcy White Turk' as identification of Old Hautboy, and opted for a third variation in the spelling of 'Pearson'. There were no anomalies in the three versions of Bay Bolton's ancestry, if they were all read as they were intended to be read, but punctuation in the eighteenth century was far from standardised, and Pick was by no means the first to create confusion in the interpretation of pedigrees by his individual style – researchers are still trying to unravel some of the more convoluted sentences of Cheny, Heber and Pond – and failing to agree on their meaning.

The *General Stud-Book* showed the least detail in the case of Bay Bolton (and in many other instances from this period), but its versions were also the easiest to follow. By concentrating on developing the female line and including just the sire of the dam in each generation, Towers was obviously aware that he was omitting a great deal from the background of each individual, but he could claim, justifiably, that his book contained everything that other publications had, and a whole lot more besides. His was more than a reference to selected individuals; it dealt with all the horses for whom he could find a reliable record, and his data were presented according to an original plan that could be readily understood by anyone capable of reading. His format allowed no misinterpretations, was foolproof, and neatly brought to fruition two of his principal aims – 'to afford an opportunity of seeing what racers of note are related to each other, and of further judging by what stallions the mares bred the best produce'.

The Towers format was soon accepted as the best and most natural way to keep breeding records. It suited breeders, who were all inevitably mare-owners and only a few of whom also owned stallions; it showed them how other breeders had acted, and how they were acting currently; it pointed up relationships, and it had the potential to disclose how success might be achieved. Its efficacy was readily recognised by William Pick, who adopted the style in his first *Turf Register* volume of 1803, and in due course, when other nations found the need for a stud book, virtually all copied the Towers prototype.

However, what was undoubtedly the best and most natural way to keep breeding records remained – and remains – an ingenious, convenient device. It is unlikely that its originator would have promoted it as the optimal, less still the only, way to interpret pedigree, but it was a scheme that automatically made the female line a focal point, and in time that would bring negative repercussions. A convenient device for displaying records was all it was ever intended to represent; its later adaptation as part of a formula for successful breeding was a mistake that still hinders understanding after more than two centuries.

CHAPTER 5
THE FIRST ANALYSTS HAVE THEIR SAY

The *General Stud-Book* of 1793 contained a wealth of information, both current and historic, and though there were numerous gaps in the record of former times, the account of breeding activity over the previous thirty years was as complete as the diligent William Towers could make it. There were clearly lessons to be learned from it, but they seem to have taken a while to digest, if the dearth of Press comment was any guide. The *Sporting Magazine* became increasingly preoccupied with matters of the Turf, but current racing provided its main focus of concern, while pedigrees and performances of past equine heroes, and lists of covering stallions (all freely lifted from the pages of Pick or Weatherby, or both) formed almost the sum total of its breeding content.

Perhaps it was a sense of disappointment over the failure of his groundbreaking innovation to attract Press attention that prompted James Weatherby to commission one Gilbert Ironside to pen *A Dissertation on Horses*, which was bound in with the Supplement to the *General Stud-Book*, published in 1800. Whatever the reason for allowing Ironside to fill thirty pages of that update, it cannot be said to have resulted in the first intelligent printed commentary on the subject of bloodstock breeding; amid his tedious ramblings, which included lengthy (untranslated) quotations in French and Latin, and occasionally strayed into areas far removed from the horse, he made only two observations that might have caused a curious reader to sit up and take notice.

One was a eulogy to the Godolphin Arabian, whom he credited for having:

> …communicated to the English horses that vigour and energy of spirit which distinguishes their intrinsic goodness, and renders them, next to the

Arab, far superior to any other race. For the English, constantly crossing their own with the breed of every other country, produce a kind, though by no means so beautiful as the Arab, yet always far surpassing him in strength, and generally in swiftness.

It is impossible to know whether Ironside formulated that view himself or acquired it from another, but credit is due to him for having expressed it. His recognition of the Godolphin's paramount importance to the breed, at a time when the horse still had great-grandsons at stud, suggested that he was more than capable of sound judgement on occasions. However, such an assessment might flatter him unduly.

He was neither so complimentary, nor so accurate, in his verdict on the influence of Flying Childers, declaring:

It is remarkable that scarcely any fleet coursers sprang from the celebrated Childers, though himself the swiftest horse ever known; on the contrary, his race have proved eminently defective, declining, like our modern nobility, with an uncommon precipitation of degeneracy.

Those opinions, the right and the wrong, are equally revealing, and for the same reason. They indicate a cast of mind that was already prevalent at the turn of the nineteenth century, and is still common. Ironside chose to ignore the several 'fleet coursers' that sprang from Flying Childers in the first generation, despite the fact that Towers had faithfully recorded their names in 1793. He clearly disparaged that son of the Darley Arabian because he did not establish a successful male line, but was able to enthuse over the Godolphin Arabian because the line through his son Cade and the latter's son Matchem continued to flourish. A twenty-first century Ironside, aware that 95 per cent of all Thoroughbreds descend in tail-male from the Darley Arabian, would erroneously condemn the Godolphin as a failure.

There is little evidence, in the form of published works, to indicate what breeders believed in, and tried to practise, before 1800. The Duke of Newcastle's expressed preferences (in 1658) pre-dated most recorded racing and virtually all recorded breeding, so are scarcely helpful. The second James D'arcy, who undoubtedly achieved success, vouchsafed nothing of his *modus operandi* beyond that craving for an outcross, in his 1689 plea to King William III, because he felt that so many in his stud were similarly bred. The eighteenth century's great authority on animal breeding, Robert

Bakewell (1725-95), most celebrated for the advances he promoted in the selection, breeding and management of sheep and cattle, also wrought improvement in draught horses, but as strictly a farming man, he left racehorse breeders to their own devices.

Because of the dearth of information in the contemporary public prints, we are heavily dependent on inferences from those early editions of the *General Stud-Book* for an insight into what breeders believed in as the Thoroughbred evolved. From our twenty-first century perspective, with our knowledge that the entire breed traces back in the male line to either the Byerley Turk (foaled about 1685), the Darley Arabian (1700) or the Godolphin Arabian (1724), the fad for stallions from the East comes as no surprise. What the Duke of Newcastle advocated in the mid-seventeenth century continued to find favour until well into the eighteenth, but only the *General Stud-Book* could reveal how many stallions (upwards of a hundred) were imported, and how few appeared to exert any significant enduring influence.

The horse from the East was clearly deemed a prerequisite for stallion duty by a number of breeders at the outset, but no distinct patterns could be discerned for many years afterwards. It was all about trial and error, with breeders constantly experimenting, sometimes favouring the Eastern horse, sometimes an English-bred son, particularly if he had found success on the racecourse. The one factor which seems to have influenced almost all breeders was racecourse performance; they bred for racing, using stallions who promised to deliver effective runners.

A trend away from the imported horse, who was invariably untested as an athlete, and towards the English-bred who had made his mark in competition, is clearly detectable in John Cheny's 1743 *Racing Calendar*, the first to contain a substantial number of pedigrees. Trusting like to beget like, breeders were by then preferring to patronise home-bred horses who had form they knew and respected, and the results they obtained justified their actions. Reginald Heber's list of sires with winning products in his annual ten years later was overwhelmingly dominated by locally-bred stock, the Godolphin Arabian being the only import to make a significant impression.

The Godolphin was, by a long chalk, the most successful of all the Eastern stallions, with a tally of notable runners far exceeding those of the Byerley Turk and Darley Arabian put together, and he surely earned the accolade that Gilbert Ironside granted him. However, by the time of his death in December 1753 he ranked as the great exception to an established rule, and though his triumphs naturally prompted a fresh spate of importations, those later arrivals made little impact on a scene where the home-bred horse held sway.

Of the imports in the second half of the eighteenth century, such as the Damascus Arabian, the Coombe Arabian, the Sedley Arabian (aka the Compton Barb), Wilson's Chesnut[1] Arabian and Ali Bey, all had ample patronage and achieved some modest success, and the last hurrah was sounded with the arrival in 1803 of the Wellesley Grey Arabian, who became the maternal grandsire of an Oaks winner (Lilias), a Derby second (The Exquisite) and two Oaks runners-up (Dandizette and Translation) in the 1820s. However, all were minor contributors to a breed that had essentially attained fruition and its distinct identity through the exploits of the Godolphin.

The frustrations suffered by such as Pick and Towers when they tried and failed to identify so many of the earliest notable runners have been felt equally by later researchers as they have sought an insight into the mindset of early breeders. Those pioneers unquestionably believed in the superior potency of the male; they clearly came to trust the horse with good racing form more readily than any other; and they quite soon expressed faith in male lines, relying on a son to emulate a successful father. No more sophisticated strategies can be discerned.

However, one particularly notable example of an incestuous mating is recorded, relating to the celebrated Flying Childers (foaled 1714). According to John Cheny, the grand-dam of the first great racehorse was sired by Spanker out of Spanker's own dam, and neither Pick nor Towers chose to query the pedigree. In the absence of better knowledge, that version has been widely accepted, and though Charles Prior expressed doubts, he produced no convincing contrary evidence. What nobody preserved for posterity was a reason for the mating, and Lady Wentworth's assertion that such unions were common is not borne out by study of the *General Stud Book*. Examples are rare, and it is possible that more were the results of accidents or expediency than of deliberate policies. If that was the general rule, the most striking exception to it is that of Jigg of Jiggs, a frequent winner of minor races in the 1750s, produced by a mating of

---

[1] The descriptive inclusion of 'chesnut' in this name prompts us to explain that this spelling of the colour (normally 'chestnut' elsewhere) is traditional in respect of Thoroughbreds, as will be evident from further references throughout the text.

mother and son. Towers ignored Pick's reference to that in his first edition, but included it later, and more recent researchers have attributed similar matings to the same eccentric breeder.

Confirmation that incestuous unions were anything but the norm is found in *The History and Delineation of the Horse* (1809), one of the first works to treat the subject of breeding at length – and to apply the term 'Thoroughbred' to the English racehorse. Its author, John Lawrence (1753-1839), alluded to the fact that it had been common practice to use parent stock from different backgrounds 'with the view to an interchange of requisite qualifications', and he noted a prejudice against close inbreeding. However, it was his view that if 'like produces like, we ought to follow form and qualification. If a brother and sister, or a father and daughter, excel in those respects, we may enjoin them with good expectations'. He pointed out that cattle breeders had enjoyed success from such matings, and Jigg of Jiggs was his example of a good racehorse bred that way. (He omitted to notice that the 12th Earl of Derby had bred two Oaks-placed fillies, Maud and Margaret, from brother-sister matings in the previous five years – a successful experiment which never came into vogue.)

Like Ironside, Lawrence was a fervent admirer of the Godolphin Arabian; he was adamant that no subsequently imported horse had come up to scratch at stud; and he stressed his belief that the contemporary English racehorse was far superior in all respects to his Eastern ancestor. He made many observations about stallions, albeit none too profound, and somewhat fewer regarding mares, but he did not neglect the female of the species, which was a fault he found in others. He opined:

> In our racing studs, not sufficient attention is paid to the form of the mare, and fashionable blood and the supposed necessity of a cross have, perhaps, generally too decided a preference to correctness of shape. We derive our best assurance of success from a junction of the best shapes, or the greater number of good points we can combine, both in the horse and the mare.

A prolific writer over a long period under his own name and a variety of pseudonyms (notably A Bit of a Jockey), Lawrence was a respected authority on both racing and breeding, but his weighty tome had less to offer the practical breeder than the slim volume issued under the title *Genealogy of the English Racehorse*, which appeared in 1810. Its author, Thomas Hornby Morland, professed to having had 30 years experience as 'an attentive observer' of the scene and in this, his only published work, he revealed himself an astute judge of racing form, an expert in stud management, and an enlightened student of pedigrees. In addition, although he was never a member of the Jockey Club, he displayed considerable knowledge of the way that body was run.

This obviously well-connected man was, in fact, a noted practical breeder, owner of a stud at Finchley, in Middlesex. His readers might well have taken his high opinion of the stallions Eagle and Haphazard ('whose colts are large, beautiful and racing-like') with a pinch of salt, aware that both horses stood at his farm, but they would certainly have found food for thought in the remarks he made about other horses – and would have recognised a man who at least practised what he preached. His imaginative and highly innovative work undoubtedly took commentary on racehorse breeding up to a new level.

Morland's advice on the fundamentals might well be repeated, with some minor adjustments only to language, style and punctuation, for the benefit of twenty-first century breeders. He asserted:

> The breeder who selects his stallions with peculiar care, nice discrimination, and particular regard to pedigree, justness of proportion, size, powers, temper, constitution, and the essential qualities of speed and bottom [stamina], at the same time crossing his mares judiciously; endeavouring also to remedy the personal defects, deficient properties and inferior qualities of the mare, by the beauty, admirable properties and brilliant qualities of the horse or vice versa; will be more likely to succeed in producing a beautiful and unexceptionable race of horses than the person who pays little or no attention to all or any of the particulars I have enumerated. It is the interest of every breeder, in forming a stud, to purchase such mares as are free from all hereditary infirmities and have produced winners; and to select stallions which not only are of acknowledged celebrity on the turf, but which have also proved themselves good stock-getters.

None of the progress in science and our understanding of pedigree over the last 200 years negates any part of the Morland doctrine. From practical experience he was able to recognise basic facts that even now continue to be ignored or misconstrued.

Morland was unafraid of contradicting other authorities, and did so convincingly. He took issue with the assertion by the renowned French naturalist, the Comte de Buffon, that the male always had more influence than the female on the appearance of their young, insisting that he knew of mares 'which invariably produce the likeness of themselves to every description of stallions'. He also roundly rebutted Gilbert Ironside's denigration of Flying Childers, citing that horse's position in the background of both the outstanding sire Herod and the outstanding sire of broodmares, Snap.

The innovation which must have most intrigued Morland's public was his division of the breed into what he referred to as the three classes – the descendants in the male line of Herod, Matchem and Eclipse. He presented tables showing the links through the generations down to the horses in the contemporary stallion population, and he gave his views on the characteristics they tended to exhibit. His researches persuaded him that 'stallions and mares of the same class should not be permitted to copulate', and that 'the descendants of Matchem and Eclipse cross better with the Herod blood than with each other'.

Morland was clearly an assiduous student of the *General Stud-Book* and of the *Racing Calendar*, extracting data from both and presenting them in a form never previously published. In addition to his classification of the sire lines, he had some rudimentary statistics, showing the number of winners in each year by prominent sires, and he even compiled a table of leading sires of broodmares, identifying the most notable progeny of their daughters.

Parts of Morland's book – the list of imported horses and obituary of stallions – were blatant cribs from the works of Towers and Pick, but it was his adaptation and interpretation of the material provided by his forerunners, allied to his own observation and experience, which made the *Genealogy* such an important contribution to breeding literature. When, five years after its publication, Filho da Puta, a colt he had bred on his recommended lines – by Haphazard (of the Herod class) out of a mare by Waxy (Eclipse) – won the St Leger, Morland's reputation as an authority was underlined.

CHAPTER 6
WIDENING THE DEBATE

When subscriptions closed in June 1807 for a new edition of the *General Stud-Book*, compiler and publisher must have been highly gratified by the response; the list exceeded 250, indicating a healthy growing demand for their product. In his Preface to that volume, dated March 25, 1808, Towers allowed himself the satisfaction that his book would be found to contain 'in the most concise and most approved form, a greater mass of authentic information respecting the pedigrees of horses, than has ever before been collected together'.

Whether Towers ever saw his largest and last volume in its printed form is not known. What we do know is that he died soon after penning that Preface, and we may surmise that his death was unexpected, although he had reached the age of 68; it is clear that nobody had been trained to succeed him in his role. When the final supplement to what became known as Volume 1 of the *General Stud-Book* was published in 1814, James Weatherby expressed his apologies for its late appearance, and remarked on the very severe loss he had sustained by the death of the inventor and author of the previous editions. He confessed that work previously carried out on a daily basis had been at a standstill from the spring of 1808 until the winter of 1812, when he had finally found the time to devote to it; he was also forced to admit that he had found the task 'more tedious and difficult than he expected'.

Weatherby was neither the first nor the last employer who failed to appreciate the difficulties experienced by one of his hired servants, and it is regrettable that when he at last acknowledged Towers' contribution and realised the severity of the burden that he had been made to take on himself, he refrained from mentioning the 'inventor and author' by name. But for a chance mention in the January 1824 issue of the *Sporting*

Magazine that sent late twentieth century historian Patrick Saward in dogged and ultimately successful pursuit of his identity, the originator of the *General Stud-Book* would still be unknown.

The eventual identification of Towers was all the more remarkable because that one solitary clue might never have been published. It came in an article written in September 1794, supposedly by 'an eminent breeder of racehorses', and intended for submission to the *Sporting Magazine* at that time. For some reason it was not sent, but was discovered among the writer's papers at his death almost thirty years later and then forwarded by his executors to the magazine's editor. When it finally achieved the light of day, the brief reference to 'Towers' Introduction' appeared, tucked away in a fascinating piece entitled 'Candid Observations upon the present Breed of Running Horses and their Ancestors', which provided several valuable insights into the thinking of late eighteenth century breeders generally and one anonymous one in particular.

Whoever it was who penned the piece, under the *nom de plume* of 'Ben Beacon', he was a man of decidedly forthright views – and, like many who came after him – he told half-truths, had prejudices, lacked consistency, and displayed faulty judgement. He dated the expansion of breeding from 1753, the year of William, Duke of Cumberland's entry into racing, and asserted that: 'the Godolphin Arabian's, Childers's and Partner's blood was only resorted to by the most scientific and accurate breeders, and continued most indisputably prevalent until the august appearance of Eclipse'. Both statements might reasonably be contested.

Having lauded the Godolphin Arabian and his sons, and declared his line successful 'to this day', he proceeded to be scathing about the influence of his most important grandson, Matchem, who 'for 20 years covered all the best-bred and most-approved mares in England'. Now, he asked, 'Is there from Matchem one horse or mare capital as a stallion, or to be coveted as a broodmare?' Many would have answered him in the affirmative. Similarly, his apparent reverence for Partner was forgotten in his dismissal of his grandson Herod's stock as 'weak and tottering in the forelegs' and while he grudgingly admitted that an exception might be made of Highflyer, he could not resist citing the observation of 'a most approved rider and trainer' that 'he got the most bad horses he ever knew'. That last comment, he said, was 'founded in truth, and verified in experience'.

The mystery critic went out of his way to belittle Highflyer:

> He has repeatedly covered most, if not all, the best mares in England…yet in every year, and in all contests, Highflyer is too seldom the sire of the winning horse. All studs from north to south, from east to west, great and small, have sent to Highflyer, but where is the effect of that confidence?

He conceded that his best son, Sir Peter Teazle, had his good points, but he expressed doubts about his prospects of making the grade as a sire. He deplored the prevailing vogue for big horses, coupling the name of Eclipse's prominent son, King Fergus, with that of Highflyer as examples of individuals whose greater height gave them a want of symmetry.

The author's second thoughts about submitting his article for publication in 1794 had been wise, and he would not have welcomed its appearance in print thirty years later. By that time Highflyer and Sir Peter Teazle had headed the sires' list twenty-three times between them; King Fergus had also been champion. Of his two recommended stallions, both small and symmetrical to his eye, Mercury had quickly faded from prominence, and Javelin had failed to make an impression.

Readers of the *Sporting Magazine* in January 1824 probably enjoyed a laugh and recalled the already-old adage about nothing making a fool of a man like a horse; mere benefit of hindsight would have made that easy. Whether they would have fully realised the reasons for an apparently knowledgeable and experienced writer's lack of sound judgement is, however, debatable.

The plain fact is that most of the mistakes he made have been made by many people of subsequent generations – failure to recognise that even the best sires get a majority of indifferent stock, that no sire transmits the same qualities or attributes to all his products, that success tends to generate success, that fashion frequently dictates events, and that fickle fortune always has a role to play. Expressions of dogmatic views about horses generally return to haunt those who utter them.

Criticism of Highflyer's perceived faults was by 1794 quite futile, and not just because the horse was already dead. He had been the best-patronised stallion in the country from the outset of his stud career, covering larger books than all of his contemporaries, and allusions to his failures could not detract from the regular successes which ensured his continued fashionable status. Once he had died, breeders naturally turned to his best son, and Sir Peter Teazle duly delivered; quibbles over a supposed want of symmetry in their stock counted for nothing while racecourse results proclaimed that handsome was as handsome did.

Racing and breeding had both evolved rapidly – so rapidly that evolution almost amounted to revolution. The introduction of foreign horses had been deemed necessary to bring quality and refinement to the resident stock. They came in, small individuals chosen for their looks, with neither verifiable pedigree nor experience of racing, and were trusted to sire stock capable, in their maturity, of carrying heavy weights over long distances in competition. Within a few generations – no more than two in the case of the Godolphin Arabian – their descendants were required to supply a markedly different demand, for earlier-maturing products who could compete over short distances. The old order had to change.

The speed of the transition is best exemplified by the cases of the great triumvirate whose male lines have survived to the present day. Matchem, Herod and Eclipse all began their racing careers at 5 years of age, and each owed something of his racing reputation to victory over the severe Newmarket Beacon Course of 4 miles, 1 furlong and 138 yards. Each also owed something of his stud reputation to stock who were able to win the new Classic races for 3-year-olds at 1½ miles or less.

Races in 2-, 3- and 4-mile heats were still programmed at the end of the eighteenth century, but they were much less common, and generally of little value. The Derby, Oaks and St Leger, all for 3-year-olds, already carried the most prestige, and there were even lucrative prizes for 2-year-olds at Newmarket. The horses who contested such events had to be different from their forefathers, and they were; taller, faster, more precocious, these beneficiaries of superior nutrition and training had left their Arab roots far behind. They had attained the distinctive character of the Thoroughbred.

Thomas Hornby Morland recognised how the breed had evolved, and was astute enough in 1810 to place Matchem, Herod and Eclipse at the head of his three 'classes'. Nicholas Hanckey Smith, whose *Observations on Breeding for the Turf* appeared in 1825, was also acutely aware of how the racing schedule had changed and the breed had adapted to it, but he was not happy about either development. In his somewhat turgid, rambling narrative, he opined that degeneracy had set in because races no longer provided a sufficient test of a horse's constitution, and he argued for a fresh wave of imported stallions.

He proved a poor advocate for his cause, admitting that the most recently imported stallions had met with little success, that any new Arab horses would find it hard to attract respectable mares, and that his own experience in Arabia and India had taught him that owners prepared to sell

Arabs would invariably lie about their pedigrees. His concession that 'our present blood is superior to our former for the present purposes' effectively rendered much of his book a waste of space, and the sporting publications which reviewed it chided him severely for having propounded an argument so lacking in substance.

The reviewers were also less than complimentary about some of Smith's other ideas, and in truth his work did seem to be the product of one who had devoted a lot of time to study, but had emerged from the process not much wiser. He did grasp one essential fact better than his predecessors, but lacked the clarity of expression to put that point across adequately.

He presented a long list of dams of good runners who had themselves never raced or had never been trained, supposedly suggesting that he had unearthed a successful formula, but provided no reference to poor runners out of likewise untried mares, who would surely have represented a majority. Similarly, he gave numerous examples of closely inbred notable winners while offering no data on bad horses produced on the same pattern.

What seems to have caused most offence to Smith's contemporaries was his approval of incestuous matings, which he expressed with the familiar cases of Flying Childers and Jigg of Jiggs as two of his justifying examples. However, lucidity and consistency were not his strong points. Having stated that 'when the breed is continued incestuous for three or four crosses, the animal degenerates', he later remarked, 'I cannot take it upon myself to say how often an incestuous breed may be carried on before a degeneracy takes place, as I am not aware of that being the case in any instance'. Elsewhere, he gave his readers to understand that his preferred methodology was to inbreed in the first generation, outcross in the second, and to alternate thereafter.

If we categorise Smith as a woolly thinker on the matter of Thoroughbred breeding, we must acknowledge that many of his successors belonged – and still belong – in the same camp. Inbreeding, line-breeding, outcrossing, and even incestuous mating are meaningless concepts *per se*. No methodology employed in the union of horse and mare has meaning without reference to the individuals who are potentially contributors to the offspring. Smith was sometimes appropriately specific, but he was inclined to lapse into generalisations, a fault perhaps forgivable in one whose world knew nothing of genetics; those who have made the same mistake in more recent times can offer no such excuse.

It was easy for the reviewers of 1825 to find fault with *Observations on*

Breeding for the Turf, and no more difficult for the twenty-first century reader to concur with their verdict. However, we can recognise in one aspect of the work a development which represented progress, yet was not identified as such at the time. To illustrate his points on inbreeding, Nicholas Hanckey Smith presented pedigrees in diagrammatic form, rather than expressing them in the long sentences, often convoluted and easily misunderstood, that his predecessors had invariably employed.

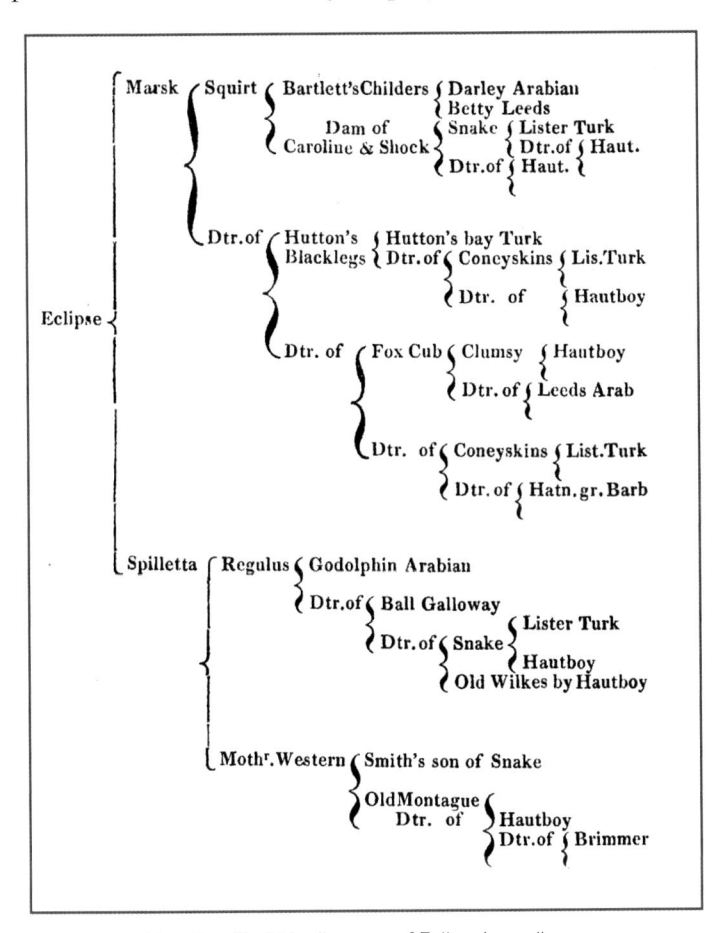

```
Eclipse ┌ Marsk ┌ Squirt ┌ Bartlett's Childers ┌ Darley Arabian
        │       │        │                    └ Betty Leeds
        │       │        │ Dam of              ┌ Snake ┌ Lister Turk
        │       │        └ Caroline & Shock    │       └ Dtr.of ┌ Haut.
        │       │                              └ Dtr.of ┤ Haut.
        │       │
        │       └ Dtr.of ┌ Hutton's      ┌ Hutton's bay Turk
        │                │ Blacklegs     └ Dtr.of ┌ Coneyskins ┌ Lis.Turk
        │                │                        └ Dtr. of    ┤ Hautboy
        │                │
        │                ├ Dtr. of ┌ Fox Cub ┌ Clumsy ┤ Hautboy
        │                │         │         └ Dtr. of ┤ Leeds Arab
        │                │
        │                └ Dtr. of ┌ Coneyskins ┌ List.Turk
        │                          └ Dtr. of    ┤ Hatn.gr.Barb
        │
        └ Spilletta ┌ Regulus ┌ Godolphin Arabian
                    │         │ Dtr.of ┌ Ball Galloway
                    │         │        │                    ┌ Lister Turk
                    │         │        └ Dtr.of ┌ Snake     ┤ Hautboy
                    │         │                 └ Old Wilkes by Hautboy
                    │
                    └ Mothr.Western ┌ Smith's son of Snake
                                    │ OldMontague ┌
                                    └ Dtr. of     ┤ Hautboy
                                                   └ Dtr.of ┤ Brimmer
```

Hanckey Smith's diagram of Eclipse's pedigree.

The example reproduced here is crude in its design, and six years later William Youatt would display an Eclipse pedigree that was easier on the eye in *The Horse*, a popular reference work that was revised and enlarged by other editors several times over the next half-century. Youatt's more widely read book (into its third edition by the 1860s) probably deserves the principal credit for the development of the tabulated pedigree as the standard method for the display of a Thoroughbred's ancestry, but Smith was the pioneer, and he used it in a way that opened up new avenues for research and speculation.

Hitherto the 'Old Testament' plan, linking the generations solely through the male line succession (Abraham begat Isaac, etc.), had always found favour with breeders, and Morland's division of the breed into classes descending, father-to-son, from Matchem, Herod and Eclipse, confirmed the common belief in its significance. Towers' plan in the *General Stud-Book*, adopted solely for reasons of convenience, had provided a focus for the female line which would eventually lead to a concept of 'family' that its originator never intended.

Smith, for all his faults, did at least draw attention to the fact that pedigrees had other components and, in the case of Eclipse, his methodology enabled him to propose a theory that would have far-reaching repercussions.

Among his considerations of horses of former times, he wondered why many good racehorses had failed to produce good stock, while a number of poor runners had managed to deliver offspring of genuine quality; Eclipse's parents provided his prime example of the latter phenomenon. He condemned Marske, his sire, as 'certainly not a first-rater, or if he could be so called, he was about the worst of his day', and he pointed out that Spilletta, his dam, had been beaten in her only race. So why should their union have produced such a magnificent champion? Smith found his answer in his tabulated pedigree, concluding, 'we may justly infer that his speed arose from the repeated crosses of the Lister Turk and Hautboy…blood that always hit or suited each other'.

A counter-argument would not be difficult to mount, on several grounds, but that is not the point. Here was an original thinker, prepared to look beyond the traditional, simplistic modes of interpretation. He knew nothing of genes and chromosomes, but he recognised the potential of all ancestors, from whatever point in the pedigree, to influence the character of their descendants. The reviewers who were so swift to criticise *Observations on Breeding for the Turf* did him less than justice when they ignored – or failed to appreciate – the most significant message he had to impart.

CHAPTER 7
FRESH IDEAS AGAINST A BACKGROUND OF CHANGE

Only about eight of William Youatt's 472 pages in the first edition of *The Horse* were devoted specifically to the Thoroughbred, but he nevertheless provided a little food for thought. There was, he said, much dispute over its origins, noting that:

> 'by some he is traced through both the sire and dam to Eastern parentage, while others believe him to be the native horse, improved and perfected by judicious crossing with the Barb, the Turk or the Arabian'.

This was not an argument in which Youatt cared to become involved, probably because he thought that by 1831 it scarcely mattered either way, but he inclined to the view that the Thoroughbred was of largely foreign extraction, 'improved and perfected by the influence of the climate and by diligent cultivation'.

As for the suggestion, by Nicholas Hanckey Smith and others, that the breed had suffered degeneration in recent times, Youatt disagreed, opining:

> Thoroughbred horses were formerly fewer in number, and their performances created greater wonder; the breed has now increased twenty-fold, and superiority is not so easily obtained among so many competitors.

On the other hand, he did concede that some horses were ruined by the 'absurd and cruel habit' of racing them too early.

Not the least interesting of Youatt's observations was his remark that 'racing is principally valuable as connected with breeding, and as the test of breeding'. That acknowledgement of the existence of an industry based on the sport perhaps stands as the model for the high-falutin notion that passed into cliché about the purpose of racing being the improvement of the breed.

Another commentator at around the same time as Youatt, the little-known C.F. Brown, also made breeding a minor feature of his *Turf Expositor*, published in 1829, but he had a new angle, or so he fancied, suggesting: 'as I am not aware that it has ever been treated physiologically, at least through the medium of the press, I will venture to record my ideas on it'.

In fact, it took him a while to get around to the Thoroughbred, but *en route* he suggested that in Nature, birds avoided close inbreeding, that cattle breeders had found such a system to be defective, and he asserted that repeated incestuous breeding in the gun dog would result, within few generations, of 'an inferior animal…utterly without sagacity, diseased, most likely, and altogether as worthless as possible'.

He even ventured into thoughts on the human race with comments that might not have passed as politically correct even in 1829. In some of the villages of Leicestershire and Derbyshire, he claimed to notice dire effects of local inter-marriage, including lunacy and early death, whereas in Lancashire he found 'the finest, the most robust, and strongest race of men and women in the united kingdom'. Lancashire, he reminded his readers, was the great manufacturing area of the country, which had attracted immigrants from Wales, Scotland and Ireland, who had settled and merged with the local population. Shifting into sexist territory, he attributed 'the proverbial beauty of the Lancashire women' to the effects of 'that intermixture of blood'.

When he eventually got around to considering the Thoroughbred, Brown said little that had not been said before, and some things which were not beyond dispute. He might easily have been contradicted on his assertion that the 12th Earl of Derby had overdone his infatuation with his outstanding stallion Sir Peter Teazle (see Chapter 6), and his observations on the optimum age for breeding-stock – he disliked the idea of two old parents – would not have stood the closest scrutiny. On the other hand, he echoed Morland's logical advice to avoid matings in which both parents had the same physical fault, but rather to breed with a view to accentuating good points and eliminating defects. In addition, he was firmly against the use of roarers, or those who were afflicted with disease, as breeding-stock. He regarded soundness as of paramount importance.

His – quite enlightened – view on the possible merits of a fresh importation of Arab stallions was that the current Thoroughbred stock was 'immeasurably superior to [those from] the source from whence they sprung'. He opined that a better bet might be the interchange of current Thoroughbred stallions between different parts of the country, who had been differently treated and 'breathed a different atmosphere'.

Brown had so little to say about individual horses that his thoughts probably had little impact on the minds of breeders of his day. However, Brown was cute enough to notice the way that Nature behaved – and behaved similarly with a number of different species. In his – inevitable – ignorance of realities about inheritance, he at least applied common sense. Many reputable scientists were to remain unconvinced for years of the virtues of Mendel's discoveries, and it was research into the Thoroughbred, conducted through the pages of the *General Stud Book*, that finally enabled them to accept as fact what Brown seemed to be on the way to recognising, if only by supposition, seventy-five years earlier.

By the time of Youatt and Brown, the Thoroughbred was certainly much more than a sportsman's plaything. In his Preface to the first edition of Volume 2 of the *General Stud Book*, in 1821, new editor Charles Weatherby referred to the avidity with which the English breed of horses was sought by foreigners, noting, 'The exportation of them to Russia, France, Germany, etc for the last five years has been so considerable as to render it an object of some importance in a commercial point of view'.

That process continued unabated, persuading Weatherby to include a section listing exported stallions in his Volume 3 of 1832; he named thirty-three who had left in the past decade, with America, Jamaica, Sweden, New South Wales and Van Dieman's Land [Tasmania] among the destinations not previously mentioned. Although there was no corresponding account of exported fillies and mares, the tally was certainly in three figures.

While breeding-stock departed in numbers overseas, and other countries adopted racing on the English plan with a view to establishing industries of their own, a new development at home gave further emphasis to the increasingly commercial aspect of Thoroughbred production. There was nothing new about breeders selling their wares, and auctions had had quite a high profile since John Pond sold Eclipse in 1765 and Richard Tattersall founded his firm a year later. What was novel was the idea of breeding expressly for the market, and Alexander Nowell became a trend-setter when he had the entire yearling crop from his Underley Stud in Cumberland sold under the Tattersall hammer in October 1826. The experiment proved a decided success, with keen competition among bidders, and after 1830, when Priam, acquired as a 2-year-old at Newmarket for 1,000 guineas, won the Derby, and Variation, bought out of the third annual Underley yearling draft for 200 guineas, won the Oaks, a fad for commercial stock was understandably instilled.

The rise of market breeding was just one of a number of developments in an environment where the wind of change gusted forcefully and not always beneficially to the sport. From the 1820s onwards, racing began to attract a different kind of owner, and what had been very much the province of the nobility and gentry was invaded by *nouveaux riches* from the lower classes, some of whom were less scrupulous in their conduct than might have been desired. Tales of sharp practice, rare in the era when Princes, Dukes and Earls had dominated, became commonplace when tradesmen, bookmakers and professional gamblers moved into the territory. Rumours of fixed races, generally by bribery of jockeys or stable-lads, abounded and the motives of owners of horses in big betting contests were regularly questioned by an increasingly attentive and vigilant Press which did not shrink from making allegations of corruption.

Proof of malpractice was not often forthcoming, and sanctions against supposed miscreants were rarer still, but confirmation of criminal activity was not necessary; the rumours were enough to ensure that racing's image was damaged. Unsurprisingly, in a scenario which encouraged distrust, there were hints that skulduggery sometimes stretched to the running of horses under false pedigrees, typically with an older individual substituted for one engaged in a race confined to a single age-group. Although some of the instances which aroused suspicion may have derived from mere malicious gossip, a genuine scandal did develop in 1844, when a 4-year-old colt called Maccabeus, masquerading as 3-year-old Running Rein, finished first in the Derby.

The colt's identity had been openly challenged when he won a minor race for 2-year-olds – and landed some hefty bets for his owner – at Newmarket in the previous October. The *Sporting Magazine* had no compunction about asserting: 'to speak plainly, the colt is as well furnished as many of our *bona fide* three-year-olds'. Underlining his suspicions, the editor placed inverted commas around Running Rein's name. Bets were settled under protest on that occasion, but it was a different matter when the Derby came along. Jonathan Peel, owner of second-placed Orlando, objected to the winner on the grounds that he was above the age stipulated for the race, a high-profile court case ensued, and a crude attempt at fraud was ruthlessly exposed. The defendant's refusal to produce his colt for tell-tale examination of his teeth amounted to a virtual admission of guilt.

The substitution of an older horse for a younger one obviously involved the falsification of pedigree, but at least a ready means of establishing that kind of fraud was available. The deliberate, or accidental, recording of an incorrect pedigree where age was not the issue presented a different sort of problem, and it was one that had embarrassed Charles Weatherby in the case of another Derby winner, Bloomsbury, five years earlier.

Information supplied to Weatherby for publication in the first edition of Volume 4 of the *General Stud Book* in 1836 indicated that Arcot Lass had been covered by both Tramp and Mulatto in the previous year. However, when Arcot Lass's 1836 colt-foal, Bloomsbury, was entered for races, including the 1839 Derby, there was no mention of a Tramp covering, and he was described as being by Mulatto. The rules of racing required that in the event of dual covering, both putative sires should be named in entries, and an inadequately identified horse was liable to disqualification.

Bloomsbury's Derby victory caused an immediate kerfuffle, with the owner of the runner-up lodging an objection, and the settlement of bets held in abeyance. Investigation of the affair was prolonged, with reliable witnesses thin on the ground, and not the least alarming revelation was that the stud records of Bloomsbury's breeder, Robert Ridsdale, had apparently been destroyed on his being declared bankrupt in 1836. Recourse to law was taken, and it was not until August 22 that Bloomsbury was confirmed as the winner of a race run on May 15. The weight of evidence proved strongly in favour of an inadvertent human error over the original claim that Arcot Lass had been covered by Tramp in addition to Mulatto.

The unfortunate Bloomsbury episode and the scandalous Running Rein experience were both damaging to the image of racing, but along with the ill wind came decided good, in that justice was done on both occasions. Deliberate or accidental misrepresentation of pedigree was clearly detectable, and that served as a deterrent to would-be cheats while providing a reminder to all breeders of the need for meticulous record-keeping over the activities of their stock. It is no mere coincidence that recorded instances of false pedigrees declined rapidly in the wake of those two events; confidence in the accuracy of information contained in the *General Stud Book* has rarely been jolted since the appearance of Volume 5 in 1845.

Of course, suspicions of errors in pedigree records had not deterred commentators from formulating opinions and theories on the basis of the best information available to them, and that would always have to be the case, but the heightened perception that *General Stud Book* data were reliable, together with the increased commercial activity in Thoroughbred breeding, undoubtedly encouraged writers to focus more on specific horses and less on generalisations.

Cornelius Tongue, who employed the *nom de plume* Cecil, did not go far down that road in his 1851 book *The Stud Farm*, the Preface of which promised more than the succeeding pages supplied. Having noted that good horses currently commanded high prices, and that those who produced them should devote their attention to breeding from the right stock, he failed to develop that theme very satisfactorily. In what was, for the most part, a work on practical horse husbandry, he devoted only two chapters to breeding, and in them had little of value to offer those whom he presumed to advise.

Tongue even led his readers astray in some instances. To illustrate his point that Nature was apt to behave mysteriously, he remarked that 'the union of a black horse with a chesnut mare may give birth to a grey foal'. Unsurprisingly, he did not cite an example, and it hardly mattered that he was wrong, but he did choose to relate an anecdote concerning a mare who had produce by a quagga (a relative of the zebra, extinct since 1883), and whose subsequent foals, by 'the best bred horses' all exhibited a stripe down the back. That assertion, once bandied about, gave rise to a widespread erroneous belief in a phenomenon for which a word had to be invented. Telegony – the notion that the influence of a previous sire may be seen in the progeny of a subsequent sire from the same dam – was commonly credited, and many breeders embraced the idea in determining their mating policies.

Not content with spreading those fallacies, Tongue also declined to argue with the opinion of 'an extensive breeder' who believed that a mare should be sent to the same stallion throughout her stud career. His reasoning was that 'a mare having bred foals by different horses entertained a greater predilection for one partner than another, and that on subsequent occasions, having reminiscences of past events, the produce was affected thereby'.

By quoting and evidently accepting the views of a crank, albeit a romantic crank, Tongue might be accused of placing himself in the same category, but on safer ground, from observations within his own experience, he was able to generate a little light. He provided convincing final rebuttal of the theory that the Thoroughbred required new Arab crosses. On the matter of conformation, he wisely asserted that 'the production of a happy medium by the union of two extremes is scarcely, if ever, realised'. He surpassed himself in the astute reflection that the maxim 'like begets like' is 'more frequently applicable to defects than perfections'.

CHAPTER 8
MODEST PROGRESS TOWARDS ENLIGHTENMENT

Of those whose views on breeding we have examined thus far, only Thomas Hornby Morland was a practical Thoroughbred breeder of any repute; the others, from Lawrence to Tongue, were observers of the scene, devotees as much of hunting as of racing, and John Henry Walsh (1810-1888), who wrote as Stonehenge, was no more a specialist than they. At the age of 34 he became a Fellow of the Royal College of Surgeons, and he spent eight more years following that profession before a love of country life induced him into a long career as a writer on all its aspects. His *Manual of British Rural Sports*, the first edition of which appeared in 1855, covered shooting, hunting, coursing, hawking, boating and pedestrianism in addition to racing, and it revealed him as a genuine authority on all.

Walsh's racing section amounted to a book on its own, stretching to some 170 pages, and his observations on breeding made it the most valuable work published on the subject up to that date. To facilitate understanding, he presented tabulated pedigrees of notable horses, in some cases up to six generations, and his commentary provided insights to their breeding background and racing characteristics that went far beyond anything that Morland had managed forty-five years earlier.

Among his remarks on the horses who headed the three Morland 'classes', Walsh noted that whereas Herod was generally considered to be a representative of the Byerley Turk (as a product of his male line), his pedigree actually contained twice as many crosses of the Darley Arabian; similarly, Eclipse was supposedly a scion of the Darley tribe, yet the Godolphin Arabian was a closer antecedent. While allowing that the laws which regulate breeding were mysterious, Walsh was persuasive in promoting the tabulated pedigree with 'all the recent ramifications presented to the eye at once, so as to grasp all its bearings at a glance, and thus estimate the relative importance of the various elements composing it'.

As a qualified surgeon, Walsh was entitled to have a good working knowledge of what was then understood on the matter of heredity in the mammal, and so it proved. He particularly stressed that bad qualities are as easily transmitted as good ones, so it was necessary to take care that a male selected for his good points should also be free from bad points. He also noted that whereas incestuous breeding was 'injurious to mankind and has always been forbidden by the divine law', it prevailed extensively in a state of Nature with gregarious mammals. If not carried further by Art than Nature teaches by her example – by which he meant two consecutive crosses – the practice should not prove prejudicial, he felt.

Yet, for all his clear understanding of how parent stock contributed to their offspring and his lucid exposition of the process, Walsh allowed himself to be convinced by the tale of the quagga (see Chapter 7) and that telegony was a reality; the question was 'settled without a doubt', he declared, though he used less emphatic terminology – perhaps because the idea still confounded his sense of logic – when observing that 'the influence of the first impregnation seems to extend to the subsequent ones'.

In the years that followed, the presumed superior knowledge of the scientist and the experience of the practised horseman stood in diametrical opposition. How was the novice breeder to act? One view had it that a mare's first mating was vitally important and should be with a top-class horse, because his influence would be seen in her later foals, while the other insisted that as first foals tended to be weedy, the choice of the mare's first mate was of no consequence. When it was noted that many more second foals than first foals had won the Derby (a statistic that still holds true, and now stands in the ratio of four to one) how was that to be interpreted?

Walsh did not just concern himself with thoughts on how heredity worked. On the contrary, he dealt at length with many individual horses, commenting on their stud performance, and he provided lists of those who had been produced from inbred matings and those who were outcrosses; his preference was for the inbred horse, but he conceded that many good runners and sires had resulted from the other method. He also devoted a section to the characteristic features of racehorses descended from various ancestors, promoting the claims of the Waxy line above all others, crediting its representatives for 'great gameness and true running' though they had less bone and substance than the descendants of Orville. The line of Buzzard he associated with speed rather than stamina, while the Blacklock tribe he denigrated for their 'plain, vulgar appearance, their calf-knees, flat foreheads and general plebeian look, often accompanied by legginess'.

Walsh was decidedly a trend-setter in adopting this approach to considerations of pedigree. Many who came after him, including some down to the present day, have operated in the same way, assessing background in terms of inbreeding or outcrossing, and making sweeping generalisations about the characteristics associated with ancestors several generations back. In common with those who followed, Walsh concerned himself solely with horses who had distinguished themselves, neglecting to notice the indifferent and poor horses who inevitably had many of the same antecedents. It was a pity, too, that one who recognised the potential influence of all a Thoroughbred's ancestors should finally fall back into perpetuating the notion of 'lines of blood' which encouraged the belief that male lines were special, distinctive and hardly affected by other factors present in the pedigree.

Walsh was undoubtedly familiar with many of the horses he wrote about, but that would not have applied in many other cases where the immediate products of such as Waxy, Orville, Buzzard and Blacklock were concerned; and where two or more of them featured in pedigrees, it could hardly have been realistic to tar all their descendants with the same brush, attributing their principal characteristics to the male-line ancestor. What he preached in connection with the pedigrees of Herod and Eclipse, he did not practise when considering the horses of his own era.

Indeed, Walsh's view of pedigree tended to focus on the influence of horses from the past rather than on current stock. A decade later the Anglo-Irish small-time breeder R. H. Copperthwaite was not so reticent about commenting on the stallions and mares of his own day in his *The Turf, The Racehorse And Stud Farm*, but he did prove all too reluctant to present a balanced view of their respective merits. Four months before the publication of his book, which appeared in May 1865, the author had spent fourteen days in prison, with hard labour, for having caused a disturbance while drunk at a hotel in Cheapside, and for assaulting the police who came to arrest him. Had he taken a drop of that Dutch courage as he sharpened his quill, he might have served his readers more ably, but instead he contrived to be complimentary about almost every horse he mentioned, even the proven failures, and found cause to advocate the virtues of every breeding system, without proper examination.

Copperthwaite's contemporary, Dr Joseph Henry Shorthouse, was an altogether different sort of commentator, one never afraid to express his opinions, and frequently ready to provoke an argument. Entering the world of the Thoroughbred from a cattle- and sheep-breeding background, he became a contributor to several sporting publications in the early 1860s, and in January 1864 he gave the *Sporting Gazette* his decided view on the subject of telegony. Perhaps he was a recent convert, because he was certainly a firm advocate, declaring:

> It may be regarded as a law that a male animal that has once had fruitful connection with a female may so influence her future offspring begotten by other males as, to a greater or less extent, to engraft upon them his own distinctive features, his influence reaching to the subsequent progeny of the female in whose conception he himself has no share.

In view of this law of Nature, he opined, it was obviously vital that a female's first mate must be carefully chosen.

Shorthouse underlined his point by reference to the human race, observing:

> It by no means happens that a child necessarily resembles his father; indeed if his mother have previously had fruitful intercourse with another man, and that other man be of a different race, it is almost certain that the child will not in the slightest degree resemble his own father, but his actual progenitor. This is a fact so well known, and of such unquestionable importance, that in any discussion of breeding it behoves us not to lose sight of it.

Whereas the trained biologist Walsh had seemed to accept the idea of telegony against his better judgement, while owning a convincing grasp of the workings of heredity, the doctor who became so convinced of the phenomenon could sum up his own science with: 'the male parent chiefly determines the external or locomotive organs, and the female the internal or vital organs'.

Having a taste for expressing his views with vehemence, and perhaps on occasions having been frustrated by circumspect editors, Shorthouse launched his own weekly newspaper, the *Sporting Times*, in February 1865 and at once set about bombarding his readers with forthright opinions on current racehorses and breeding-stock, as well as on sires of the past, regularly rewriting their reputations, generally to their detriment. His favourite *bête noir* was always Blacklock, whom Walsh had denigrated in rather moderate terms, but whose name Shorthouse could hardly deign to mention without the accompanying epithet 'accursed'. He claimed to have traced the pedigrees of 3,000 horses, and that in every case where Blacklock's name occurred three or more times he or she was 'a detestable wretch'.

In fact, Blacklock's name even once, especially in the male line, was a hindrance to any horse's prospects, according to Shorthouse, who gave his readers plenty of food for thought in the early issues of his paper. He was particularly fond of querying – even denying – the recorded pedigrees of famous horses, including the 1847 Derby winner Cossack (allegedly switched with Old Port) and the 1835 Oaks and St Leger winner Queen of Trumps ('definitely by Camel, and not Velocipede, who never got near her'), while Ratan, the 1844 Derby favourite, was not only not by Buzzard, his reputed sire, but not by any Thoroughbred. In his comments on Gladiateur, the colt who in the following months would win the Triple Crown, he sarcastically referred to his being 'reputed to have been foaled in 1862'. That last insinuation so persisted that an objection was lodged to Gladiateur's running in the St Leger, and he competed only after an examination of his mouth confirmed that he was a 3-year-old.

Shorthouse was undoubtedly keen on gaining circulation in a competitive marketplace for sporting publications, and he did not shy away from causing controversy, yet there are good grounds for believing that his views were honestly expressed, and in his day he was seen not just as an opinionated writer, but as a writer who helped to shape public opinion. When he cast aspersions on the integrity of the *General Stud Book*, he had his reasons, and there were many who took him at his word.

However, one who chooses to be outspoken must expect to acquire enemies, and there were plenty who rejoiced when Shorthouse got what they regarded as his comeuppance in December 1869. In the preceding month Shorthouse commissioned an article from one Alfred Geary and by chance fell ill on the very day it was submitted, so did not vet it prior to publication. The piece appeared, under the *nom de plume* 'Caustic', and it turned out to be a scandalous libel on the prominent owner and breeder, Sir Joseph Hawley, who had little option but to sue. To his considerable credit, Shorthouse – who had sent an apology to the obviously offended party as soon as he had read it – declined to name the author of the article and insisted on bearing himself whatever punishment should ensue. He was fined £50 and imprisoned for three months.

On his release from that chastening experience, Shorthouse resumed his chair at the *Sporting Times*, which became a distinctly blander publication. His readers, who had been accustomed to polemic on matters of the Thoroughbred, soon had to get used to the front pages of the paper being given over to medical matters, under the heading of The Common Sense of Medicine, by J. H. Shorthouse, M.D. Typical titles in this long series were 'Concerning Cholera' and 'Appertaining to Infantile Diarrhœa'.

Shorthouse's period of influence as a writer on the Thoroughbred was clearly over. He sold the paper, which revived under the enlightened editorship of John Corlett and is now remembered chiefly for its famous 1882 obituary of English cricket, announcing that the ashes had been sent to Australia. The Shorthouse era ended shortly before the 1875 Derby was won by the mighty Galopin, a horse with three crosses of the accursed Blacklock, and sire in due course of the mightier St Simon.

We can now date Shorthouse's heyday as an influential, if misguided, commentator on inheritance in the Thoroughbred from the first appearance of his *Sporting Times* on 11 February 1865. By an extraordinary coincidence, it was in the very same week, far away in Brünn (now Brno), the provincial capital of Moravia, that a 42-year-old monk rose to deliver a lecture to the local Society for the Study of Natural Sciences on the results of some experiments he had been conducting with garden peas.

It would be a long time before anyone appreciated that Gregor Mendel had found the key to understanding the process that Shorthouse could not begin to discern.

CHAPTER 9

MISSED EVIDENCE AND A FALSE DAWN

While it is easy to understand why generations of writers on Thoroughbred breeding, including a number of experienced breeders, proved so inept in their efforts to explain the workings of heredity, it does seem odd that they missed one clue that had always stared them in the face. From Volume 1, the *General Stud-Book* had recorded the colour of every registered horse, and from 1846 the annual *Racing Calendar* had provided a list of foals under their sires, complete with colour and sex. Nobody seemed to realise that there were lessons to be learnt from such data.

It was not that colour was ignored; in fact, it almost invariably featured when physical descriptions of horses were given. Yet in 1855 the evidently studious and comparatively wise Walsh confined his remarks on colour to the observation that the Thoroughbred was 'now generally bay, brown or chesnut, one or other of which will occur in 99 cases out of 100'. Grey and black were uncommon, he said, while roans, duns and sorrels were 'now quite exploded'. He had noticed that certain colours, frequently seen in the eighteenth century Thoroughbred, had died out, but it did not occur to him to consider why the colours currently expressed had survived.

It seems scarcely credible that breeders had failed to recognise that a mating of two chesnuts always produced a chesnut, that there was never a grey who had no grey parent, and that there were certain bay or brown horses – and mares – who invariably produced bay or brown offspring. Walsh's failure to remark on such facts suggests that none was common knowledge in his day, and it seems that ignorance prevailed for quite a while afterwards.

In 1873, in his *Newmarket and Arabia, An Examination of the Descent of Racers and Coursers*, Roger Upton remarked that the progeny of the recently deceased prominent bay sire Newminster had been 'chesnut, bay, brown and grey, some large and some small', as though he were providing information out of the ordinary, instead of describing the norm. Copperthwaite, for all the flaws in his 1865 work — and there were many — at least cottoned on to one colour-related point when discussing the pedigree of the chesnut 1860 Derby winner Thormanby, who was officially described as being by Melbourne or Windhound. He gave several reasons why he believed that Windhound was the true sire, and all bar one might have been discredited, but it had not escaped his notice that Melbourne had no other chesnut progeny, and that made his deduction absolutely correct.

While we credit Copperthwaite with that one spark of inspiration, that is all it was. To the best of his recollection, the bay King Tom was a chesnut, which said little for his memory, and in common with all his contemporaries, he failed to deduce anything from the readily available evidence showing that other prominent sires such as Voltaire, Ion, The Flying Dutchman, Voltigeur and his own favourite horse, Vedette, got nothing but bay or brown products.

Voltigeur, the Derby and St Leger hero of 1850, was a brown horse who sired only bay or brown progeny. Almost half a century passed before Mendelian genetics explained the reason.

The Upton work, alluded to above, did nothing to increase the sum of human knowledge on the development of the Thoroughbred; quite the reverse. The author, a former Captain in the 9th Royal Lancers, was steeped in lore of the Arabian horse, and so much in awe of it that his judgement of the breed which had evolved, in part, from those origins was seriously flawed. His readers must have found it hard to imagine how he could claim, on page 7: 'Those who have expressed the opinion that our horse attained its highest perfection in Flying Childers I believe were perfectly correct'. If they bothered to read as far as page 101, they would have been astonished to be posed the question: 'What have we to guide us to the assumption that our present horse is superior, even to Eclipse?' It was Upton's view (page 105) that for 150 years the racehorses we had been breeding were no better than impure half-breds, and in his concluding chapter (pages 199-200) he seriously suggested: 'The sportsman who loves racing for the sport itself may yet carry off the Blue Riband of the Turf with a horse of pure Arabian blood, and know he is conferring a lasting benefit on his country.'

Could there really have been, in 1873, any practised horsemen who might side with Upton over a view that had been largely discredited for a century? Perhaps there were, but not after July 1885, when Asil, the best pure-bred Arab in the country, was matched over 3 miles at Newmarket with Iambic, one of the worst Thoroughbreds in training, unsuccessful in all his nine races, and despite an allowance of 4st 7lb at the weights, was beaten in a canter by 20 lengths.

By 1885 no fewer than fifteen volumes of the *General Stud Book* had been published, representing a massive store of data on the evolution of the breed. For more than a century and a half performance records had also been kept, showing how the products had fared in competition. Breeders had used those resources chiefly to do what was obvious – trust in like to beget like, and hope to produce good horses by employing proven good parent stock. It did not always work, but it had always seemed the logical way to proceed, and there was now no doubt that they had wrought substantial improvement in the creature that their forefathers had fashioned with the help of those Eastern importations.

The contributions of those who had made a particular study of pedigrees did not amount to much. They had devised the tabulated display, which at least encouraged breeders to consider all the elements in a horse's background, but they had continued to emphasise male lines, thereby suggesting the paramount importance of the father-to-son chain of inheritance. They were virtually unanimous in preferring inbreeding to outcrossing, but that view had been founded on developments in the eighteenth century when the population was so small that inbreeding was unavoidable. In what, by 1885, had long been a closed breed, the horse with no ancestor duplicated within four or five generations was still an exception to the rule, so inbreeding was producing many more bad horses than good, although the pundits advocated it as a formula for success.

Charles Darwin was, by this date, already dead and buried, and nobody had considered whether anything in his *On the Origin of Species* (1859) or *Descent of Man* (1871) had applications to a study of the Thoroughbred. Darwin's cousin, Francis Galton, had expressed views on ancestral contribution in the early 1870s, but they, too, had passed unnoticed by those who presumed to offer their views on breeding the racehorse in the public prints. They passed on their vague notions that combinations of certain ancestors seemed to work – something they had acquired from the days of Herod and Eclipse – and made suggestions as to others that *might* work, and all they managed to pick up from what they regarded as science was the folly of telegony. When they dared to become dogmatic about what they believed, Shorthouse and the others of his ilk were soon exposed as no wiser than the rest.

In such circumstances, anyone who came along with a fresh approach to analysing all the accumulated evidence, specifically with regard to the Thoroughbred, was guaranteed a hearing, maybe even a following. It was perhaps not too surprising that, while the home-based scribes seemed to be stuck in a rut, the next significant developments came from abroad, in the works of an Australian and two Germans. Racing had by now become established all over the world, with breeding industries sprouting up as a natural consequence. Several countries had started to compile and issue their own stud books, and fascination with pedigrees had long since become a global phenomenon.

Bruce Lowe's fascination began before the publication of the first volume of the *Australian Stud Book* in 1877, and initially it was data from the mother country that he absorbed, focusing on female lines and tracing them back to the earliest root that he could find. Of course, the plan adopted by Towers for his *Introduction to a General Stud-Book*, which had been followed in every subsequent volume, facilitated that process to some extent, but it was inevitably time-consuming, embarked on as a labour of love.

Lowe's labours were contemporaneous with those of the equally diligent German researchers, J. P. Frentzel and Hermann Goos, who set themselves similar tasks, acting independently, though aware of each other's work. Frentzel had compiled family records for Trakehnen, the leading Prussian stud, as early as 1864 and was responsible for the first volume of its stud book fourteen years later. His study of maternal lines, in sheep as well as horses, suggested to him that some were more successful than others in producing sound and strong stock, and he was encouraged to extend his researches to the Thoroughbred, with the aim of discerning whether that tendency was expressed in terms of racing merit. Frentzel's study included 4,605 mares who appeared in the three most recently published volumes of the *General Stud Book*, and he identified ninety-seven families, employing a somewhat arbitrary definition of the tap-root as 'the mare who was the first in her family to have her year of birth recorded'.

While Frentzel could see no point in going back to what he called 'prehistorical time', Goos and Lowe endeavoured to do just that and, unsurprisingly, they identified far fewer distinct families. Goos, who based his classification of the families on the winners of major races in Britain, France, Germany, Austria-Hungary and Scandinavia, came up with a figure of fifty-nine, and he was the first into print with the results of his researches, publishing his *Family Tables of English Thoroughbred Stock* in 1885. Frentzel was then magnanimous enough to acknowledge errors in his own work and to encourage study of the Goos tables, which he felt would result in 'a better insight into the science of breeding'. He obtained no reward for the work on his own tables, as he died, aged 55, in 1886, three years before their publication.

The Goos and Frentzel compilations initially attracted little notice outside Germany, and they were still quite unknown to Bruce Lowe when, in 1894, the Australian felt that he had made significant discoveries, of which revelation to the world would 'to a great extent revolutionise the present methods of mating Thoroughbreds'. Unlike the Germans, Lowe had the benefit of access to the fifth (1891) edition of Volume 1 of the *General Stud Book*, which indicated that a number of mares, hitherto regarded as unrelated, came from the same root. That enabled him to reduce the number of founder-mares to forty-three, and he classified their families in an order based on the number of successes they had recorded in England's Derby, Oaks and St Leger (see Table opposite). In fact, he found winners of those races only in families 1 to 34, and those designated 35 to

THE ALLOTMENT OF FIGURES.

No. 1.	Tregonwell's Natural Barb mare	Whalebone, Minting.
No. 2.	Burton's Barb mare	Voltigeur, Blacklock.
No. 3.	The dam of Two True Blues	Stockwell, Sir Peter.
No. 4.	Layton Barb mare	Matchem, Thormanby.
No. 5.	Dr. of Massy's Black Barb	Gladiateur, Hermit.
No. 6.	Old Bald Peg	Priam, Diomed.
No. 7.	Darcy's Black Legged Royal mare	West Australian, Donovan.
No. 8.	Bustler mare (dam of Byerly Turk mare)	Marske, Newminster, Sultan.
No. 9.	Old Vintner mare	Mercury, Bendigo, Peter.
No. 10.	Dr. of Gower's stallion	Blair Athol, Hampton.
No. 11.	Sedbury Royal mare	Regulus, Birdcatcher, St. Simon.
No. 12.	A Royal mare (Montagu mare)	Eclipse, Sterling, Prince Rudolph.
No. 13.	A Royal mare (dam of Turk mare)	Highflyer, Orlando.
No. 14.	The Oldfield mare	Touchstone, Macaroni.
No. 15.	Royal mare (dam of Old Whynot)	Soothsayer, Jerry, Foxhall.
No. 16.	Sister to Stripling by Hutton's Spot	Ormonde and Agnes family.
No. 17.	Byerly Turk mare	Pantaloon, Yattendon.
No. 18.	Old Woodcock mare (dam of Old Spot mare)	Waxy, Trenton (Aus.).
No. 19.	Dr. of Davill's Old Woodcock	Isonomy, Sir Hugo.
No. 20.	Dr. of Gascoigne's Foreign horse	Citadel, Traducer (N.Z.), Ghuznee.
No. 21.	Moonah Barb mare	Sweetmeat, Lonely.
No. 22.	Belgrade Turk mare	Gladiator, St. Blaise.
No. 23.	Piping Peg	Ossian, Barcaldine.
No. 24.	Helmsley Turk mare	Camel, The Baron, Hindoo (Am.).
No. 25.	Brimmer mare	Y. Melbourne, Comus, Sefton.
No. 26.	Merlin mare	Herod, Promised Land.
No. 27.	Spanker mare	Saunterer, Pero Gomez.
No. 28.	Dr. of Place's White Turk	Emilius, Dalesman.
No. 29.	Natural Barb mare (dam of Basset Arab mare)	Landscape, Ashton.
No. 30.	Dr. of Duc de Chartres' Hawker	Paris, Delpini, Stamford.
No. 31.	Dick Burton's Barb mare	Ruler, Fazzoletto.
No. 32.	Barb mare (Dodsworth's dam)	Nike, Fitz-Gladiator.
No. 33.	Sister to Honeycomb Punch	Sergeant, Dungannon.
No. 34.	Hautboy mare	Antonio, Birmingham.
No. 35.	Dr. of Bustler	Haphazard, Bustard (Castrel).
No. 36.	Dr. of Curwen's Bay Barb	Economist, Old Engineer.
No. 37.	Sister to Old Merlin	Dr. Syntax, Little Red Rover.
No. 38.	Thwaits' Dun mare	Pot-8-os.
No. 39.	Bonny Black	Dagworth (Aus.).
No. 40.	Royal mare (dam of Brimmer)	Boston (Am.).
No. 41.	Grasshopper mare	Bagot, Portrait.
No. 42.	Spanker mare	Oiseau, Cestus.
No. 43.	Natural Barb mare (Emperor of Morocco's gift)	Balfe, Underhand.

Lowe's list of families.

43 were chosen arbitrarily. (He misplaced one Derby winner – Sir Thomas – in family 18 instead of family 38.) As can be seen from the Table on page 67, he listed his families by showing the original mare and some of her most notable descendants.

By virtue of the fact that his families 1 to 5 were the principal sources of the major winners mentioned above, Lowe called them his running families; he further identified five families – his 3, 8, 11, 12 and 14 – as the strongest in producing sires of note. He claimed that every great racehorse and sire of the nineteenth century would be found to have, within three generations, one or more representatives of those nine families.

Lowe had devoted more than twenty years to his researches, he had incorporated evidence from Australia, New Zealand and the USA into his data, and he had travelled, both to England and to America. At home, his only confidant, New South Wales breeder Frank Reynolds, had put some of Lowe's theories into practice at his Tocal Stud, supposedly confirming their validity. Utterly convinced that he had found the key to successful breeding, Lowe determined to publish his findings, and, aside from his views on families and sires, they included a belief in telegony, which he referred to as 'saturation'.

Displaying a hopeless grasp of what was then known about sexual reproduction, Lowe theorised that: 'with each mating and bearing, the dam absorbs some of the nature or actual circulation of the yet unborn foal, until she eventually becomes, as it were, saturated with the sire's nature, or blood, as the case may be.' Like others before him, he alluded to cases in the human race which, he believed, defied explanation if telegony were not a fact, and he claimed: 'the majority of practical physiologists have accepted the absorption theory'.

It did not seem to cross Lowe's mind that if telegony were a fact, just about all of his other theories on breeding were rendered nonsensical. However, that also did not cross other minds, including that of William Allison, to whom Lowe entrusted the completion and publication of his work, if anything should happen to him. Lowe's prescience of early death proved correct, and Allison, who had corresponded with Lowe and had met him on his last trip to England, duly undertook to carry out his friend's wishes.

Allison wrote as 'The Special Commissioner' of the Sportsman newspaper, acted as a bloodstock agent, and had long been a director of the Cobham Stud, where a number of stallions, mostly of little consequence, were resident over the years. In the table of prominent horses under their families, shown on page 67, the one name which stands out as not really belonging is that of Prince Rudolph, a moderate runner mentioned alongside the exceptional Eclipse and notable sire Sterling as a representative of family 12. Prince Rudolph stood at Cobham, so Allison was understandably delighted with Lowe's expressed approbation, and no less so to be able to place that horse's name in such exalted company, and to have the excuse to feature a full-page photograph of him in the book. In fact, Prince Rudolph turned out to be a bad sire, and was exported to Canada in 1899.

Allison proved the staunchest of advocates for Lowe's theories, and claimed, in his Preface to the work published in 1895 as *Breeding Racehorses by the Figure System*, to have arrived at similar conclusions to those propounded by Lowe. 'I think his views on the sire families and running families are sound, as also his theory of saturation', he remarked. Six years later, in his own *The British Thoroughbred Horse*, Allison developed Lowe's theme and provided numerous 'proofs positive' of its correctness. The figures, he said, were irresistible, and for him judgement by results counted for more than anything the scientists were now beginning to unravel.

Allison had been taken in, hook, line and sinker, by the Lowe doctrine, and his promotion of the so-called Figure System was a key factor in its long-term acceptance. Better knowledge came swiftly, and was soon made public, but Lowe's ideas suited breeders and seemed to offer them the route to success. They were to die hard, if, indeed, they have died yet.

CHAPTER 10

THE THOROUGHBRED'S PART IN THE BIRTH OF GENETICS

If Bruce Lowe had lived to witness the reaction to his book, he would not have been surprised that there were dissenters. His hypothesis was bound to be challenged, and he knew that one of its opponents would be Joseph Osborne, an Anglo-Irish writer (under the *nom de plume* 'Beacon') who had been breeding Thoroughbreds before Lowe was born. Osborne was decidedly long in the tooth by 1898, when he brought out the fifth edition of his *Horse-Breeders' Handbook*, but he proved that he was still game for a verbal fight by devoting some fifteen pages of its Introduction to a denunciation of Lowe's work.

In fact, Osborne hardly needed to go to so much trouble, because he had said enough in his first two paragraphs to make his point, but presumably he felt that as Lowe had stretched his theory to 250 pages, a brief rebuttal might seem inadequate. Lowe's book, said Osborne, could be summed up in two words: 'presumption and assumption'. He was right on that score, and though some of his own arguments were unnecessarily convoluted, and challenges to Lowe's views on individual families were irrelevant, his most basic criticism – that it was ludicrous to assume that descent in tail-female from an eighteenth century ancestress was all-important, when so many other factors must have parts to play – hit the nail on the head.

However, in a world where a multiplicity of religions have adherents, and myths are frequently accepted as fact, a logical cast of mind and a cogently expressed denial do not serve to satisfy those who want to believe. Lowe had a theory that Osborne – and many others, particularly in America – did not like, but where was *their* theory? All they had to offer was disbelief. The plain fact was that many breeders had wanted something to believe in, and Lowe gave them something that was at least plausible; he showed them a way, which nobody else had done, and they were ready to accept it. Lowe's conviction that he had found something that would 'revolutionise the present methods of mating Thoroughbreds' was not far wrong.

When Hermann Goos's genealogical tables were updated and re-published in 1897, they were made to fit the Lowe design, following his numbered sequence. The 1900 edition of William Hall Walker's *Stallion Register* featured five-generation tabulated pedigrees with family numbers of every individual included. William Chismon's *Stallion Record* of 1901, which showed three-generation pedigrees of all the notable horses to have stood in Britain and Ireland in the nineteenth century, also added the family number to every name. Chéri Halbronn's equivalent volume aimed at French breeders, *Les Étalons de France au XIXème Siècle*, followed suit in 1904. The world over, it seemed that no horse was properly identified unless the Lowe family number was attached. Americans felt the need to comply, as did the Australians and New Zealanders; in cases where horses descended from roots not mentioned by Lowe, they fell in with his plan and instigated their own form of notation, employing an 'A' (American) plus a number or a 'C' (Colonial) plus a number.

These developments did not always mean that there was universal acceptance of everything that Lowe stood for, but because the believers included the numbers, the non-believers felt obliged to include them also; it was additional 'information' which readers could employ or ignore as they chose. Inclusion in stallion reference books was followed by inclusion in sale catalogues, and numerous countries around the world persisted in citing the numbers – up until the 1960s in America and France.

Inevitably, the rapid acceptance, then continued use of the Lowe numbers in publications led newcomers to believe that they were there for a reason and had to be significant. When Allison brought out a second, expanded edition of *The British Thoroughbred Horse* in 1907, he did not have to apologise for having been Lowe's chosen apostle; his reworked gospel found a ready market, and in many cases he was preaching to the converted – those who had sufficient faith in the doctrine of running and sire families to make it the basis of their breeding policies.

Osborne and the others who had found fault had been overruled; it was going to need something more than rejection on intellectual and logical grounds by lucid thinkers to curb the enthusiasm of those who had found the new religion. As it happened, something more was now available, because a major scientific breakthrough had occurred and, ironically, what provided the scientists with their *quod erat demonstrandum* was evidence derived from the *General Stud Book*. When William Sidney Towers devised his plan for the presentation of data on the breeding of Thoroughbreds, he had unwittingly played a role in the recognition of a new branch of science. Gregor Mendel, the Augustinian monk who gave that lecture entitled 'Studies on Plant Hybridisation' in Moravia back in 1865 had died nineteen years later, remembered as a well-loved cleric (finally Abbot of his monastery), an amusing companion, and a fellow who had developed theories about his hobby that nobody could really comprehend. However, in the years that followed, others got involved with experiments with plants and, in 1899, a botanist named Robert Allen Rolfe came across some papers that Mendel had left and found that he could relate Mendel's studies to his own. At a London conference that year, Rolfe dropped Mendel's name into his speech, sparking an interest in what the long-dead monk had discovered.

It was all hopelessly recondite, far beyond the ken of anyone engaged in the breeding of Thoroughbreds, but there was no reason to bring it to their attention at that time anyway. Yet the feeling grew, among some enlightened scientists, that Mendel had made significant discoveries about the workings of heredity. It was Mendel's use of the terms 'dominant' and 'recessive' that proved particularly intriguing and for some, notably the Cambridge academic William Bateson, the theory potentially held the answers to a number of the questions that troubled the inquiring mind. Others were not so impressed, among them Oxford Professor of Comparative Anatomy, Raphael Weldon, who had fallen out with Bateson in 1895; the former college friends never spoke to one another again, and in their continuing enmity each collected disciples who would readily argue a case against the other camp. The war raged for five years, with the pro-Mendel faction desperately seeking proofs for its case, while the opposition insisted that no such proofs could exist.

One of those who supported Weldon was Francis Galton, whose first pronouncements on ancestral contribution in the early 1870s had failed to satisfy the scientific community, but who returned to that theme with renewed vigour when he learnt that Sir Everett Millais, son of the famous pre-Raphaelite painter, had kept meticulous records of the characteristics of the many Basset hounds he had bred over a twenty-two year period up to 1896. The large sample, and the fact that only two colour varieties were involved, soon enabled Galton to formulate his Law of Ancestral Heredity, which he outlined to the Royal Society in June 1897. His researches had led him to conclude that parents contributed one half to the heritage of their offspring (a quarter each), the grandparents one quarter (one-sixteenth each), and so on. The theory was actually a bit too simplistic and would not stand the closer scrutiny that came much later, but when Bateson picked up on it he saw it in terms of dominants and recessives, in line with Mendel's observations, and told Galton so; Galton was evidently unconvinced, and ignored Bateson's letter.

Undeterred, and now with a powerful ally in distinguished Dutch botanist Hugo de Vries, Bateson pressed on with his search for proofs of Mendel, and finally they came. Galton's work with the Basset hound turned out to be an 'own goal' against the Weldon camp. Where else were there records of a breed, compiled over a long period, that might furnish the crucial evidence? A staunch Batesonite, poultry and rabbit breeder Charles Chamberlain Hurst, discovered the *General Stud Book*. It was all there, as plain as a pikestaff, how bay and brown behaved, how chesnut behaved – dominants and recessives working unfailingly, just as Mendel had described. He submitted a paper on the subject to the Royal Society, seeking permission to deliver it. Weldon and Bateson soon saw it, the former reacting with rage, the latter with no more than lukewarm appreciation, because he felt that young Hurst was apt to jump to conclusions and would face a formidable foe when presenting his case.

Nevertheless, the 35-year-old Hurst was granted leave to read his paper on 7 December 1905 and, in the month before that date, Weldon delved into the Bodleian Library's set of the *General Stud Book*, seeking the anomalies that would destroy his opponent's argument. Hurst was not fully prepared when the big day came. Once he had sat down, Weldon rose and identified the anomalies he had noticed. 'Mere clerical errors', Hurst insisted, but he could not cite chapter and verse. Weldon claimed victory, and Bateson, with no evidence to support his disciple, told Hurst that unless he could clear up the apparent discrepancies, he would have to withhold his paper from publication in the proceedings of the Royal Society.

Some of the anomalies, from the distant past, were never going to be resolved to anyone's satisfaction. Who could say whether a single rogue reference was fact or fiction? Ultimately, the key to resolution of the problem was a single horse, the registered chesnut Ben Battle, who had died in 1894 after a long stud career in which he had regularly sired bay or brown foals from matings with chesnut mares. Ben Battle became central to Weldon's argument and a problem for Hurst. If horsemen had been party to this row between scientists, it would have been swiftly resolved. As it was, Hurst did not take the obvious step of checking racing records until early in 1906, when he was delighted to discover that throughout his career on the racecourse, Ben Battle had been described as brown. His bay and brown offspring from chesnut mares demonstrated his colour dominance. A jubilant Bateson declared that Hurst's paper could now be published, along with a footnote explaining apparent anomalies. A distraught Weldon drove himself harder in his quest for flaws in his opponents' argument, poring ceaselessly over volumes of the *General Stud Book* until a severe bout of influenza assailed a weakened constitution. He died, a disappointed man, on 14 April 1906, aged only 46.

It was not just the thought that arguing against Mendel was not worth dying for that caused previously unconvinced members of the scientific community to now ally themselves with Bateson. Those *General Stud Book* records amounted to confirmation of Mendel's hypothesis; hidden secrets to the workings of heredity had been revealed, and a new branch of science, which Bateson labelled genetics, was born.

Although Thoroughbred breeding had played a huge part in exposing those hidden secrets to scientists, it was a while before breeders became exposed to the new revelations. Allison was still gaining converts to Lowe with the second edition of his book a year later, and there was no way that laymen were going to grasp such esoteric concepts as dominance and recessiveness until they heard it or read it all from one of their own, in terms they could understand.

The self-appointed educator of the Thoroughbred breeding world came along in the shape of James Bell Robertson (1858-1940), a Yorkshireman who had spent five years as a rancher in Minnesota, qualified as a vet on his return to Britain and, after some years in practice, abandoned that occupation in favour of racing journalism, taking the title of 'Professor' with him. Beginning with a series of articles under his own name in the *Winning Post* from November 1909 and continuing under the *nom de plume* 'Mankato' in the *Sporting Chronicle* from the following year, he set himself the twin tasks of demolishing the bogus Lowe doctrine and inculcating the principles of Mendelism into the minds of his readers. He was pitting the wonders of modern science, cogently expressed, against the whims of an Australian fantasist who had built castles in the air, and his English interpreter whose only professional qualification lay in law. It should have been no contest.

Robertson attacked Lowe at every opportunity, and when the first periodical directed specifically at breeders, the *Bloodstock Breeders' Review*, made its début in 1912, he was hammering away at 'The Figure Fallacy' in its first issue. The *Review*'s editors needed no encouragement to present the argument for science; one of them, Robert Bunsow, nailed his colours to the Mendelist mast in that initial number, but ironically he did so in an article which showed him to be in conflict with none other than Charles Chamberlain Hurst. Having found the key to genetics through the Thoroughbred, the former poultry and rabbit breeder had by now become an adviser to the British Board of Agriculture on horse breeding, and was associated with an experiment designed to prove that jumping ability was a dominant Mendelian character.

Bateson had been right about Hurst after all. He was impulsive – a maverick, the Americans would have called him – and Robertson must have despaired to note how the man who had been a prime mover in advancing the cause of science had taken a backward step. Breeders now did not know what to think, observing these professed Mendelists arguing among themselves, and, when all was said and done, the scientists still had not provided a practical plan for breeding, as Lowe had.

Robertson was still finding the need to rail against Lowe in his eightieth year, and in the *Bloodstock Breeders' Review* of 1940, which contained his obituary, the tabulated pedigrees of that year's leading winners were still adorned with their Bruce Lowe numbers, and the convention of displaying the sire families in bold type was upheld. Genetics had not yet provided the great breakthrough, and by now there were other theorists whose views were commanding attention.

CHAPTER 11

FROM MUMBO-JUMBO TO COMMON SENSE

The essential point about Bruce Lowe's system was that any fool could understand it, and every fool did – many even acting on its principles. Jean-Joseph Vuillier, by contrast, might have come from another planet. He published his *Croisements Rationnels dans la Race Pure* (Rational Cross-Breeding in the Thoroughbred) in 1903, and brought out a second, revised edition two years later, but a quarter of a century passed before many people took much notice of his ideas. By then he was associated with the Aga Khan's breeding programme, and when that stud thrived the thought occurred to some that perhaps it might be worth the effort to examine his convoluted system.

Vuillier dismissed Lowe's ideas in the Foreword to his first edition, and he had overhauled and refined his own system by the time of his last, in 1928. What he substituted for the Lowe doctrine was to some extent an exercise in mathematics, which doubtless impressed those who appreciated a scheme based on a branch of science, but to the last he never let genetics intrude. He was certainly a remarkable student of pedigree, and for him the conventional tabulation of five generations was not enough. He analysed the backgrounds of some 650 prominent racehorses to twelve generations, observing that certain ancestors featured more often than others, and drew conclusions about the elements contained by what he termed 'a standard good horse'.

This was the birth of 'dosage', which would have two later reincarnations, modified first by the Italian Franco Varola, and subsequently by the American Steven Roman. In the final Vuillier version, fifteen stallions (Birdcatcher, Touchstone, Voltaire, Pantaloon, Melbourne, Bay Middleton, Gladiator, Stockwell, Newminster, St Simon, Galopin, Isonomy, Hampton, Hermit and Bend Or) and one mare (Pocahontas) were identified as key individuals. In the twelth generation of a pedigree there are 4,096 names

– not all different, of course – and for each instance at that degree Vuillier gave the ancestor one point; an appearance in the eleventh generation earned two points, and so on down to the first, where each parent received 2,048 points. His sixteen key individuals were supposed to attain the standard figure – the dosage – allotted to them, and where there were deficiencies, he advised matings that would result in a product closer to the standard dosage for each ancestor. In the sense that Vuillier advocated the creation of a balanced pedigree, his ideas had some appeal. Correcting by adding what was missing seemed reasonable; this was outcrossing with a logical, definite purpose.

Or was it? The fact that his mathematics were in conflict with Galton's Law of Ancestral Heredity need not matter, because Galton could have been wrong – and he was. No, what really concerned critics of the scheme was that it was all so arbitrary. Was it really possible that Nature worked according to Vuillier's grand plan? What if he had devoted his time to researching the twelve-generation pedigrees of 650 bad horses, or 650 indifferent horses, instead of the good ones? Would he not have found that their standard dosages were much the same? These were ancestors common to the breed as a whole.

Breeders may have found genetics rather difficult to understand, but they could see that there was no science whatsoever in Vuillier. He was just juggling with names in pedigrees and trying to make them fit his arbitrary pattern. Needless to say, like Shorthouse and Lowe before him, Vuillier was not to be fazed by criticism. 'Denial will not alter it, for it is in nobody's power to prove that truth is in error', he insisted.

The successes of the Aga Khan's breeding programme were bound to bring Vuillier a measure of credibility, but dosage was only one of the factors employed in that stud's mating strategy, and a quality broodmare band, allied to the use of top stallions, provided an adequate explanation for its achievements. Other leading breeders of the period, such as Federico Tesio, Marcel Boussac and the Earl of Derby, paid no heed to the Vuillier plan.

Besides, the Vuillier plan could not be followed in perpetuity. The breed is in a constant state of flux, and just as he had had to make adjustments as his key ancestors began to disappear off his twelve-generation map, those who took up his ideas and adapted them have needed to identify new key ancestors in their own arbitrary ways.

What Varola did was to develop the dosage idea along lines of aptitude, classifying his so-called *chefs de race* (influential sires) under five headings –

brilliant, intermediate, classic, stout and professional. He confessed to being a 'humanist' rather than a geneticist, and held that 'dosages are the study of the differentiation of functions within the Thoroughbred, and not magic formulae'.

In the Roman version, a product of the computer age, dosage has gone further down that route, and a degree in applied mathematics might be required to comprehend it, but for the fact that modern technology can readily produce the dosage profile of any given horse. Dosage today has followers in America, and virtually nowhere else. Its fundamental flaw is obvious, in that it still favours juggling ancestral names over acknowledging genetics, but it is no less important to recognise that it has drifted far away from Vuillier's original intention. It is no longer a scheme designed to help the breeder produce a good horse, and cannot be applied that way. What it does is to attempt to predict the aptitude, specifically the degree of stamina, in any horse, and that is why it is employed more by the American betting public than by American breeders. One must hope that it delivers winners to punters, as it has no validity for any other purpose.

During the period when Lowe's star remained – with Allison's aid – in the ascendant, Vuillier was first advancing his dosage theory, and the proofs of Mendel were still awaited, an Italian based in England came up with another new plan: love. Edoardo Ginistrelli (1833-1920) had experienced apparently insurmountable problems with his once-notable race-mare Signorina, who had produced only one live foal in a long career at stud. The story goes that, on her daily exercise, her path crossed with that of an undistinguished stallion called Chaleureux, and the pair could hardly be dragged away from one another. Ginistrelli, in true Latin romantic fashion, declared it a love match and determined that they should be mated. The product of their union was Signorinetta, who won both Derby and Oaks in 1908, her Wednesday and Friday triumphs coming either side of Ginistrelli's own 75th birthday.

The happy outcome of that episode hardly amounted to a viable formula for practical breeders, yet even Federico Tesio was seduced by the idea. In his *Breeding the Racehorse* he remarked:

> In the case of Signorinetta it is not unlikely that the issue was affected by the circumstances of the unplanned encounter between her parents. The arrows of the equine Cupid roused the sexual urge to a maximum of tension which endowed the resulting individual with exceptional energy.

That was something, he said, that could never be achieved with artificial insemination 'because the parents are cheated of their pleasurable spasm with its violent nervous release'. The master breeder was not immune to fanciful notions.

No less eccentric than Ginistrelli, William Hall Walker (1856-1933) found consistent success at the same period, breeding several classic winners, including Minoru, who was leased to King Edward VII and won the 1909 Derby. It was well known that Walker routinely consulted an astrologer for predictions about his own life and those of his horses, but there is no evidence that the seer played a part in the mating policies, which were conducted very much on conventional lines. The astrologer's job was to forecast the future of Walker's foals from scrupulously kept records that detailed time of birth to the minute, and he did so, often in the bluntest terms. His report for the foals of 1911, which has been preserved, included the observation that White Man had Moon in the 12th and Mercury in the 8th, which was bad news, and he would be no good for racing until 1916, 'if not previously converted to cat's meat'. The prediction proved partly correct, because although White Man won as a 2-year-old, he did die later that year of a twisted gut. The filly Dolabella had 'the grave obstacle of Saturn practically opposing the M.C. with Jupiter therein'. She was due to fail as a 3-year-old 'after having romped over everything as a 2-year-old'. In fact she achieved nothing at 2 and scored her only win in May 1914, a month when she was supposed to be 'not much good'.

In 1917 Walker abruptly sold his stud at Tully and all the stock he owned to the British government, possibly on account of a prophesy of doom from the astrologer. If that was the case, he should have used his own better judgement. Some notable results were achieved at what became the National Stud from the produce of the mares sold in that package, including Dolabella, about whose breeding prospects no prediction had been offered; she became the grand-dam of Big Game, winner of the 2000 Guineas and later a successful sire. The exceptional sire Blandford and outstanding race-mare Sun Chariot were others who descended from stock acquired from Walker.

As our record has shown, it was never necessary to be a genuine eccentric to offer odd ideas about breeding, and when those with theories to peddle clashed, they tended to expose their frailties – and no little arrogance. The German Friedrich Becker and England's James Bell Robertson were both avowed opponents of Bruce Lowe, but they also did not care much for each other's ideas, would not give an inch in argument, and their bickering was probably one reason why Lowe's ideas attained a longer lease on life.

Becker lashed into Lowe in the first barely comprehensible sentence of his *The Breed of the Racehorse*, published in 1935, and kept the vitriol flowing over many turgid pages. In fact, he was with Lowe up to a point, because he was emphatic that the female of the species was more important than the male. The original stallions in the breed probably numbered around a hundred, but the lines that sprang from them had swiftly been whittled down to three. By contrast, there were around fifty families at the outset, and branches had sprouted from virtually all of them; they were still vibrant and delivering success. Lowe's nonsense, Becker said, was the idea that just five families were responsible for sire power, either through the direct tail-female line or through inbreeding to them. There was scarcely a Thoroughbred in existence who was not inbred to one or more of families 1-5, so Lowe's idea was ridiculous. Yet this was a man who did not feel able to contradict Lowe's ideas on saturation, and who, like Lowe, saw breeding that was essentially about male lines and female lines. Moreover, he claimed that he was no theorist, but an exposer of facts.

Robertson, of course, was the fellow who had sought to bring Mendelism to the attention of breeders, who spent thirty years advocating science over fantasy, yet even he, towards the end of his life, revealed a reluctance to accept one of the fundamental revelations of genetics. In an article in the 1937 edition of the *Bloodstock Breeders' Review*, he pointed to the fact that the X chromosome is present in both male and female, and is thus not tied exclusively to the mother-to-daughter chain, whereas in the case of the Y chromosome there was continuity. That was another stick to beat Lowe with – and presumably Becker, too – but the natural inference from his remarks was that, after all, he was inclined to believe in a certain significance, and superiority, of the father-to-son chain. As a disciple of Galton, and one who had become a Fellow of the Eugenics Society, Robertson was not above venturing into a perversion of science.

After the strident rantings of dogmatists like Vuillier and Becker, and the selective science of Robertson, the wit and wisdom of Joe Estes (1903-70) came as welcome relief. Estes, for twenty-eight years editor of the U.S. weekly *Blood-Horse*, knew genetics and was one of the first writers on breeding in America to draw attention to its possibilities. He also had a healthy scepticism towards the theories of pedigree pundits, which he felt were almost invariably the products of limited and inconclusive evidence. He preferred to deal in hard facts, and his own articles were always models of logic and common sense, his views formed by thorough research. Unlike many who came before him – and some who followed him – he had no pet theory to peddle, and though he knew pedigrees as well as, or better than, the next man, he recognised that they told only part of the story, stressing the importance of good land, management and veterinary care to those who sought to produce good stock.

While he had no breeding theory as such, Estes did develop what has come to be regarded as a significant tool for measuring racing class in the Thoroughbred. His Average Earnings Index, unveiled in 1948, was the product of what had to be a monumental research job in the pre-computer era. The two key figures he needed to establish were the total amount of prize money earned in a year, and the number of horses who competed for it. Dividing the first by the second gave him the earnings of the average horse, a par figure which he set at 1.00; if the average horse earned $1,000, while horse A earned $2,000 and horse B $500, A would have an index of 2.00, B 0.50. The system was applicable in any country, and a cumulative index could be readily computed for horses who raced over several seasons. In addition to its usefulness as a measure of racing class, the AEI had obvious applications in the evaluation of sire and broodmare performance. It was Estes' view – and he had done the research to verify it – that the best athletes tended to be the best producers of athletes, and that meant that the individual counted for more than its pedigree. He even went so far as to say, in a 1952 column:

> Pedigrees are useful only when we are ignorant of the merit of the individual, and not very useful then. The more we know about the individual and its progeny, the less we need to know about the pedigree. When we have a moderately complete record of the individual and its progeny, the pedigree becomes useless.

For some that was heretical, or at the very least, mischievous. Others recognised that no commentator on the bloodstock business ever provided more consistently sound advice to breeders.

An observer of no less intellect than Estes was Phil Bull (1910-89), a former teacher who did not entirely abandon that profession when he embarked on a career that brought him renown as the publisher of

Timeform, Britain's premier betting advice service. The advice was not always just about punting, and in *The Best Horses of 1947* he expressed some forthright views about the ways in which pedigrees were commonly misunderstood. He wrote of 'the pernicious habit of looking at pedigrees and treating one or two particular "lines" as if they were continuities in fact in the same way that they are continuities on paper'. He insisted that it was wrong to regard a pedigree as stamped by, or characterised by, a particular pattern in it, and expanded on the theme as follows:

> Every individual in one generation of a pedigree is potentially of the same importance to the student of the pedigree as every other individual in that generation. To see only a couple of 'lines' forming a particular pattern, and expect the product of the mating to conform to that pattern, is to ignore the possibilities presented by the rest of the pedigree. Every mating presents an astronomical number of different possibilities in the offspring, and our business as pedigree students begins and ends with an attempt to envisage the more probable of these possibilities. After that we must turn to the horse himself to tell us, by his conformation, his action and his racecourse performances, which of the many possibilities presented by his pedigree has, in fact, actually materialised in him. If we don't understand the rudiments of Mendelian heredity we have no right to be talking or writing about pedigrees at all.

Estes, over decades of devotion to the cause, and Bull, within a few short paragraphs, had introduced more common sense into the debate on the breeding of Thoroughbreds than all of those who had preceded them put together. Of course, that did not mean that common sense would necessarily prevail in the long term.

CHAPTER 12
ENLIGHTENMENT REMAINS ELUSIVE

There were reasons why the outbreak of common sense from the likes of Estes and Bull failed to budge others from their traditional, entrenched positions. Bull relished an intellectual argument and almost never lost one; he was not the sort of man anyone wanted to argue against. If he had encountered real opposition to his brief outburst about those who interpreted pedigree in terms of blood, lines and families, it might have been different, but he had said his piece, and that was that. He rarely touched on the subject in print again. If Estes had written in the brash Bull style, accentuating the very real positives he had to offer, and had eliminated the negatives more forcefully than in the gentle mocking tones he routinely employed, that might have made a difference.

The upshot was that the ghost of Bruce Lowe continued to haunt the scene. One did not have to subscribe to all his ideas, but it was hard to get away from the notion of female families as somehow especially significant. Harry Keylock's *Dams of Winners* series, and his *Thoroughbred Pedigree Charts* focused on female line inheritance, employing the Lowe figure system. In 1932 the Society for the Promotion of Horse Breeding in Poland had issued *Tabulated Pedigrees of Thoroughbred Horses*, a work on the pattern that Frentzel and Goos had set over forty years earlier, and which would have a reincarnation in 1953 in Kazimierz Bobinski's more familiar *Family Tables of Racehorses*.

None of these publications actively promoted the theory of the mare's greater influence; their chief function was as a convenient reference for students of pedigree, rather than to provide guidelines to breeders. That, however, was not how they were generally perceived, nor how they were always employed. They provided further grist to Lowe's mill, and the fact that Bobinski, an English-based Pole, found the need to sub-divide the families (as his compatriots had done two decades earlier) gave rise to another misconstruction. The branches established by Bobinski, designated by a letter added to the Lowe number, were identified by the mare at the head of the branch; this had no significance whatever, and was determined simply by the constraints imposed by his book's format. Half a century later the names of mares who, of necessity, had to head a new Bobinski page, are regularly treated as though they have their own mystical qualities.

Still, it was not necessary to be a pedigree buff, and to acquire books which focused on the tail-female line. By long-standing convention, the only area of a pedigree elaborated upon in sale catalogues was – and still is – the mother-to-daughter chain. What appears in that elaboration, for many readers, tends to act as a definition of the pedigree as a whole, and since the introduction of black type (to denote stakes-winners in the female line) its impact has been accentuated. The reason why sale catalogue pedigrees are displayed as they are is rarely considered, but it merely reflects the fact that whereas it is generally reasonable to assume that all of the other individuals in a horse's background have earned some distinction, either by dint of superior racing performance or as the producer of a worthy performer, those in the bottom line may be non-achievers, employed as broodmares for no better reason than that it is customary to give all mares an opportunity at stud. The pedigree page is an advertisement, and the detail on the dam's female line is all about providing a justification for her being in the breeding population.

What breeders needed was guidance toward a more scientific approach to their art, preferably from someone with a 'horsy' background, but it was not forthcoming. It could not come in Dennis Craig's 1964 work *Breeding Racehorses From Cluster Mares*, which turned out to be a new angle on an old theme, once again focusing on female lines. More significantly, it could not come from another book published in the same year, Sir Rhys Llewellyn's *Breeding to Race*. This book's author came from a family which had been involved with Thoroughbreds, and he had made a study of genetics over a thirty-year period, but he was able to draw attention only to experiences with cattle, sheep, poultry and the like. By page 11 he was already hedging his bets about what might occur in the horse, regretting that: 'research into horse genetics has been very limited and the laws relating to the inheritance of genes which influence speed, stamina, fertility, maturity, temperament, conformation, etc., have yet to be studied'.

Therein lay the problem for anyone seeking instruction; there was too little knowledge available. An accomplished writer on breeding matters, such as Peter Willett, could tell it as it was in a number of fine books, notably *An Introduction to the Thoroughbred* (1966), but he could not carry the story forward. Similarly, the outstanding amateur rider, authoritative writer and successful breeder John Hislop was unable to advance the cause. Hislop's principal achievement in the last-named role was the production of Brigadier Gerard, arguably the best miler seen in Britain in decades. The colt was out of a mare whose own dam had been purchased expressly because she was a tail-female descendant of Pretty Polly, and though her breeder understood genetic realities, he liked to entertain the romantic notion that the great race-mare from the first decade of the century had played a significant role in his creation. That prompted the rationalist Bull to break his silence over breeding affairs and observe prosaically: 'So far as I am concerned Pretty Polly is merely one of 32 individuals in the fifth generation of Brigadier Gerard's pedigree.'

Llewellyn's remark about the limited research into the genetics of the horse was all too true in 1964, and there was little change in that situation for another quarter of a century. It seemed so ironic that the Thoroughbred, which had provided the proofs of Mendelism and been instrumental in the birth of genetics, had received next to nothing in return for its gifts. The few horsemen who thought about it, and who regularly heard of the triumphs of geneticists with pigs, sheep and cattle, began to suspect that science had a blind spot where the athletic animal was concerned. Meanwhile the old adherence to male and female lines was maintained, vague notions about inbreeding, outcrossing and nicking (of which, more in Chapter 22) persisted, and other ideas were emerging which seemed to have little or no foundation in science.

Among these other ideas were the two reincarnations of dosage, the first outlined by Franco Varola in *Typology of the Racehorse* (1974) and elaborated further in his *The Functional Development of the Thoroughbred* (1980), the second finally committed to print, years after its divergence from the prototype, in Steven Roman's *Dosage, Pedigree & Performance* (2002). Neither version seemed to concern itself much with genetics, except in its dependence on the prepotent qualities, in terms of aptitude, of a group of arbitrarily chosen sires, the so-called *chefs de race*. No doubt the arrogant Jean-Joseph Vuillier would have been appalled at the way Varola adapted *his* dosage; Varola certainly considered Roman's further adaptation an abortion.

All the promoters of dosage had to spend a lot of time fending off opposition from sceptics, and when Rommy Faversham and Leon Rasmussen brought out their *Inbreeding to Superior Females* in 1999, they were on the defensive in the opening pages of their Introduction. The pair were aware that what they were about to propose had already been dismissed as unproven – and therefore not worthy of belief – by Joe Estes in 1942, and though their begging to differ occupied 500 pages, their argument, replete with references to sire and dam lines, family numbers, *chefs de race*, and other discredited notions was never going to convince.

Works which failed to add to the sum of human knowledge on the subject of breeding, generally through want of science, have appeared regularly, and there have even been a few which purported to have a basis in genetics, yet succeeded only in dispensing misinformation. One privately published book of 1979 by an English author was predicated on a complete misunderstanding of coat colour genetics, and in the 1990s an American writer produced two books expounding theories about the X chromosome which bore little relation to the way that factor behaves in the Thoroughbred (see Chapter 18). When the latter author's ideas gained some acceptance among pedigree pundits who advised breeders on matings, it became more apparent than ever that a little science was a dangerous thing. None of the writers whose views have been featured in this book could fairly be described as a charlatan. They all believed what they wrote, many with total conviction, and perhaps none was more self-assured than Harold Hampton, an English-born, long-time New Zealand resident who first came to notice in December 1954 with the publication of a forty-page pamphlet entitled *The First Scientific Principles of Thoroughbred Breeding*. The fact that it carried a dedication to 'the Blessed Virgin Mary, without whose perpetual succour this research would never have been published' gives a clue to the character of the author, who apparently felt that his eleven years of research had been conducted under divine inspiration, and that he had revelations to bestow to mankind.

In fact there was not one shred of science in Hampton's document, unless one counts a single occurrence of the word 'genes'. Remarkably that appeared in a startling sentence claiming that 'it is at last possible to concentrate in a foal the genes that make for speed, courage and endurance'. Just how the breeder was supposed to achieve that was not adequately explained, but it seemed that the author was disposed to believe in nicks, he favoured line-breeding over its closer form, inbreeding, and the version of line-breeding which most appealed to him involved the coupling of different-sex representatives of the same parent, or better still, both parents. Most of the examples he chose to illustrate these phenomena sprang from the early-to-middle nineteenth century and, of course, they all involved superior racehorses. He gave no indication, presumably because he did not know, as to whether bad horses, or indifferent horses, exhibited the same features in their backgrounds.

It was all hopelessly unscientific, and it seems extraordinary that what might be termed 'the breed according to Hampton' acquired followers. Yet that is what occurred, at first very much on a local basis, with wider recognition following the emergence of Bonecrusher, a product of an unfashionable mating arranged by Hampton, as a runner of high repute in both New Zealand and Australia. That gelding's parents also combined to produce several nonentities, but that hardly signified, and suddenly the creator of that wonder was hailed as a guru.

What ensued, aided by the arrival of the home computer age and technological advances which facilitated pedigree research, was an upsurge in interest in Hampton's methodology and, before long, acceptance throughout Australasia of ideas for which genetics could provide no justification. Moreover, that was the part of the world where Bruce Lowe retained most adherents, and soon there was literature advocating line-breeding to nineteenth-century brother and sister ancestors, in conjunction with some numbered family.

This was way out, off-the-wall stuff, but in a sense it was the fault of the geneticists, who had taken so long to move into the area of the Thoroughbred, conduct the appropriate researches, and deliver the guidance required. It got worse before it could get better, with South Africans inventing new pseudo-scientific but meaningless terms such as 'genetic sibling', which conveyed the idea of a close relationship where only a remote relationship existed. Genetically, full brothers, whilst on average sharing 50% of their genes, may in extremely rare cases have nothing in common (see Chapter 13), yet Owen Tudor and Royal Charger, with only two common ancestors within three generations, were described as genetic siblings.

A 2003 American-published work by a Hampton disciple brought a deluge of references to nineteenth-century ancestors, continued insistence on the relevance of Lowe families, misattributions to the workings of the

X chromosome – in fact, every kind of assumption that could find no support in terms of equine genetics. It was simply playing with names in pedigrees, without regard to the characteristics of the individuals or those they imparted to their products. Joe Estes would have dismissed it in a few gently mocking words, but knowing intuitively or intellectually that something is not right, and saying so, cannot always suffice. He was powerless to prevent the follies that came after him.

Without categorical proof that they are wrong, fallacies may retain their status as received wisdom, and in Thoroughbred breeding wrong ideas tend to be put into practice – a sorry state of affairs in the twenty-first century, when science is able to provide wiser counsel. At the 2003 Annual Awards Dinner of Britain's Thoroughbred Breeders' Association, the manager of one of the world's largest studs announced that among its mating strategies was one that sought to involve line-breeding to Sainfoin and Sierra, a brother and sister combination from the 1880s, some dozen generations distant from the present population.

This was not something that many in the audience of (largely) practical British breeders would ever have considered, but a few recognised it as a theory propounded in the past by Ken McLean, an Australian whose advice to prominent breeders in various parts of the world had delivered a good deal of success. It was to get a fresh airing in McLean's subsequently published work, *Designing Speed in the Racehorse* (2005). Perhaps there was something in it, granted that its proponent had evidently been responsible for the production of a number of high-class runners with this factor in their background? Sadly for would-be believers, in this era of computerised programmes capable of producing pedigrees extended to twelve generations, it takes little time to establish that Sainfoin and Sierra appear together in a multitude of pedigrees; good, bad and indifferent horses are bred with those ancestors in combination, often several times over, and it would probably now be difficult to devise a mating in which both did not appear.

If the title of *Racehorse Breeding Theories* (2004), an American publication edited by Frank Mitchell, led buyers of the book to fancy that it would yield secrets to success, they were mistaken, but it was nonetheless a valuable work, as it did a fine job in exposing many misconceptions. In particular, its final chapter, contributed by Western Australian veterinary surgeon Ross Staaden, made a convincing case in asserting that there was no theory based on pedigree alone that could promise the production of a better racehorse.

Hardly less significant was the chapter contributed by Kentucky-based David L. Dink, the 'statistician's statistician' of the breeding industry. Never content with the analysis of élite groups of horses, Dink extends his researches to the examination of entire foal crops over long periods. He it was who, in 1993, presented a huge body of statistical data to expose the folly of dosage in a series of articles for the US weekly *Thoroughbred Times*. His more recent work has gone much further, demonstrating – again through number-crunching on a massive scale – that assessments of pedigrees simply in terms of the names that appear in them are essentially flawed.

What can one assume about the presence of a successful and influential sire such as Nasrullah in the fourth generation of any pedigree? Knowing that he is one of sixteen ancestors in that remove would allow the belief that he is responsible for, on average, 6.66 per cent of the genes in any fourth generation descendant. The fact that he had an outstanding record at stud might suggest that his impact counted for something more. Such assumptions do not pass the Dink test, which measures not just the quality of Nasrullah's – and many other notable sires' – fourth-generation descendants, but also the degree of success obtained according to his position in the pedigree. There are eight positions in the fourth remove where Nasrullah might be found, ranging from sire of paternal great-grandsire in the direct male line to sire of maternal great-grand-dam in the tail-female line, and all points in between. Examination of tens of thousands of pedigrees provided conclusive proof of the vast potential for variation in the racing ability of the descendant, according to the position occupied by the fourth-generation ancestor.

We can debunk some myths about pedigrees through their sheer implausibility or through their defiance of logic, and a David Dink may go to extraordinary lengths to demonstrate the flaws statistically. We might feel that any deliberate coupling of ancestors several generations back is of dubious value; that inbreeding *per se* is pointless, and worthwhile only when involving an ancestor whose descendants are known to carry the factors that it is intended to reproduce; that nicks, if they exist at all, are far less common than many would like to believe; that the concept of male lines and female lines is but a figment of man's feeblest imagination; that Thoroughbred breeding should be all about the matching of individuals – the parent stock – rather than a game played with names on a page. But the layman's thoughts are futile without the backing of science.

The time has surely come for the geneticists, now deeply committed to the Thoroughbred cause and immeasurably more knowledgeable than their predecessors, to reveal what can and what cannot be credited as we ponder the ever-fascinating conundrum about how to breed a better racehorse.

CHAPTER 13
WHY THE HORSEMAN NEEDS TO KNOW GENETICS

A century on from the rediscovery of Mendel, it is still unusual to come across an article about the breeding of the horse in which the author displays an awareness of genetics. It is still the norm to treat pedigree simply in terms of the names that appear, and to speculate on which matter most. In that scenario it is perhaps unsurprising that few people in the breeding industry seem to have gone beyond Mendel and grasped the theories of complex genetic inheritance that are most relevant to the Thoroughbred, or realised the possible impact that modern molecular genetics might make on their world within the next ten years.

Professional breeding analysts, with their expertise in pedigree lore, are a well-accepted part of the Thoroughbred industry. They play an important role in many of the major studs worldwide, having a strong influence on determining which mares visit which stallions. From the scientist's perspective, genetics is really only another word for pedigree, but one that potentially provides more detailed and accurate information about the chances of producing the desired outcome than that of names on a page, the analyst's usual stock-in-trade.

Through much of its history, the Thoroughbred horse has been selectively bred by incorporating the limited scientific knowledge available and reflecting the fashionable ideas of the day. Numerous different approaches have been applied, as described in the earlier chapters of this book, none of them paying specific heed to genetics. One of the aims of this work is to examine the different breeding schemes that have been employed in terms of what we currently know about genetics, and to suggest possible strategies for the future.

It is no exaggeration to say that there has been a revolution in our understanding of genetics as a result of the human genome project. This new knowledge is rapidly being extended into our domesticated farm, pet and leisure animals. The different breeds of domestic species were initially created and developed by selective breeding. Milk and meat yields are being significantly increased through the application of molecular genetic techniques to identify breeding stock better able to pass on these traits.

The Thoroughbred horse world, being by nature tradition-based, is far less receptive to revolution, so that change in response to new ideas tends to be slow. Horsemen are comfortable with a *status quo*, concerned that an 'invasion' of their territory by scientists might constitute a threat, and that the whole subject is far too complicated. Their natural response is to bury their heads in the sand and hope it will go away. Judging by progress in other farm species, this 'it' is unlikely to go away, and it will become increasingly important to understand the new concepts.

Some may argue that the genetics behind milk and meat production has little relevance to the genetics behind the unique physiological demands placed on successful Thoroughbred horses. While athletic performance in Thoroughbreds is undoubtedly complex, involving the respiratory and circulatory systems, together with an efficient musculoskeletal system, conceptually it is similar to many aspects of farm animal production. This idea is reinforced through the finding that as more mammalian species, including the horse, have had their genetic sequences completely determined, it has become increasingly clear that mammals by and large possess a common set of genes. Variation within those genes, rather than the possession of an alternative species-specific set of genes, is responsible for the distinct features of each species.

The basic ideas are not difficult to understand, dealing, as they do, largely with odds, which is something for which most Thoroughbred people have a natural affinity! In fact, new genetic data can easily be incorporated into the traditional approaches, and actually provide the tools for pedigree experts to test their theories about the importance of certain individual ancestors and combinations of them. The results may disprove some pet notions, but there is little doubt that they will lead to the generation of many more answers to the fascinating puzzle of Thoroughbred horse breeding.

From a scientist's perspective, the Thoroughbred presents a fantastic resource for genetic studies, and most of the basic genetic principles can be illustrated by using well-recognised traits that should aid the horseman's understanding. The origins of the breed, from the foundation stallions and mares, and its subsequent expansion to a population of about half a million individuals worldwide, are nearly completely documented in the volumes of the *General Stud Book*, from its initial issue of 1791 up to Volume 46 of 2009, and in similar publications compiled in other countries. Recent molecular research from Ireland investigated the authenticity of the stud book records, and though a number of discrepancies were found, much of the data was substantiated.

Scientific studies have attempted to estimate the contribution of genetics to racing performance in the Thoroughbred. Most suggest that about one-third of racing ability is genetic, with the remaining fraction being made up of numerous components labelled as environmental. These environmental aspects represent in large part the art and skill of the horseman, through, for example, nutrition and training. The genetic components are likely to include differences in the genes which code for the components of heart, lungs, muscles, bones, tendons, and, not least, temperament. Genetic studies into Thoroughbred performance are increasingly complemented by research into human athletic ability, often undertaken on Olympic athletes.

As mentioned earlier in this book, a number of writers have provided horsemen with clues about genetics, one of the most remarkable being Chapman Pincher, a contributor to early issues of the *British Racehorse*. In the early 1950s, before the discovery of the structure of DNA, he clearly described the state of knowledge regarding the shuffling of chromosomes that takes place in the formation of individual eggs and sperm, and showed that, following reproduction, the fertilisation of egg with sperm generates a unique genetic entity. Many horse breeders today still do not understand this concept, with the result that they often entertain unrealistic expectations about the chances of replicating success when repeating a mating that has previously generated a top-class runner. They also seem to have difficulty in understanding the real contribution that a famous ancestor, five generations ago, is likely to have made to the individual horse under study. The chapters that follow will put these topics in perspective.

The principles are shown in the diagram overleaf using a simplified example with only three pairs of chromosomes. The six different chromosomes in each of the cells have been given a different colour. When

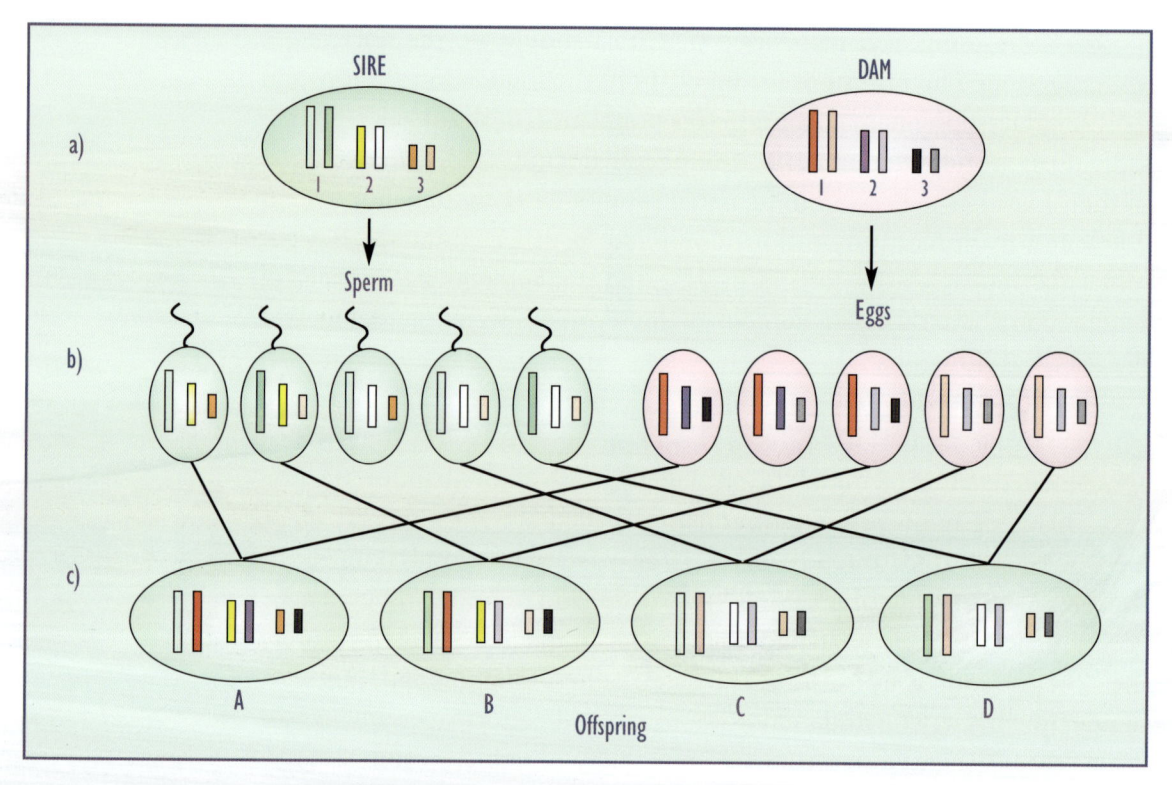

The independent segregation of chromosomes ensures that each offspring is unique.

a) The sire and dam are shown with only three pairs of chromosomes, 1, 2 and 3 for convenience. All six chromosomes are coloured differently.

b) When the sire produces sperm and the dam produces eggs, one chromosome from each pair is randomly introduced into each sperm or each egg. Each sperm and each egg shown contains a different coloured set of the three chromosomes.

c) Sperm and eggs are fused to generate new full-sibling offspring, A, B, C and D, each of which has a different set of chromosome pairs. Whilst offspring A shares some chromosome material with offspring B and C, it does not possess any of the chromosomes present in offspring D. Whilst this example shows the inheritance for only three pairs of chromosomes, the horse has thirty-one pairs of chromosomes and the additional sex chromosomes X and Y. The number of possible combinations when repeating matings between the same sire and dam is therefore enormous.

the stallion produces sperm, only one of the largest pair of chromosomes enters each sperm. Which one of the pair of chromosomes is used is essentially random, such that half the sperm will contain one, and half the other. This process is repeated for each pair of chromosomes with the choice being independent for each pair of chromosomes such that 2^3 (2x2x2=8) different combinations of chromosomes are produced. A similar process takes place in the dam during formation of the egg, and again eight different chromosome combinations are produced. In the simplified example illustrated, 2^6 – that is sixty-four different chromosome combinations – are possible in the progeny. In the horse there are thirty-two 'pairs' of chromosomes in each cell, such that 2^{32} different combinations are possible for the sire and dam, and any one of 2^{64} different chromosome combinations could be present in the offspring. If a mating has been successful in producing a highly-rated racehorse and it is repeated, it is virtually impossible that the same genetic make-up will be produced. Indeed, full-siblings on average share only 50 per cent of their genetic material.

When half-siblings to successful horses are sold at auction, auctioneers put great emphasis on the relationship, but in reality it accounts to on average only 25 per cent shared chromosomal DNA. This mixing up of chromosome combinations is thought to be one of the main benefits that come from sexual reproduction, in that the new combinations of variation obtained have the potential to be better adapted to their environment,

Siblings frequently differ widely in racing ability, a fact readily explicable by a knowledge of genetics. However, Persimmon (above left), winner of the 1896 Derby and St Leger, had a younger full-brother, Diamond Jubilee, who won England's Triple Crown in 1900. Likewise, Galtee More (above right), the Triple Crown hero of 1897, was half-brother to Ard Patrick, successful in the 1902 Derby.

Generation	Ancestors in that Generation	Average % Contribution From Each	Average Number of Chromosomes Transmitted per Ancestor
1	2	50.00*	32.00*
2	4	25.00	16.00
3	8	12.50	8.00
4	16	6.25	4.00
5	32	3.13	2.00
6	64	1.56	1.00
7	128	0.78	0.50
8	256	0.39	0.25
9	512	0.19	0.12

Contribution of chromosomes down generations.

*Actual contribution

which also changes over time. In reality, the picture is even more complex as the members of each chromosome pair are not inherited intact when passed down through generations. Instead they go through a reciprocal 'cut and paste' process called recombination during the formation of each egg and sperm, which vastly increases the number of possible genetic variants that are produced.

Some also seem to have difficulty in understanding the real contribution that a famous ancestor, say five generations ago, is likely to have made to a contemporary horse under study. The genetic contribution is shown in the table above, where it can be seen that an offspring must get thirty-two chromosomes from each parent, via the egg and sperm, which come together to form the normal thirty-two chromosome 'pairs' in each cell of the horse. At the parental generation the number of chromosomes received is fixed, but in the other generations the genetic contributions are based on average transmission. This occurs as, in some cases, one grandparent may by chance have contributed more chromosomes than another. When building the genetic map of the horse, where we were able to follow the chromosomal origins of each chromosome, it was possible to see just this sort of variation amongst the offspring that were being tested. While many of them contained roughly 25 per cent of their genetic material from each grandparent, within the seventy or so individuals examined two had combinations where the ratios of DNA from each of the four grandparents was 35 per cent: 15 per cent: 16 per cent: 34 per cent.

At the sixth generation, an individual has sixty-four ancestors, who on average will each have contributed one chromosome – or, more accurately, as a result of recombination – one sixty-fourth of the genetic material. In such a situation, it is likely that some of those sixty-four ancestors did not contribute *any* genetic material to the genetic make-up of the contemporary individual. These basic rules of genetics do not always sit easily with traditional approaches to Thoroughbred breeding, though they are well established and supported by a mass of experimental data.

In another telling piece of writing, Howard Wright's excellent biography of Phil Bull, the founder of *Timeform*, his subject claimed, as one of his major lifetime achievements, to have put Thoroughbred breeding on a sound footing by demonstrating the illogical nature of many so-called 'breeding systems'. The evidence that he provided lessons on that topic undoubtedly exists, but the proof that they were heeded remains sadly lacking half a century later. There are still a surprising number of dubious mating systems in existence, and still plenty of people prepared to experiment with them.

It has already been mentioned that the beginning of this millennium has seen a revolution in molecular genetics, exemplified by the human genome project. It is now possible to examine in detail, rapidly and cheaply, the genetic make-up of individuals, and to represent that information accurately in relatively simple diagrams. In the case of the Thoroughbred horse we are beginning to understand the flow of genetic information through the pedigrees that fascinate us. It may even be possible to examine the genetic make-up of many of the most famous Thoroughbreds in history, through analysis of DNA extracted from the bones and hooves of those individuals kept in museums and private collections. That lucid writer Peter Willett, responsible for several valuable works on breeding, once described the study of genetics of the Thoroughbred as like looking at a jigsaw puzzle in which one could see only the edge pieces. With the application of molecular genetics to the horse, it is now possible to view quite large internal areas of the picture and to obtain a better understanding of the combinations of genetic pieces making up individual horses.

The chapters that follow aim to synthesise knowledge of traditional genetic theory with modern molecular genetics, 'from Mendel to molecule', in ways directly relevant to those interested in the Thoroughbred horse. Many of the answers to the enigmas of racecourse and breeding success remain unknown, but the experimental routes to such knowledge are becoming progressively clearer – and horsemen have plenty to offer through their detailed observation of the animals in their care. Genetics is a dynamic science that keeps developing. For certain observations that scientists would have dismissed as impossible only a few years ago, the genetic mechanisms are now becoming explainable. There will undoubtedly be more surprises in the future.

It is hoped that by understanding in greater detail the building blocks he is working with, and the rules that apply to them, the horseman will be better equipped to pursue his art. The wise application of new technologies promises to lead to the continued improvement of the Thoroughbred, and to ensure that the breed continues to raise the pulse of onlookers for centuries to come.

CHAPTER 14
THE EQUINE GENOME

Federico Tesio, probably the greatest breeder of the twentieth century, was famously quoted as saying:

> The Thoroughbred exists because its selection has depended, not on experts, technicians, or zoologists, but on a piece of wood: the winning post of the Epsom Derby. If you base your criteria on anything else, you will get something else, not the Thoroughbred.

This was Tesio the philosopher, another side of Tesio the creator of Nearco, Ribot and many other champions, and his statement could not be taken literally. Nevertheless, his allusion was to the race that for nearly two centuries had represented the ultimate goal for Thoroughbred breeders; the Derby was why they did it, and therefore a key environmental factor in the development of the breed. Derby winners were highly prized as stallions, regularly employed to mate with high-quality mares, and they made a huge contribution as the breed evolved.

Practical breeders would no doubt have preferred some insights from Tesio as to how he achieved such exceptional results over half a century, but they were not forthcoming. The observations contained in his book *Breeding the Racehorse* have been scrutinised by countless eager readers, and interpreted in a myriad of ways by many commentators, but nowhere did he provide a ready formula for success. The breeder, whether he has aspirations of Derby glory or more modest goals, starts from scratch with that crucial decision over which individuals to breed from and thereby, knowingly or otherwise, he is involving himself in a genetic experiment. This chapter and the two following seek to provide a clear understanding of the underlying genetic realities taking place when breeding a new foal.

At different periods in the history of the Thoroughbred, the perception of the relative importance of the stallion and mare in the contribution that each makes to the offspring of their union has ranged widely. Some of those ideas have featured in earlier pages of this book. In the early days of the breed the mare was commonly regarded as merely providing the receptacle for the good qualities of the stallion. Later the opposite view was held, with the mare seen as the key to successful breeding. By considering the scientific facts of the contribution of each parent as outlined below, it is possible to see that stallion and mare make approximately equal genetic contributions. However, those facts do not settle the argument conclusively, as we shall see later.

Genetics and molecular genetics are no different from many other specialised disciplines in that any discussion inevitably involves the use of jargon. Brief definitions of some of the most common terms employed should facilitate understanding of the key concepts we are going to examine.

The **genome** is the term used for all the genetic material present in an organism. It has been referred to as 'the book of life', containing, as it does, the instructions on which the shape and function of the organism under consideration are encoded. The genetic instructions, however, are subject to constant interaction with the environment, and the finished product is the sum of Nature plus Nurture. Indeed, when considering Thoroughbred racing performance, the balance seems to be about one-third Nature and two-thirds Nurture.

The genetic message is contained in what is commonly abbreviated to **DNA** (the full, unwieldy, version is deoxyribonucleic acid) which has an 'alphabet' comprising only four 'letters', representing the simple building blocks, the **nucleotides** A, C, G and T. The famous double helix structure of DNA was determined at Cambridge in 1953 by James Watson and Francis Crick. They and others were awarded the Nobel Prize for their discovery, which also helped to explain how DNA could be copied accurately in the cells of the body to preserve the precious information it contains.

In mammals the length of the DNA 'book' is approximately three billion letters, roughly equivalent to the number of letters in 1,000 copies of the Bible. One of the outstanding scientific achievements of all time was recorded in 2003 with the completion of the entire human genome sequence. Since then genome sequences for several other mammalian species have been completed, including chimpanzee, mouse, dog and cattle.

THE EQUINE GENOME

In 2006 it was announced that the horse genome was being sequenced at the Broad Institute in Cambridge, Massachusetts, the individual chosen being a Thoroughbred mare, Twilight, from Cornell University. That project has been completed and the DNA sequence of Twilight is publicly available on the internet, annotated with gene locations based on DNA sequence comparisons with other mammals.

The book analogy is helpful again in recognising **chromosomes**, into which the genome sequence is partitioned, as 'chapters'. Chromosomes can be seen, counted and distinguished by microscopy, so we know that in the horse there are thirty-three different types – the X (female) and Y (male) chromosomes that determine the sex of the individual, and thirty-one non-sex chromosomes known as **autosomes**. Most cells in the body contain two complete sets of chromosomes, making a total of sixty-four – two sets of thirty-one autosomes, plus either two X chromosomes in a female, or an X and a Y in a male. In the same way that not all the chapters

The Thoroughbred mare, Twilight – the individual chosen for the sequencing of the horse genome at the Broad Institute in Cambridge, Massachusetts.

in a book are the same length, the chromosomes vary greatly in size, but in this case the autosomes are numbered in part according to size, chromosome 1 being the largest and chromosome 31 the smallest. The sex chromosomes are close to the extremes of the size range, with the X being approximately the same size as chromosome 1, while the Y is even smaller than chromosome 31.

In addition to the chromosomes, there are other structures within cells that contains DNA, known as **mitochondria**. In contrast to the three billion bases of DNA of the chromosomes, the mitochondria contain a small circle of DNA of about 16,000 bases that is inherited only from the mother. There are thousands of copies of mitochondrial DNA within each cell, and the genes encoded on this small circle are chiefly involved in the process of energy generation.

The information content of DNA is encoded in **genes**, the units of inheritance. In every individual in each new generation (with the exception of identical twins), unique combinations of gene variants are assembled from those present in each parent. The inheritance of genes follows certain rules, which are the subject of the next two chapters.

Over the last decade or so there have been many surprises as the structure and organisation of the mammalian genome has been revealed. One of the initial unexpected findings concerned the structure of the gene, which in simple bacteria is a continuous stretch of DNA sequence. It was assumed that the same arrangement for the gene would be found in more complex organisms, but in this case the gene sequences were interrupted by large stretches of DNA sequence called **introns**, which only rarely seemed to have a useful function. These might be compared to the advertisements which regularly interrupt the story in a television programme; with our video recorder we can choose to skip the adverts, and in much the same way the cell has the ability to edit out the introns and retain only the useful information.

A second major surprise concerned the proportion of DNA that codes for the useful information in genes. A lot of energy is required to copy DNA each time a cell divides, so it was supposed that, during evolution, selective forces would have ensured that DNA was densely packed with genes. In fact, it turned out that less than 10 per cent of the genome encodes genes, with most of the rest being made up of tens of thousands of relatively short repeated sequences, frequently referred to as 'junk DNA'. As that name implies, it has no function that has been recognised to date.

During the human genome sequencing project, scientists made bets – they are not as boring as they may seem! – as to the final number of genes that would be present. The variation in estimates was huge, with the majority in the range of 75,000 to 100,000. As the sequence neared completion it became evident that the number of genes present was dramatically lower than predicted, the actual figure being about 20,000. It was found that many genes were able to generate slightly different products by putting together different pieces when they spliced out the introns. Even though scientists now have the complete sequence, the question of the number of genes is still not fully resolved, as there is an ongoing philosophical debate as to the precise definition of a gene.

There was also speculation as to what proportion of genes was likely to be unique to each mammalian species, and how many would turn out to be common genes shared by most mammals. Since scientific evidence points to all mammals sharing a common evolutionary ancestor, it is to be expected that all would therefore share many of the genes that control the basic properties of mammalian cell biology. When the DNA sequence of these conserved genes is compared between different mammals, the level of DNA identity (the number of times the same letter of the DNA code is present at the same position in the sequence) is a measure of the times at which the different species branched off their common evolutionary tree. When the genes of humans and chimpanzees are compared, the level of DNA identity is very high, often about 99 per cent, reflecting the relatively recent divergence of these two species. Comparison of the same gene sequences between man and horse reveal a much lower level of identity, often around 80 per cent, indicating that our two species diverged a considerable time ago.

Given the wide range of shapes and sizes of different mammals, it seemed reasonable to suppose that each species would carry a set of genes that were unique to it, defining, as it were, the 'essence' of that species. Speculation on the proportion of unique genes that would be found again produced a wide variety of estimates, ranging up to 25 per cent. When the mouse genome DNA sequence was obtained, and a detailed comparison with the human DNA sequence carried out, all estimates were again shown to have been wide of the mark. The proportion of genes in common between man and mouse was found to be 99 per cent; a mere one-hundredth part was unique to each species. That finding has been reinforced as further mammalian genome sequences have become available.

During the copying of DNA when cells divide, very rare errors are introduced into the DNA sequence, producing **mutations**, which might be regarded as spelling mistakes in the 'book of life'. When these mutations take place in the cells that produce sperm or eggs, they may be transmitted to the next generation, producing **genetic variation**. It is the presence of mutations that makes individuals different.

Darwin's theory of natural selection proposed that, in Nature, certain variants would be more successful than others in particular environments, i.e. by producing more progeny than the less successful variants. With the selective breeding employed in the Thoroughbred industry we are replacing natural selection with artificial human selection to determine which individuals will produce the most progeny.

In this chapter we have outlined the basic genetic building blocks that go to make up a mammal such as a horse. We can now move on to show how they are transmitted from generation to generation, and to consider how the inheritance of genes follows rules that enable us to make some predictions about the outcomes of matings between particular stallions and mares.

CHAPTER 15
COAT COLOUR 1 – GREY, A DOMINANT TRAIT

Originally, wild horses appear to have been brown or dun in colour, to judge from the evidence of European cave paintings dated between 15,000 and 30,000 years ago. Strong natural selection would have militated against the propagation of colour variants that might have made an individual more visible to predators. Strange as it may seem, it is thought that the distinctive striped black and white pattern of the wild horse's relation, the zebra, was also to its selective advantage by spatially distracting predators during a chase. In contrast, domestication and captive breeding have led to the appearance and maintenance of colour variants, not only in the horse. Another notable example concerns the silver fox, bred for generations in Russian fur farms; studies have charted many variants in coat colour.

The horse was probably domesticated about 5,000 years ago, and we know that over the ensuing millennia variations in coat colour appeared. The tomb of Userhat, excavated in Egypt and dated to the fifteenth century BC, featured paintings showing a chariot pulled by a chestnut and a grey.

Approximately 3 per cent of Thoroughbreds are greys and nearly all of these carry a single copy of the grey mutation. Several authorities on the origins of the Thoroughbred, including Lady Wentworth, have suggested that all grey Thoroughbreds can be traced back to a single horse, Alcock's Arabian, supposed to have been born in 1700. However, the story is somewhat confused, and, as mentioned earlier, in those days the name of a horse was changed as the horse changed ownership, almost as a matter of routine. Alcock's Arabian may be represented in the *General Stud Book* by eleven or twelve different names (see overleaf). It cannot be stated definitively that the grey gene in the Thoroughbred population has a single origin, but we have enough evidence to assume that this is the case.

> **Possible Alternative Names for Alcock's Arabian**
> The Suffolk Arabian
> Akaster Arabian or Turk and Ancaster Arabian
> Brownlow Turk
> Dorchester Turk
> Pelham Arabian
> Honeywood's Arabian
> Turner's White Arabian
> Williamson's White Arabian or Turk
> Holderness Turk
> Duke of Beaufort's Grey Arabian
> Duke of Beaufort's White Arabian

Traditional accounts of the origins of the Thoroughbred horse have long concentrated on three stallions – the Byerley Turk, the Darley Arabian and the Godolphin Arabian – as the male founders of the breed, but the facts conflict with the myth. Those three were the only founding stallions to have established male lines that have survived, but numerous other horses were major contributors to the evolving breed, most notably the Curwen Bay Barb, whose male line quickly petered out, but who is estimated to be the source of 6 per cent of the genes in the twenty-first century Thoroughbred. However, Alcock's Arabian, whose own male line delivered one Derby winner – the non-grey Aimwell in 1785 – before it disappeared is much the more conspicuous influence on the breed of our era, simply by virtue of his being the ancestor of every grey Thoroughbred.

Grey coat colour in horses is an interesting trait, in that individuals are generally born coloured, progressively turn grey and, granted sufficient longevity, frequently become white. Foals destined to turn grey frequently show an eye ring of light-coloured hairs soon after birth, but evince no other signs that their coat colour will undergo such a dramatic change, usually within a year. We believe that a normal function of the gene involved is to transport pigment from the hair follicles into the hair shaft. In grey horses this transport is disrupted, such that pigment fails to get into the hair, resulting in grey/white hairs being produced. The mutation may also have a negative effect: in later life many grey horses acquire melanomas, skin tumours that are usually benign, that may result from the disruption to the normal transport of pigment caused by the grey mutation.

Grey coat colour is inherited as a dominant Mendelian trait; the possession of a single copy of the grey mutation results in an individual having grey hair. Individuals with two identical copies of a gene are called **homozygous** for that gene, while individuals with copies of a gene that differ in some way are referred to as **heterozygous**.

Heterozygous grey stallions, with a single copy of the grey mutation, will pass the grey gene to half of their offspring on average, and if mated to non-grey mares, on average half of the foals produced will be grey (see diagram overleaf). In a mating when sire and dam are both heterozygous greys, three-quarters of their offspring, on average, will be grey, and only one in four on average will not receive a copy of the grey gene. Of the three grey horses produced, one would be expected to be homozygous for the grey mutation, meaning that this horse has inherited two copies of the grey gene.

Homozygous greys have the same appearance as heterozygous greys, but appear to turn white more rapidly than horses with a single copy of the grey mutation. There is also a significant difference when they are used for breeding. A homozygous grey can produce only grey offspring, however he or she is mated. Two copies of the grey gene in a parent ensure that greyness is expressed, as all offspring will inherit at least one copy. A notable present-day example of a Thoroughbred stallion with two copies of the grey gene mutation is Linamix, champion sire in France in both 1998 and 2004.

It is relatively straightforward to trace the grey gene through pedigrees, as every grey horse must have had at least one grey parent from whom the coat colour was inherited. In the case of a homozygous grey, such as Linamix, the grey gene is inherited from both sire and dam. The passage of Linamix's grey genes through his pedigree is presented in the diagram on page 109. Both Linamix's sire, Mendez, and his dam, Lunadix, were grey.

When we trace the grey genes for Mendez and Lunadix we find that both of Mendez's parents were also grey, so the grey gene goes back down both sides of his pedigree, via Bellypha to his dam Belga, and through Miss Carina to her sire Caro. Extending the pedigrees of Belga and Caro, we find that their greyness has descended from their common ancestor, the celebrated stallion, The Tetrarch, who was foaled in 1911.

On Lunadix's side we see something similar; her grand-dam Mona being the product of grey parents, Abernant and Social Gulf, who both

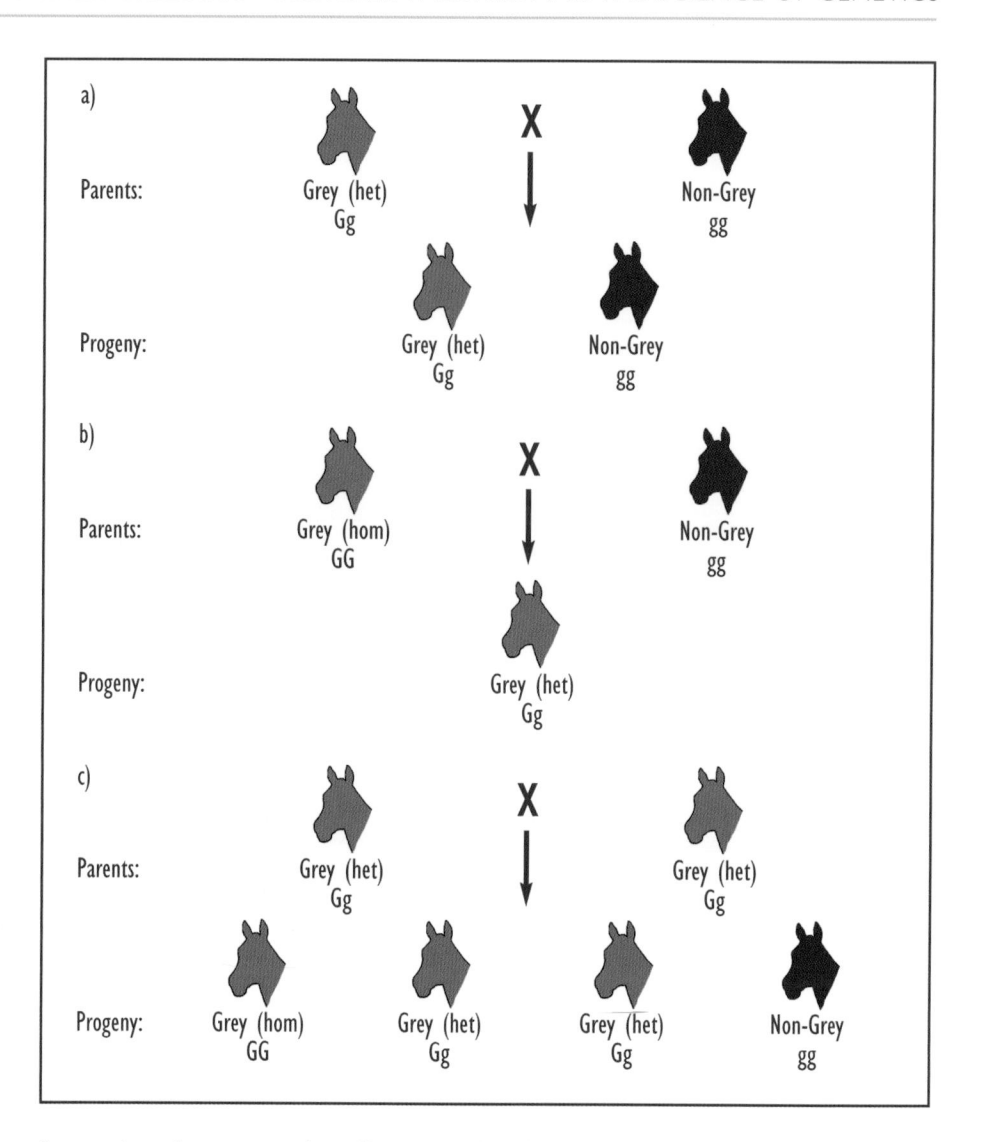

Segregation of grey coat colour. Grey coat colour is a dominant trait, such that the presence of a single copy of the gene with the grey mutation results in a grey coat colour.

a) A horse with a single copy of the grey mutation (i.e. heterozygous Gg) is mated to a non-grey horse. Half of the eggs or sperm produced by a heterozygous grey horse contain the grey mutation and so when mated to non-grey individuals half the progeny will be grey and half will be non-grey.

b) A horse with two copies of the grey mutation (i.e. homozygous GG) is mated to a non-grey horse. All the eggs or sperm produced by a homozygous grey horse contain the grey mutation, so that all the offspring will be grey.

c) When two horses with a single copy of the grey mutation are mated together, on average only one out of four offspring will not receive a copy of the grey mutation and so be non-grey. Of the three grey offspring shown, one has two copies of the grey mutation, whilst two have a single copy.

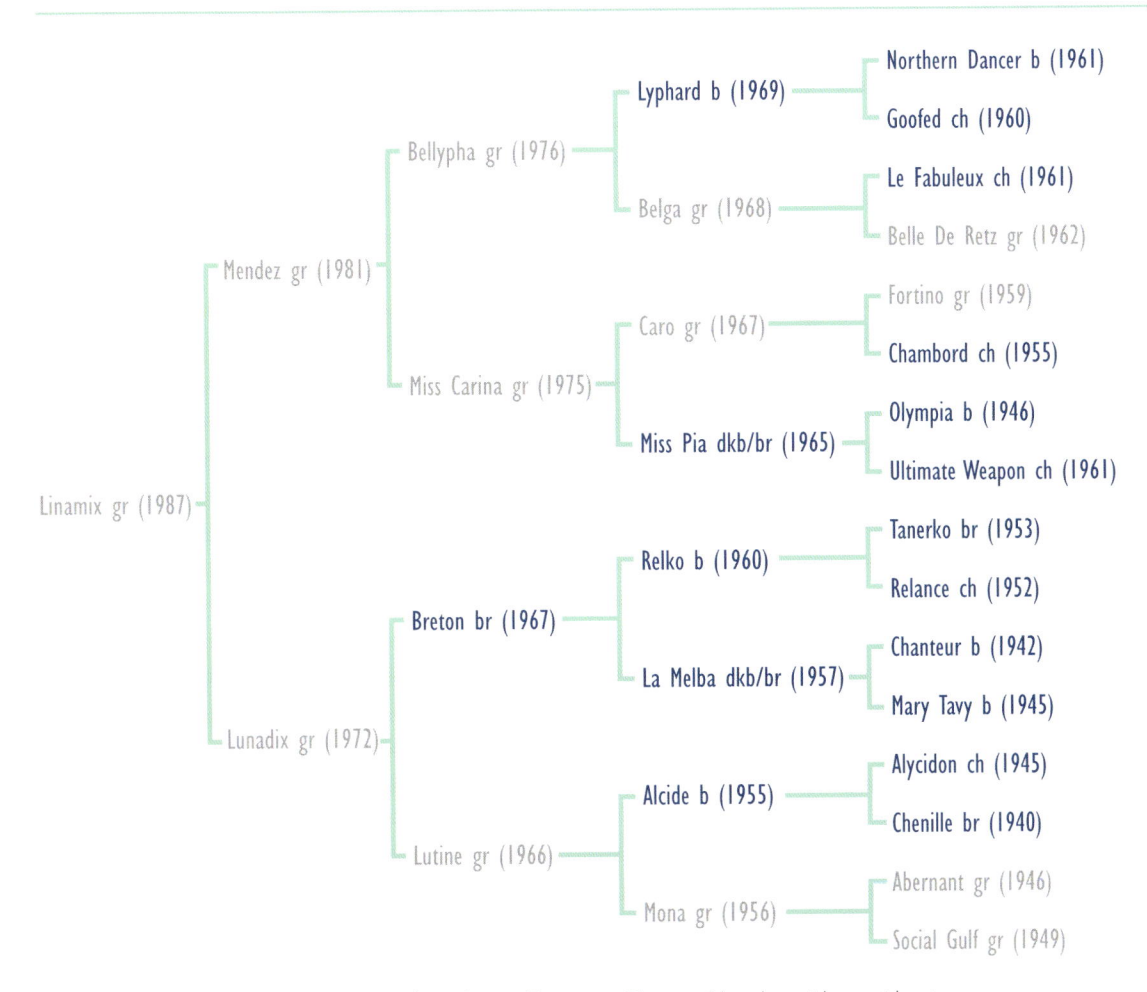

```
                                                ┌─ Northern Dancer b (1961)
                              ┌─ Lyphard b (1969) ─┤
                              │                   └─ Goofed ch (1960)
               ┌─ Bellypha gr (1976) ─┤
               │              │                 ┌─ Le Fabuleux ch (1961)
               │              └─ Belga gr (1968) ─┤
               │                                └─ Belle De Retz gr (1962)
 ┌─ Mendez gr (1981) ─┤
 │             │                                ┌─ Fortino gr (1959)
 │             │              ┌─ Caro gr (1967) ─┤
 │             │              │                 └─ Chambord ch (1955)
 │             └─ Miss Carina gr (1975) ─┤
 │                            │                     ┌─ Olympia b (1946)
 │                            └─ Miss Pia dkb/br (1965) ─┤
Linamix gr (1987) ─┤                                    └─ Ultimate Weapon ch (1961)
 │                                              ┌─ Tanerko br (1953)
 │                            ┌─ Relko b (1960) ─┤
 │                            │                 └─ Relance ch (1952)
 │             ┌─ Breton br (1967) ─┤
 │             │              │                    ┌─ Chanteur b (1942)
 │             │              └─ La Melba dkb/br (1957) ─┤
 │             │                                   └─ Mary Tavy b (1945)
 └─ Lunadix gr (1972) ─┤
               │                                ┌─ Alycidon ch (1945)
               │              ┌─ Alcide b (1955) ─┤
               │              │                 └─ Chenille br (1940)
               └─ Lutine gr (1966) ─┤
                              │                 ┌─ Abernant gr (1946)
                              └─ Mona gr (1956) ─┤
                                                └─ Social Gulf gr (1949)
```

Tracing the grey gene through Linamix's pedigree. Every grey Thoroughbred must have at least one grey parent from which is inherited the grey mutation. It is usually fairly easy to follow the path of the grey mutation through a pedigree as, in most cases, only one parent was grey and therefore the source of the mutation. In the case of an individual like Linamix, who has two copies of the grey mutation, both parents must have been grey and each passed a copy of their grey mutation to him. Linamix's sire, Mendez was also sired by two grey parents so that it becomes impossible to know whether the grey mutation he passed to Linamix traced through his sire, Bellypha or his dam, Miss Carina.

derived their coat colour from The Tetrarch. The precise route that the grey genes took *en route* to Linamix cannot be determined, because both Mendez and Mona had two grey parents, but we can be sure that Linamix derived both of his copies from The Tetrarch. There were ten generations and exactly 100 years between the birth of The Tetrarch and that of Master Robert, the Irish-bred horse now believed to be the most recently foaled ancestor of every Thoroughbred in the world today. The third dam of

Grey Thoroughbreds were comparatively rare when The Tetrarch (left), an unbeaten, exceptionally fast two-year-old, retired to stud in Ireland in 1915. The prevalence of greys in the twenty-first century is largely attributable to the influence of the so-called 'Spotted Wonder', much of it through his celebrated daughter Mumtaz Mahal (right).

Master Robert was Bab, herself the product of two greys, each a descendant of Alcock's Arabian.

Thus we see that the colour of a modern grey Thoroughbred is the result of the expression of a sequence of DNA introduced into the population in about 1700. Indeed, grey coat colour is one of the more easily grasped examples of a common truth – that nearly all of the characteristics of today's Thoroughbreds trace back to DNA sequences captured by the breed's founders.

Looking at pedigrees like this, as the transmission of blocks of DNA by the founders through generations, allows us to see other interesting features. One salient point is that there are twenty-six generations between Alcock's Arabian and Linamix over a period of some 287 years. The generation interval through that period is therefore about ten years per generation.

As the number of ancestors doubles with each generation, simple arithmetic would indicate that Linamix has upwards of 134,000,000 ancestors in those twenty-six generations, which might suggest that the odds against a single gene making its way from 1700 through to the early twenty-first century were astronomical. However, the apparent paradox is readily explained. Today's Thoroughbred population is estimated at 500,000, having grown from foundation stock of perhaps a hundred. No present-day horse has individual ancestors numbered in seven figures; early influential horses feature literally thousands of times at different points in every current pedigree.

This difference between the increasing number of ancestors of an individual horse looking back, and the increasing number of individuals in the Thoroughbred population from the foundation of the breed, is illustrated in the graph below. Tracking the grey gene through Linamix's pedigree provides an appropriate example. The Tetrarch, and therefore all of his

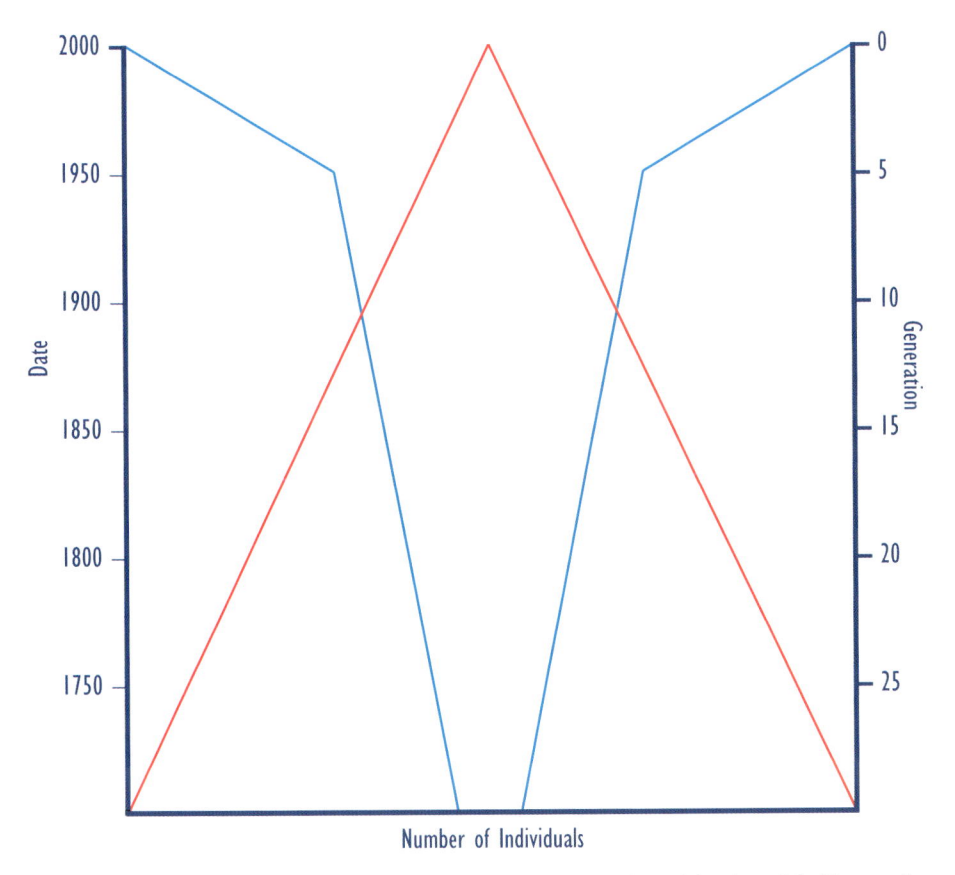

Population structure in Thoroughbreds. In blue, is a representation of the size of the Thoroughbred population through history (not drawn to scale), showing that, from a small number of individuals founding the breed in the 1700s, the breed slowly expanded until about the 1950s when a much larger expansion in the number of Thoroughbreds took place. In red, is shown the exponential increase in the number of ancestors in an individual's pedigree as we move back through the generations. The number of ancestors quickly exceeds the number of different individuals present in the whole Thoroughbred population, leading to an inevitable repetition of certain ancestors in pedigrees.

ancestors, appears at four positions in the pedigree following the possible routes of inheritance of the grey gene. Although their births were separated by only seventy-six years, The Tetrarch appears sixteen times in Linamix's pedigree, seven times on his sire's side and nine times on his dam's side. Interestingly, St Simon, who was foaled in 1881 and was Britain's champion sire on nine occasions, appears 164 times within the first twelve generations in Linamix's pedigree – and a similar number of times in the pedigrees of most current Thoroughbreds, good, bad and indifferent, reflecting both his influence as a sire and the relatively small population size at the time. The graph below shows the number of Thoroughbreds registered in the UK since the 1840s, illustrating the rapid expansion in production since the 1950s.

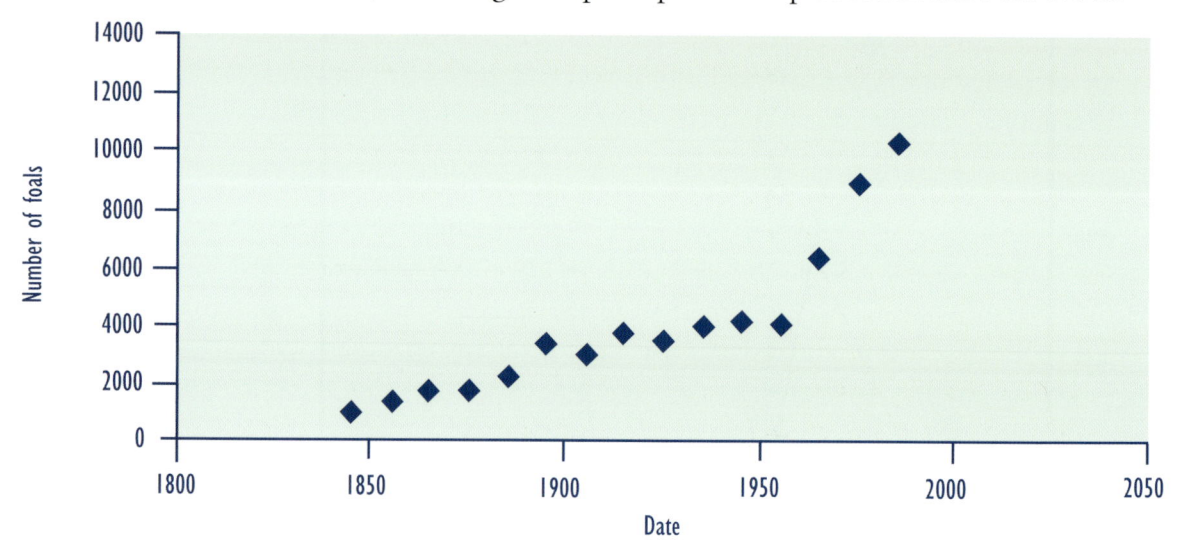

Number of Thoroughbreds registered in the UK since the 1840s.

A Thoroughbred without any duplications in the first nine generations of his pedigree – assuming that such a horse existed, which is not the case – would have a total of 1,022 ancestors to that degree. Linamix is typical of the current breed with his tally of 583 different individual ancestors.

The grey gene in Thoroughbreds has been genetically mapped to horse chromosome 25 (ECA25), in one of the first examples of trait mapping in the horse. The approach used involved testing a set of markers selected from the genetic map of the horse on a set of blood samples from the stallion Paris House, an English-based heterozygous grey, carrying one copy of the grey mutation that he inherited from his grey sire, Petong, and one copy of the non-grey gene that he inherited from his non-grey dam,

Foudroyer. Blood samples were collected from about forty of Paris House's offspring, roughly half of whom were grey and half of whom were non-grey. Samples were also collected from some of the mares in the pedigree.

The genetic markers that proved useful were those that were heterozygous in Paris House, i.e. those which had different forms on his two chromosomes. In essence, the experiment involved searching for a marker where one of the forms was passed more frequently than 50:50 to his grey offspring while the other form was passed preferentially to his non-grey offspring. About 180 markers were used, an average of about six markers on each chromosome. For one marker, nineteen of twenty-one grey offspring inherited one form, while seventeen of twenty non-grey horses inherited the other form. This type of distribution is expected for a marker close to the gene under study, whereas for a marker not closely linked to the gene it is expected that the distribution of marker forms would be random, and roughly half of the grey offspring would have inherited one form of the marker, while the other grey offspring inherited the other form. Having identified a marker on ECA25 that appeared to be closely linked to the grey gene, other markers along this chromosome were tested and also demonstrated linkage to the grey gene.

The reason why all twenty-one grey offspring did not inherit one form of the marker and that all twenty non-grey offspring did not inherit the other form is a consequence of the process called recombination which, as described earlier, takes place in the parents during the formation of sperm and eggs. Recombination is another mechanism, together with the independent segregation of chromosomes, which ensures that combinations of genes are shuffled over generations to generate new combinations. These can then be subjected to natural or artificial selection. In this case, the marker linked to the grey gene was far enough from the gene that two of the twenty-one grey, and three of the twenty non-grey offspring had undergone a recombination, uncoupling the form of the marker linked to grey in Paris House. The further a marker is from a particular gene, the more frequently it will be uncoupled by recombination; in fact, genetic maps use units of distance that relate to this recombination frequency.

When Alcock's Arabian contributed the chromosome containing the grey mutation to three of his grey offspring (identified as Alcock Arabian Mare 2, Crab and Jackson's Favourite), it may have been passed intact or it could have undergone a cross-over with his non-grey chromosome at any point along its length. Over the twenty-six or so generations that the grey gene has been passed down via his son Crab (the only one of Alcock's Arabian's offspring to contribute grey offspring to the present population), many recombinations have taken place.

The extent of DNA around the grey gene that is shared by all the current Thoroughbred horses tested was recently found to be about one million base pairs of ECA 25. This region is likely to contain at least ten genes, based on the average mammalian gene density. So, a grey Thoroughbred today expresses not only the grey gene from Alcock's Arabian, but also another ten or so genes that are likely to have been inherited in a block over the 300-odd years separating the horses.

We can also use grey coat colour to demonstrate the use of genetic markers to select a population with desired characteristics. If one wanted to produce a population of true-breeding grey Thoroughbred horses using traditional selection it would take a long time. Essentially, it would be necessary to identify a set of homozygous grey stallions and mares. The initial stages would involve mating two grey individuals which, given the frequency of the grey mutation, both appear likely to be heterozygous for the grey gene. As was noted before, a mating between two heterozygous greys will on average produce three greys and one non-grey, and only one of the three greys is likely to be homozygous. So the process slows down, because the way to identify the homozygous greys is to mate them to non-greys to check that they produce all greys. While this could be achieved in a single season for a stallion, it would take several years to establish that a grey mare was homozygous, as five or six grey offspring (all of whom would be heterozygous because the mating involved non-grey partners) would need to be produced before there was a reasonable certainty that the mare was homozygous for the grey mutation.

In contrast, using genetic markers linked to the grey gene, it is possible to identify which of the grey offspring produced are homozygous and which are heterozygous within a few days of birth. This means that we could select for a true breeding collection of grey Thoroughbreds in a relatively short time, and without the inefficiency of producing unwanted (non-grey) progeny. The technique using genetic markers is called marker-assisted selection, and it has been widely used in farm animals to increase the efficiency of selection for breeding stock with increased meat and milk yields. Its application to the selection of desired traits in the Thoroughbred has the potential for a significant impact on the industry and the breed.

CHAPTER 16
COAT COLOUR II – MENDEL AND BEYOND

There are wide ranges of coat colours and patterns found in different horse breeds, but the range is far more limited in the Thoroughbred. Stud Book authorities include coat colour in the registration process, and while they do not all apply the same definitions, the colours recorded are generally limited to bay, brown, chesnut, grey and black. (The American Jockey Club adopts the vague designations 'dark bay or brown' and 'grey or roan', while Germany employs more precise definitions for shades of the basic colours.) This chapter uses the genetics of coat colours and markings apart from grey to illustrate the basic principles of Mendelian and complex genetic inheritance and to describe concepts of population genetics using the Hardy-Weinberg equation (see also Appendix).

BAY AND CHESNUT COAT COLOURS

The historical origins of the colour varieties displayed by the different breeds of domestic horse are not known, although increasingly we are coming to understand the genes and the mutations that produce these colours. In the Thoroughbred, three basic coat colours predominate; bay, chesnut and grey. There is, however, variation within these three basic coat colours: Thoroughbreds with chesnut coats, for example, are sometimes sub-classified into golden, red and liver chesnuts. There is also a wide range in the body colour and extent of dark hairs on bay Thoroughbreds, leading to the bay/dark bay/brown/black coat complex of coat colours. (In addition, grey horses of similar ages may vary greatly in their shade of grey, and also as to whether dark dapples or white blotches are present.) The three basic Thoroughbred coat colours involve mutations and interactions in only three different genes, the extension locus (E), the agouti locus (A) and the grey locus (G).

In mammals, the pigments responsible for coat colour are synthesised in cells called melanocytes that are produced early in development in the backbone region, and then migrate to populate the skin and hair follicles. Two basic types of pigment exist: eumelanin, which produces black or brown colour, and pheomelanin, responsible for chesnut (red) coat colours. The bay and chesnut coat colours are under the control of a single genetic locus, called extension, which, in Thoroughbreds, exists in two alternative forms symbolised by the letters *E* and *e*. The *E* form of the gene produces bay markings and is dominant to the recessive form of the gene, *e*, which produces chesnut colouring when inherited from both parents. Geneticists call the different forms of the same gene **alleles**. It should be noted that, while there are only two colour types, bay and chesnut, there are three different possible genotypes, *EE*, *Ee* and *ee*. The genotypes *EE* and *Ee* both produce bay horses because the E form of the gene is dominant.

When considering the likely colour of the progeny of a mating, it is useful to consider which allele of the gene the individual is capable of putting into their sperm or eggs. For an individual who is homozygous (i.e. either *EE* or *ee*), their sperm or eggs can contain only one allele of the gene. For heterozygous individuals (i.e. *Ee*), half their sperm or eggs will contain the dominant *E* form and half will contain the recessive *e* form.

Among current Thoroughbreds, about a quarter of the population has chesnut coats, and is therefore homozygous (*ee*) for the recessive *e* allele. About 3 per cent of Thoroughbreds are grey, with the remaining 72 per cent being bay-type horses (*EE or Ee*). The proportions of offspring with particular coat colours that are produced from matings between parents of different genotypes are shown in the diagram opposite. It is possible to estimate what proportion of bay horses in the Thoroughbred population are homozygous (*EE*) and what proportion are heterozygous (*Ee*) using the Hardy-Weinberg equation. Interested readers will find the worked example of this calculation in the Appendix.

The mutation responsible for chesnut coat colour in horses was identified within the melanocyte-stimulating hormone receptor (*MC1R*) gene, a gene involved in hair colour variants in other species. Mutations in *MC1R* produce red and yellow coats in Irish Setters and Labrador Retrievers respectively, and ginger hair in humans. In horses, a single nucleotide base change causes an amino acid change in a key part of the *MC1R* molecule, illustrating how a simple, single nucleotide base change in a genome of about three billion nucleotide bases can determine whether a horse is bay or chesnut.

COAT COLOUR II – MENDEL AND BEYOND 117

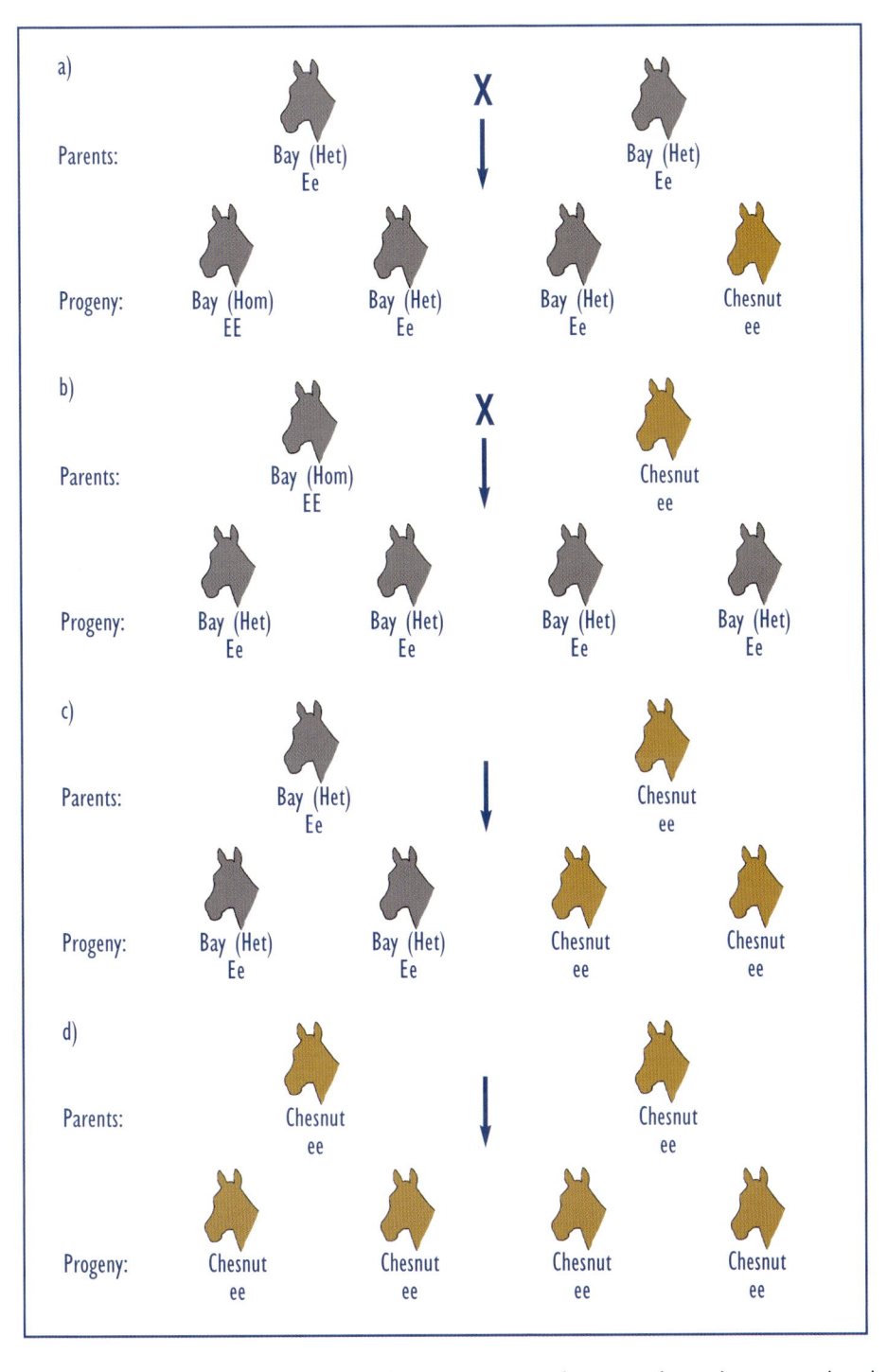

a)
Parents: Bay (Het) Ee X Bay (Het) Ee

Progeny: Bay (Hom) EE | Bay (Het) Ee | Bay (Het) Ee | Chesnut ee

b)
Parents: Bay (Hom) EE X Chesnut ee

Progeny: Bay (Het) Ee | Bay (Het) Ee | Bay (Het) Ee | Bay (Het) Ee

c)
Parents: Bay (Het) Ee X Chesnut ee

Progeny: Bay (Het) Ee | Bay (Het) Ee | Chesnut ee | Chesnut ee

d)
Parents: Chesnut ee X Chesnut ee

Progeny: Chesnut ee | Chesnut ee | Chesnut ee | Chesnut ee

Diagram to show the proportions of offspring with particular coat colours that are produced from matings between parents of different genotypes – in this example, chestnut/bay segregation.

Hyperion, the outstanding Derby and St Leger winner of 1933 and six-time champion sire, was a chestnut son of bay parents Gainsborough and Selene. He was an example of a seemingly odd, but common, phenomenon, easily understood when the workings of coat-colour inheritance are recognised.

Apart from a very slight bias against chesnut horses among some horsemen, who associate this colour with poor temperament, there has been little selection for coat colour in the Thoroughbred. Several studies have concluded that there is no association between coat colour and performance in Thoroughbred horses.

BLACK, WHITE AND ROAN

True black coat colour is rare in Thoroughbreds, one example being the Australian stallion, Lonhro, who is actually registered as black/brown. The black colour is seen only in the presence of the E allele, discussed in the bay/chesnut section above, and represents the distribution throughout the body of the black pigment normally restricted to the mane, tail and ear regions in bay horses. Black pigment distribution in the other regions of the body is controlled by a gene called the agouti gene, which has a similar function in other mammals. The dominant form of the gene, *A*, restricts the distribution of pigment and it is the recessive allele, *a*, which when present in the homozygous *aa* state produces the uniformly black horse. It appears likely that interactions between the agouti gene and the extension gene produce the range of bay/dark bay/brown/black coat colours seen in Thoroughbreds. Different coat colours may result from the different genotype combinations for these two genes (EE,AA/EE,Aa/EE,aa/Ee,AA/EeAa/Ee,aa) and additional genes that modify the intensity and distribution of the colour pigments may also exist. Very rarely, white Thoroughbreds have been accepted for registration into stud books. These exceptional individuals, which are not albino, have a dominant mutation, and most of the few tens of white Thoroughbred horses that have been registered in the past fifty years trace to a couple of individuals, for example the French-bred Mont Blanc, within whom the mutation probably arose spontaneously. These white Thoroughbreds, who are born white, should not be confused with older 'white' Thoroughbreds, i.e. grey horses who have progressively lost pigment such that they end up *looking* white.

Roan coat colour results from a mixture of white and coloured and other hairs and there is debate about whether true roans exist in the Thoroughbred population. A true roan horse does not get whiter with age,

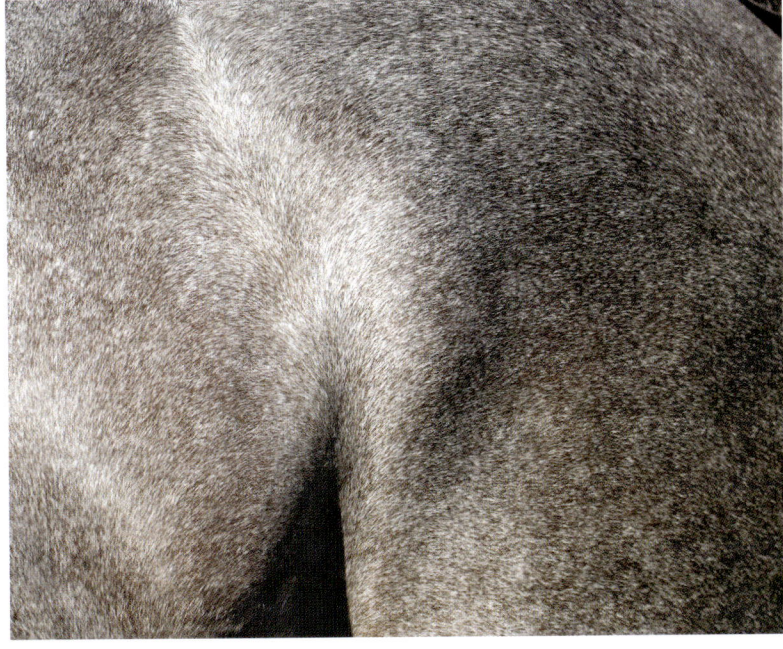

Roan coat colour.

but retains the solid base colour about head and legs throughout his lifetime. Thoroughbreds described as roan, such as the 1980 Kentucky Derby winner, Winning Colors, are invariably really grey horses who are homozygous for the chesnut mutation; the progressive greying produces an appearance of roan as the coat colour of an individual becomes de-pigmented with time. True roan coat colour in other breeds of horses has been associated with a gene called *KIT,* which is involved in coat colour variants in many other mammalian species. In other breeds the roan trait is inherited as a dominant trait, with the dominant form of the gene given the *RN* symbol, while the recessive non-roan form is given the designation *rn*.

EPISTASIS – THE INTERACTIONS BETWEEN GENES

The genetics of coat colours also offers a useful system for understanding gene series. In addition to the existence of dominant and recessive alleles of one particular gene, there can be complex interactions between the alleles of different genes. For example, if a horse has a single copy of the grey mutation it does not matter whether he is homozygous or heterozygous for the dominant bay allele, *E* – he will be grey. This illustrates that different genes may themselves be in a series of dominance relationships, with in this case the grey gene mutation 'trumping' the other colour gene mutations. The interaction between the alleles of different genes is called **epistasis**.

WHITE SOCKS, STARS, STRIPES AND SNIPS

A large proportion of Thoroughbred horses have white markings on their legs or faces and these are useful features for identifying individuals on their passports. While the inheritance of bay/chesnut and grey coat colours follows the simple rules derived from Mendel, the patterns of inheritance for white markings are considerably more complex.

As mentioned earlier, solid coat colour results from the production of pigments by specialised cells called melanocytes. Parts of the coat that are white represent areas of the skin that the melanocytes failed to reach. While genetic factors are involved, there is also an element of chance, as the migration and survival of these cells has a random component. This is best illustrated by comparing the patterns of white markings on the two identical twin mares in the photograph opposite. These two identical twins,

The two identical twins in this photograph (produced by embryo splitting) share exactly the same genetic make-up, yet one has four white socks and the other only three; the white facial markings are also significantly different.

produced by embryo splitting, share exactly the same genetic make-up, yet one has four white socks and the other only three; the white facial markings are also significantly different. Another way to think about this phenomenon is to consider that in a horse with one, two or three white legs, all four legs have the same genetic information in their cells, even though the legs are different colours.

The *KIT* gene, mentioned earlier in relation to roan coat colour, may also be involved in white face and leg markings in the Franches-Montagnes and potentially other horse breeds, including the Thoroughbred. The extent of the markings is likely to be modified by several other genes, called 'spotting' genes. White markings are therefore an example of complex genetic inheritance, where the action of several genes, together with environmental influences, interacts to give the patterns observed. The relative proportion of genetic and environmental contributions to the variation in the trait is described by the heritability of the trait. Values of heritability range between 0 and 1, with 0 representing no genetic contribution and 1 indicating that the trait is entirely under genetic control.

In studies in Arab horses, the heritability of white facial and leg markings was estimated independently, and both were found to be about 0.69, suggesting that about two-thirds of the variation in white markings resulted from the actions of genes. The same study also reported that there is a correlation between the extent of white facial markings and the presence of white leg markings, and that the extent of white markings is also influenced by the sex of the horse and the number of chesnut, *e*, alleles present.

Chesnut horses had more extensive white markings than bay horses and heterozygous bay horses with an *Ee* genotype had more markings than homozygous bays, *EE*. Male horses on average have more white markings than female horses, which suggests that one of the genes involved in white markings may be located on the X chromosome. More white markings are found on the hind legs than on the forelegs, and more markings are present on the left side than on the right side. During embryonic development, the melanocytes migrate down the left and right sides of the body independently and it is obvious that the migration path to the limb buds for the forelegs is different from that for the hind legs. The different frequencies of white markings on different legs probably reflect different rates of melanocyte survival during their migration in the early stages of embryo development, and are thus not under direct genetic control.

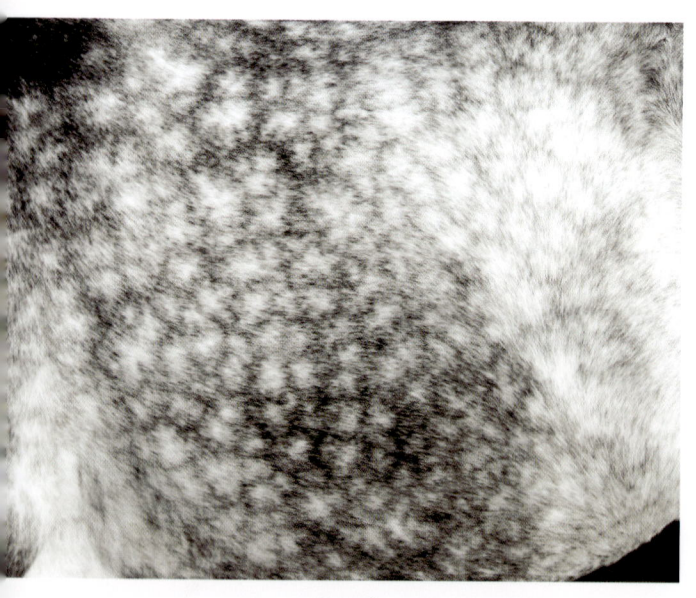

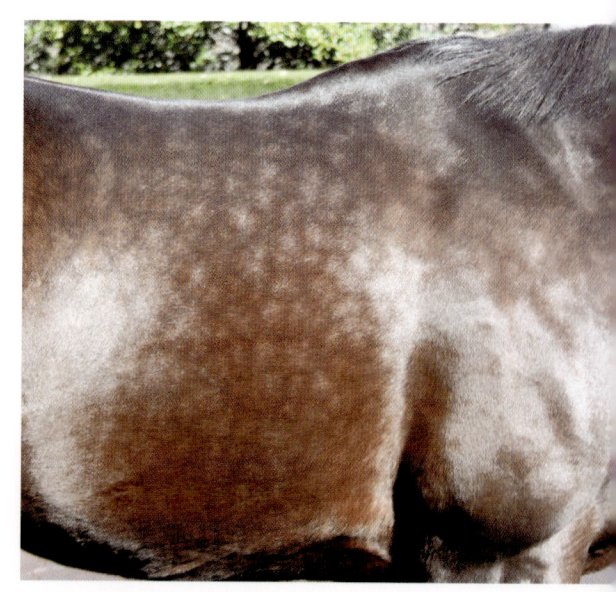

Dappling on grey and bay coats.

With a complex system such as this, two solid-colour parents can, on occasion, produce offspring with extensive white markings, while parents with white markings might sometimes produce a solid-coloured foal. In general, parents with markings will produce more foals with markings than would solid-coloured parents, but there is enough variation that it is difficult to predict the outcome of any particular mating.

One other sort of marking that is more subtle than the white markings just described is the dappling that is commonly seen in grey and bay horses (see photographs opposite). The genetic control of this patterning is not understood and would represent a good subject for future studies.

This chapter and the previous one have described the inheritance of recessive, dominant and complex traits using Thoroughbred coat colours and markings as easily appreciated characteristics. The same genetic rules apply to the inheritance of all the other traits of interest in Thoroughbred horses. Most of the more interesting traits, such as racing ability, are complex traits, and further description of polygenic inheritance (that involving interactions between multiple genes) is given in Chapter 20.

CHAPTER 17

BRUCE LOWE FAMILIES AND THE ROLE OF MITOCHONDRIA

The work of Bruce Lowe (and modern interpretations of it) still exercises a powerful influence on the thinking of some breeders and equine scientists despite the fact that his theories were attacked almost as soon as they were published in 1895. Although Lowe's work came after the discovery by microscopy of structures in the cytoplasm called mitochondria, it was not until relatively recently that a link was made between the two.

In the 1980s, scientists discovered that mitochondrial DNA was inherited maternally, that is, males and females both inherit their mitochondrial DNA from their mothers, but males cannot transmit their mitochondria to subsequent generations. Mitochondrial DNA acts as a female 'surname' and therefore follows the same pattern through a pedigree as the Bruce Lowe family number. This path through a pedigree is shown in the diagram opposite and is the tail-female line for each individual, i.e. the bottom line on a typical pedigree. Mitochondrial DNA is the only genetic material that follows the tail-female pattern of inheritance. X chromosomes are passed by males to their daughters, and the path of X chromosomes through pedigree is complex. In relation to mitochondrial DNA there is no blending of different types within the pedigree and an individual always inherits mitochondrial DNA from the mother.

The essence of Bruce Lowe's theory was that the tail-female descendants of some of the forty-three foundation mares he identified had been more successful than stock from other foundation mares in winning the English Derby, Oaks and St Leger races. The foundation mare and her descendants with the most winning descendants of these races were given

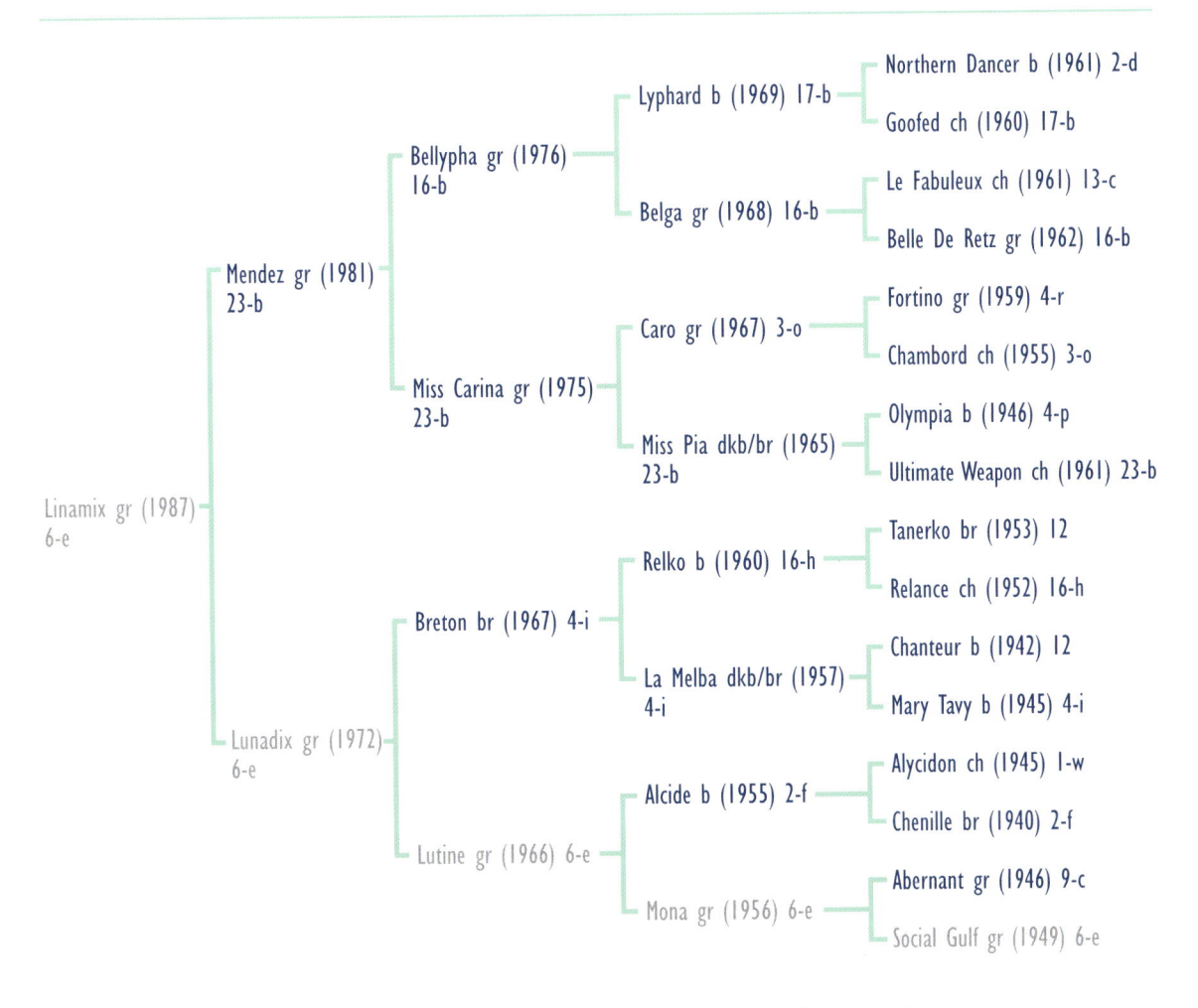

```
                                                      ┌─ Northern Dancer b (1961) 2-d
                              ┌─ Lyphard b (1969) 17-b ┤
             ┌─ Bellypha gr (1976)                     └─ Goofed ch (1960) 17-b
             │  16-b                                   ┌─ Le Fabuleux ch (1961) 13-c
             │          └─ Belga gr (1968) 16-b ───────┤
┌─ Mendez gr (1981)                                    └─ Belle De Retz gr (1962) 16-b
│  23-b                                   ┌─ Fortino gr (1959) 4-r
│            │          ┌─ Caro gr (1967) 3-o ────────┤
│            │          │                             └─ Chambord ch (1955) 3-o
│            └─ Miss Carina gr (1975)                 ┌─ Olympia b (1946) 4-p
│               23-b    └─ Miss Pia dkb/br (1965) ────┤
│                          23-b                       └─ Ultimate Weapon ch (1961) 23-b
Linamix gr (1987)
6-e                                       ┌─ Tanerko br (1953) 12
│                       ┌─ Relko b (1960) 16-h ───────┤
│            ┌─ Breton br (1967) 4-i                  └─ Relance ch (1952) 16-h
│            │          │                             ┌─ Chanteur b (1942) 12
│            │          └─ La Melba dkb/br (1957) ────┤
│            │             4-i                        └─ Mary Tavy b (1945) 4-i
└─ Lunadix gr (1972)
   6-e                                    ┌─ Alycidon ch (1945) 1-w
             │          ┌─ Alcide b (1955) 2-f ───────┤
             │          │                             └─ Chenille br (1940) 2-f
             └─ Lutine gr (1966) 6-e                  ┌─ Abernant gr (1946) 9-c
                        └─ Mona gr (1956) 6-e ────────┤
                                                      └─ Social Gulf gr (1949) 6-e
```

The mitochondrial path in a pedigree (that of Linamix) – tail-female line. Linamix is a member of Lowe's family in the branch designated 6-e by Bobinski. The family numbers of other individuals in the pedigree are listed so that the tail-female line inheritance can be followed.

the family number 1, with the rest classified according to the number of successes of their families.

In the graph of the results overleaf, updated to include the winners of the races in 2005, it can be seen that family 1 still dominates the Classic races, with the distribution of the other families still correlating reasonably well with Lowe's original assignment more than a hundred years after it was originally made. The findings are deceptively simple. It may seem clear that the route to breeding a Classic-winning Thoroughbred should start with a mare from one of the low family numbers, but Joe Estes, former editor of the *Blood-Horse* magazine, was one of many to note that the Lowe family numbers correlated closely with opportunity. If the total number of horses

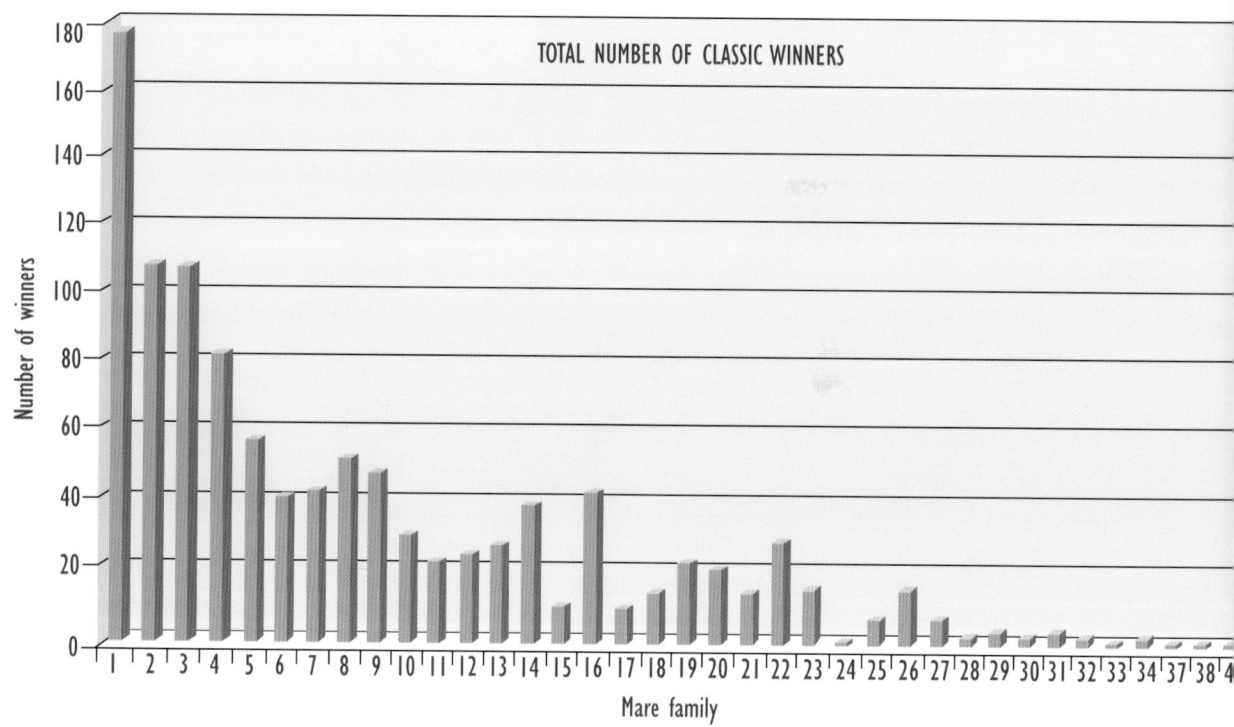

The Lowe family winners graph.

in the Thoroughbred population as a whole is plotted according to their Lowe family numbers, the graph looks similar to that of the Classic-winning individuals. The Lowe family 1 has produced more Classic winners than any other because it has most representatives and therefore most opportunity.

Despite this convincing explanation of Lowe's observations as a case of opportunity, science continues to tempt an allegiance to his basic theory, perhaps because the mitochondria are the 'energy factories' of the cell. Differences in mitochondrial function would be an obvious place to look for enhanced performance, and several inherited diseases in man which result in impaired physical ability map to mitochondrial DNA. Several thousand of these mitochondrial energy factories are found in each cell in the body. The structure of mitochondria is extremely complex, being made up of many hundreds of proteins coded for by hundreds of genes, the vast majority of which are present on the normal chromosomes, but not in mitochondrial DNA.

The mitochondrial DNA, a small circle of DNA that codes for a total of only thirty-seven genes, contributes fewer than ten proteins to the functioning mitochondria. It is possible that differences in mitochondria contribute to the differing abilities of Thoroughbred horses, and it is possible – though the odds are against it – that those differences could involve the few genes actually present on the mitochondrial DNA. It is clear, however, that there is no magic recipe for breeding success present on the mitochondrial DNA, as in each founding mare family there is the full range of good, bad, indifferent and plain useless racehorses in approximately the same proportion. In summary, while there is no evidence for positive factors coded by mitochondrial DNA, even if they were present they represent a small proportion of the multitude of factors needed to produce a superior racehorse.

Scientists have recently put Thoroughbred mitochondrial DNA to another use, in trying to understand more about the history and foundations of the Thoroughbred breed. Their approach is based on work in other species, including man, where mitochondrial DNA has been used to unravel the early origins and movement of human populations. In a popular book, *The Seven Daughters of Eve*, Brian Sykes traces man's (or, more accurately, woman's) early migration from the initial human origins in Africa. Researchers were able to answer such questions as the origins of the human populations who initially settled the American and Australian continents. The key to the use of mitochondrial DNA to unravel such questions resides in the high mutation rate of a particular section of the molecule. By examining a large number of mitochondrial sequences from current populations it is possible to reconstruct the order in which mutations occurred and thus the relationships between individuals within the different groups. Two populations who share very similar DNA sequences will be more closely related than two populations with vastly different sequences.

Emmeline Hill and her colleagues in Ireland used this approach to examine the mitochondrial sequences of 100 current Thoroughbreds that traced back to nineteen of Bruce Lowe's most common founder-mares. Individuals tracing back to the same founder-mare should share identical, or near-identical, mitochondrial sequences as the DNA passed unchanged down the thirty or so generations that separate the present from the origins of the breed. In those 300 years it is possible that one or two mutations might have occurred, but if two individuals, whose pedigrees both trace back to the same founder-mare, have vastly different mitochondrial DNA sequences, it is evident that an error exists somewhere in the pedigree.

The origins of the *General Stud Book* were described in Chapter 4, and it will be remembered that the first volume was a retrospective exercise in which the compiler sought to give identity to many horses from an earlier era when records of breeding activity tended to be kept haphazardly, if at all. The work's ethos was to substitute order for chaos, but it was impossible, despite best intentions, to verify accounts of many matings that had taken place eighty or ninety years earlier, and it was inevitable that errors would occur. In truth, the accuracy of the pedigree record can really be trusted only for the past thirty or so years, when parentage verification by blood-typing has been used. Innocent errors caused by foals swapping mares on a stud farm or mistaken double coverings could have led to incorrect pedigrees which then became fixed in the official records.

The results obtained by the Irish researchers were fascinating and have provided material for much discussion amongst pedigree enthusiasts. Of the nineteen mare lines from which they examined more than one individual they found that eight contained evidence for more than one mitochondrial DNA type, suggesting that there were multiple inconsistencies in the *General Stud Book*. Intriguingly, they were able to identify the approximate date of some of these errors by examining the pedigrees of the individuals within the different lineages and identifying the points at which they shared common tail-female ancestors. The findings indicated that several of the anomalies, such as those in families 5 and 6, were very deep-rooted and must have involved a mistaken individual in the 1700s, while other anomalies were more recent, occurring in the last two centuries. Examples of the pedigree trees based on the new knowledge are presented in the diagram opposite.

Another interesting outcome of this analysis was that several of the founding mare lines were themselves closely related; for example, six of the families (2, 7, 8, 16, 17 and 22) essentially shared the same founding mitochondrial DNA sequences, indicating that they were derived from a common maternal ancestor. Similarly, the mares at the head of families 4, 11 and 13 also appeared to derive from a single common founder, and this was perhaps not surprising, given that the three were all owned by James D'arcy and kept at the same stud at about the same time. In fact, it is possible that some of these newly discovered relationships in the founding mares could have been caused by the confusion over horses' names and involve the same individual mare under different names.

The data also showed that certain founder-mare lines that were

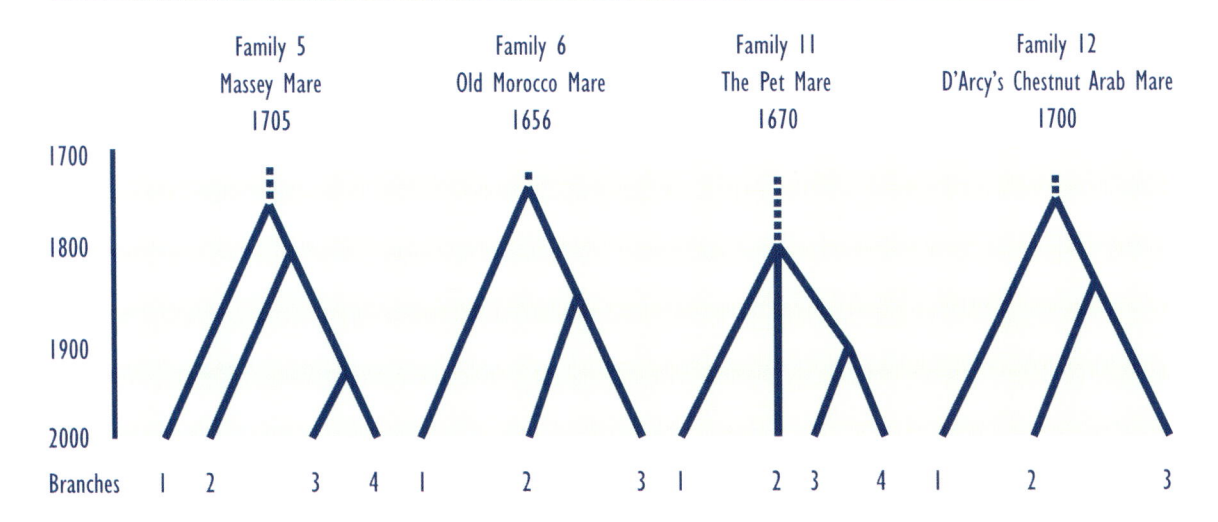

Family 5	Family 6	Family 11	Family 12
Massey Mare	Old Morocco Mare	The Pet Mare	D'Arcy's Chestnut Arab Mare
1705	1656	1670	1700

Mitochondrial family trees. Recent research has thrown up a number of anomalies in the General Stud Book.

supposedly related, according to historical records, were in fact distinct, as their mitochondrial DNA differed extensively. The researchers concluded that as few as twelve founders may have contributed to the nineteen families they examined. Interestingly, descendants of the founder of family 19, Davill's Woodcock Mare, who was at stud in Yorkshire in the 1730s, possess mitochondrial DNA that is less closely related to the other Thoroughbred mitochondrial types characterised so far.

As mentioned earlier, it was possible for researchers studying the origin of human populations to identify the geographical origins of the native populations of the Americas and Australia from mitochondrial DNA sequences. The Irish researchers examined their data to determine whether they could learn more about the geographical or breed origins of the mares that founded the Thoroughbred breed. Unfortunately, in contrast to most other domesticated farm species and man, the identification of any geographical or breed signature for mitochondrial DNA sequences in horses proved difficult. Current theories of horse domestication propose that mares were domesticated from wild horses in many places and at many different times through history and, with the high mobility that horses provided and their value as items of trade or spoils of war, it is perhaps not surprising that there has been extensive mixing of different mitochondrial types within different breeds and geographical regions.

Although the mitochondrial studies have so far failed to tell us more about the geographical or breed origins of the female stock which founded the Thoroughbred horse, the research conducted has opened a window on the early history of the breed. Further ongoing research is examining additional mare lines, and it is to be expected that some of these will also be found to contain anomalies, showing that a number are related to existing DNA types and reflect a common ancestry. By carefully selecting individuals whose tail-female pedigrees meet within the time-frame during which anomalies occurred, it should be possible to identify the discrepancies in the *General Stud Book* more precisely. Similarly, examination of American lines should make it possible to re-establish the concordance between the American family numbers and those of the English founding mares.

The improved knowledge of the relationships between mitochondrial DNA sequences and founder-mare lines will also be useful to researchers working with old bones from famous Thoroughbreds, as it will provide one level of authentication that the material they are working with is, indeed, from an individual who has the correct mitochondrial DNA pedigree.

One consequence of the recent research is that it might be used by some to re-justify their belief in the basic Bruce Lowe concept. If a significant proportion of Thoroughbreds are not from the founding mare lines to which they are attributed, how can it be certain that the opportunity argument used against it is still valid? Once more data has accumulated and we understand the positions of the anomalies in the *General Stud Book* better, it will become possible to reassign all the Classic winners to their corrected maternal families and relate this to the relative proportions of current and historic individuals within these families. Given that the experience of most breeders is that the same mare can produce good, mediocre or poor progeny despite transmitting the same mitochondrial DNA type, it would be surprising if any future analysis were to refute the view that Joe Estes formed in the 1930s.

CHAPTER 18
BIG HEARTS, THE X FACTOR AND TORTOISESHELL CATS

The racing population inevitably encompasses Thoroughbreds of widely different abilities, and there may be a multitude of reasons to account for the super-athleticism of a Secretariat and the total ineptitude of the beast who cannot get out of his own way.

BIG HEARTS

When we consider what physiological factors might be responsible for such a huge difference in racing ability, it is logical that we look first at the efficiency of the heart, the organ required to pump large volumes of blood. The haemoglobin molecules in the blood's red cells carry oxygen to tissues such as the muscles, providing an important component of the fuel needed to drive energy production. Because equine muscles have an energetic capacity that is far greater than the ability of the cardiovascular system to deliver oxygen to them, the amount of blood that can be pumped around the body during exercise is necessarily one of the limiting factors in the capacity of the muscles to sustain energy production.

While the Thoroughbred can modulate his heart rate between 20 to 240 beats per minute, heart rate does not appear to respond to training, so that heart volume is important in determining the aerobic capacity of individuals, and the significance of heart size is likely to be greater over longer distances. A Thoroughbred with a small heart might be capable of being a good sprinter over 5 or 6 furlongs, as he could run this distance anaerobically, using oxygen already stored in the blood at the beginning of the race. However, longer distances bring a heavy demand for oxygen transport from the atmosphere to the muscles, and the importance of having a large, efficient heart will become apparent.

The correlation of large hearts with superior athletic performance is supported by evidence derived from autopsies performed on a number of famous Thoroughbreds. The first such example was that of the unbeaten Eclipse (1764-89), an important sire, and a pillar of the breed whose name appears many times over in all of today's pedigrees. As a result of his remarkable ability, Eclipse was subjected to a full autopsy on his death in an attempt to learn the secrets of his success. The autopsy was conducted and published by Charles Vial de St Bel, who subsequently helped to found the Royal Veterinary College in London. The skeleton of Eclipse on which St Bel worked is now displayed in a building named after the horse at the Hawkshead campus of the Royal Veterinary College. It is reported that Eclipse's heart weighed 14lb, which is considerably bigger than the 6lb average heart weight for Thoroughbreds during Eclipse's era.

Of course, it should be borne in mind that the racecourse test for the Thoroughbred of Eclipse's era was very different from that of our own; it was even different from that of the time when many of his progeny raced. Eclipse did not have his first run until he was 5 years old, when he distanced his four opponents in the second of two 4-mile heats at Epsom. Although officially credited with eighteen victories in all, such was his exalted reputation that he had only to 'walk over' to claim eight of the prizes. However, of the ten races that were contested, seven were run in heats, so he actually faced competition on seventeen occasions and finished first every time. The shortest distance he was required to cover in a single heat was 2 miles, and in three of his races run in 4-mile heats he had to carry 12st.

Was Eclipse's large heart a significant factor in his ability to stay long distances under huge weights? Perhaps it just made him superior *per se*. Within a few years of Eclipse's retirement to stud, the English racing schedule placed more emphasis on earlier maturity and shorter distances; many of his sons and daughters excelled over a mile and 12 furlongs as 3-year-olds.

Another notable example of a large-hearted Thoroughbred was the great New Zealand-bred gelding, Phar Lap (1926-1932), whose record of thirty-seven wins from fifty-one starts included a Melbourne Cup in which he carried the burden of 9st 12lb to an impressive victory by 3 lengths. His performance in that 2-mile race is routinely cited as the best of his career, but Phar Lap was undeniably a top-class racehorse at all distances from 7 furlongs up. After his mysterious death in California, which followed hard on his victory in the Agua Caliente Handicap in New Mexico, autopsy revealed that Phar Lap's heart weighed nearly 14lb, compared with an average for the breed at that time of 9lb. It is now preserved as an exhibit in the Australian National Museum in Canberra.

A more recent example of a Thoroughbred with an exceptionally large heart is Secretariat (1970-1989), who won sixteen of his twenty-one starts, including the US Triple Crown. Though by a sire – Bold Ruler – whose stock were more noted for speed than stamina, Secretariat won the Belmont Stakes (12 furlongs) in record time by the astonishing margin of 31 lengths. As he has been widely regarded as the best horse ever to run in America, it is natural that there should be curiosity as to what might have accounted for his exceptional brilliance. Autopsy disclosed that Secretariat's heart weighed a massive 22lb. While it would be unwise to suggest that this one factor was all-important, it would also be folly to ignore a recognisable advantage expressed to such a remarkable degree.

It should, of course, be noted that the autopsies on Eclipse, Phar Lap and Secretariat were all conducted when they were fully mature horses; they do not tell us the size of their hearts when they were actually racing. However, it is surely not unreasonable to surmise that they were well above average size when they achieved their fame as athletes.

The examples of Eclipse, Phar Lap and Secretariat all suggest that the possession of a large heart may be an important factor in determining athletic performance, but we should note that indifferent and bad racehorses are not usually the subjects of intensive examination when they die. We must expect there to be variation within the Thoroughbred population, and no doubt there are big-hearted specimens incapable of winning a humble claiming race.

However, one interesting study has noted that Thoroughbreds have larger hearts, measured as a proportion of their weight, than other less athletic breeds of horses. It also reported a similar effect when greyhounds were compared to other pedigree dog breeds, supporting the idea that the size of the heart has responded to selective breeding for athleticism in both the Thoroughbred and the greyhound.

Heart size can be estimated in the living horse using an electrocardiogram machine to determine heart scores, and the development of portable equipment has resulted in pre-purchase echocardiography examinations becoming common, at least at the principal yearling sales. Experience has persuaded a number of buyers of youngstock that heart scores provide valuable information, though they have to accept that the heart is still growing and the measurements they obtain provide only an approximation of the size of the heart when the horse reaches racing age.

Several studies have examined the relationship between heart score and performance ability in Thoroughbred horses. In an early study, Irish researchers found a correlation between heart scores and *Timeform* scores for 3-year-olds, though the same correlation was not seen for 2-year-olds. In a more recent study, published in 2005, scientists in Newmarket found that left ventricular size (the size of the chamber of the heart responsible for pumping oxygenated blood to the whole body) was larger in horses involved in jump racing than in those competing over shorter distances on the Flat. The authors suggested that the differences in heart shape and size resulted largely from the heart adapting to the endurance requirements of different racing and training regimes. Interestingly, a stronger correlation between heart size and performance rating was seen for the jumping horses compared to the horses competing in Flat racing, which probably reflects the increased benefits of greater oxygen transport in the endurance events. In older Flat racehorses, the correlation between left ventricular mass and performance rating was improved when the volumes of blood ejected by the left ventricle were included. In the latter case, the heart function measurements were found to account for 25-35 per cent of the overall variation in performance.

However, we must continue to stress that, according to our present knowledge, there is unlikely to be one single factor that can identify the élite Thoroughbred, and that proviso includes heart size. Indeed, several very successful Thoroughbreds are known to have had below-average heart sizes, while many individuals with large hearts have been poor racehorses. A large heart is probably a useful attribute in races beyond sprint distances, but it cannot determine success on its own.

THE X FACTOR

The role of the heart in Thoroughbred performance has been emphasised – perhaps unduly – in two recent books by American theorist Marianna Haun, *The X Factor* and *Understanding the Power of the X Factor*, in which she proposes that a gene controlling heart size in the Thoroughbred is inherited on the X chromosome. Some of the popular online Thoroughbred pedigree websites include the option to track the X factor in the pedigrees and also distinguish between single copy and double copy mares, depending on whether the mare has one or two copies of what Ms Haun identifies as 'the large heart gene'.

The theoretical basis on which the gene controlling heart size is assigned to the X chromosome is obscure. As previously mentioned, it is to be expected that any single gene mutation having a major effect on racing performance would have been highly selected during 300 years of Thoroughbred breeding. It is likely that, at this stage of the breed's development, all horses would have the mutation if it was so advantageous. The corollary of this is that we would predict that the genetic component of the variation in racing ability that is still present in the breed is probably going to involve a large number of different genes, each of which has a comparatively small effect on its own. It is open to question, therefore, whether a simple single gene mutation causing large hearts in the Thoroughbred breed exists. If such a gene does exist, it is not clear on the evidence presented that it is located on the X chromosome.

The X chromosome is one of the longest chromosomes in mammals and carries about 1,000 genes in humans. The gene content is well conserved between different mammalian species, so we can reasonably expect that it will contain a similar set of genes in horses. The X and the Y chromosomes are called the sex chromosomes, with males and females having different combinations of these chromosomes. Males have an X and a Y chromosome, while females have two copies of the X chromosome. Sex determination in mammals is initiated by a gene on the Y chromosome called the *sry* gene, which in turn switches on a cascade of other genes that code for the differences between males and females. The majority of these other genes are not encoded on the Y chromosome, and so are also present in females, though they remain inactive because they have not been activated by *sry*. The diagram overleaf shows the inheritance of the sex chromosomes. Eggs produced by a mare contain one of her two X chromosomes, half having one of the copies while the others have the alternative X chromosome. In contrast, males have an X chromosome and a Y chromosome. Half of the sperm produced by a stallion will contain the X chromosome, while the other half contains the Y chromosome. When a sperm containing the Y chromosome fertilises an egg, the resulting progeny will be male, while sperm containing the X chromosome will generate female offspring. In this way, approximately equal numbers of males and females are produced.

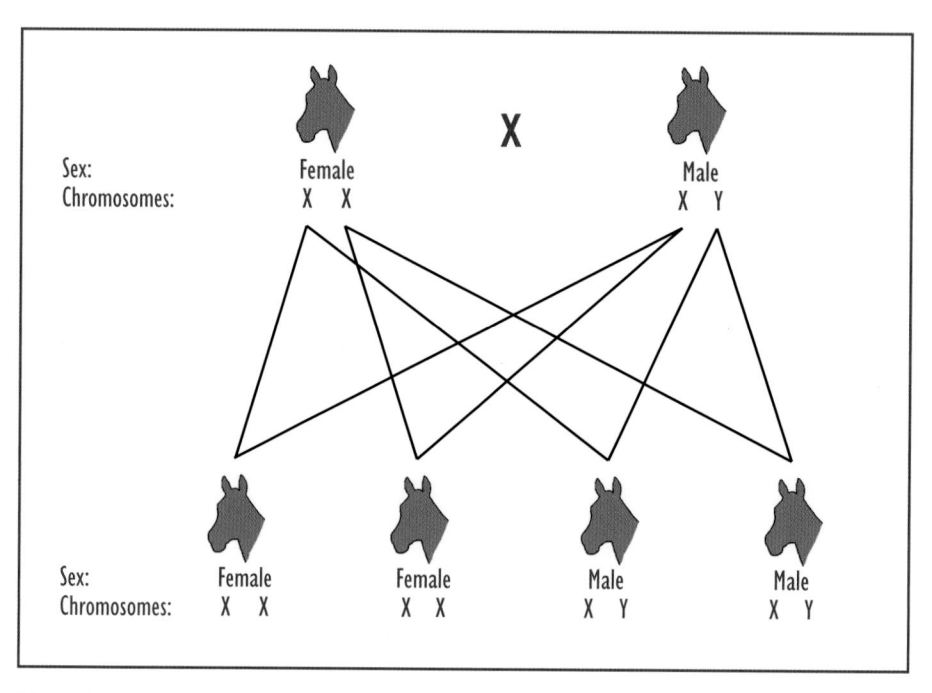

The inheritance of sex chromosomes – sex determination. The possession of a Y chromosome determines maleness.

When examining an extended pedigree, it is possible to trace the origin of the Y chromosome in any particular horse by following the tail-male line back to the origins of the breed. The path of the Y chromosome in a pedigree is shown in the diagram of Montjeu's pedigree opposite. As mentioned earlier, all present-day male Thoroughbreds trace back to one of the three foundation sires, the Byerley Turk, the Darley Arabian, or the Godolphin Arabian. The Darley Arabian male line is now dominant, as about 95 per cent of current Thoroughbreds trace back to him, while very few males descend directly from the Godolphin Arabian.

In contrast to the simple path that the Y chromosome takes through a pedigree, until recently it was not possible to follow the path of Thoroughbred X chromosomes through pedigrees with any certainty. It is clear that a stallion will transmit his single X chromosome to all his female offspring, and that none of his male offspring will acquire his X chromosome. The presence of two copies of the X chromosome in mares, each of which is passed on to her offspring at an equal frequency, ensures that it is not possible to follow the individual X chromosomes through the pedigree.

Given that, as stated above, the inheritance of sex chromosomes is common to all mammals, we can resort to man for an appropriate and

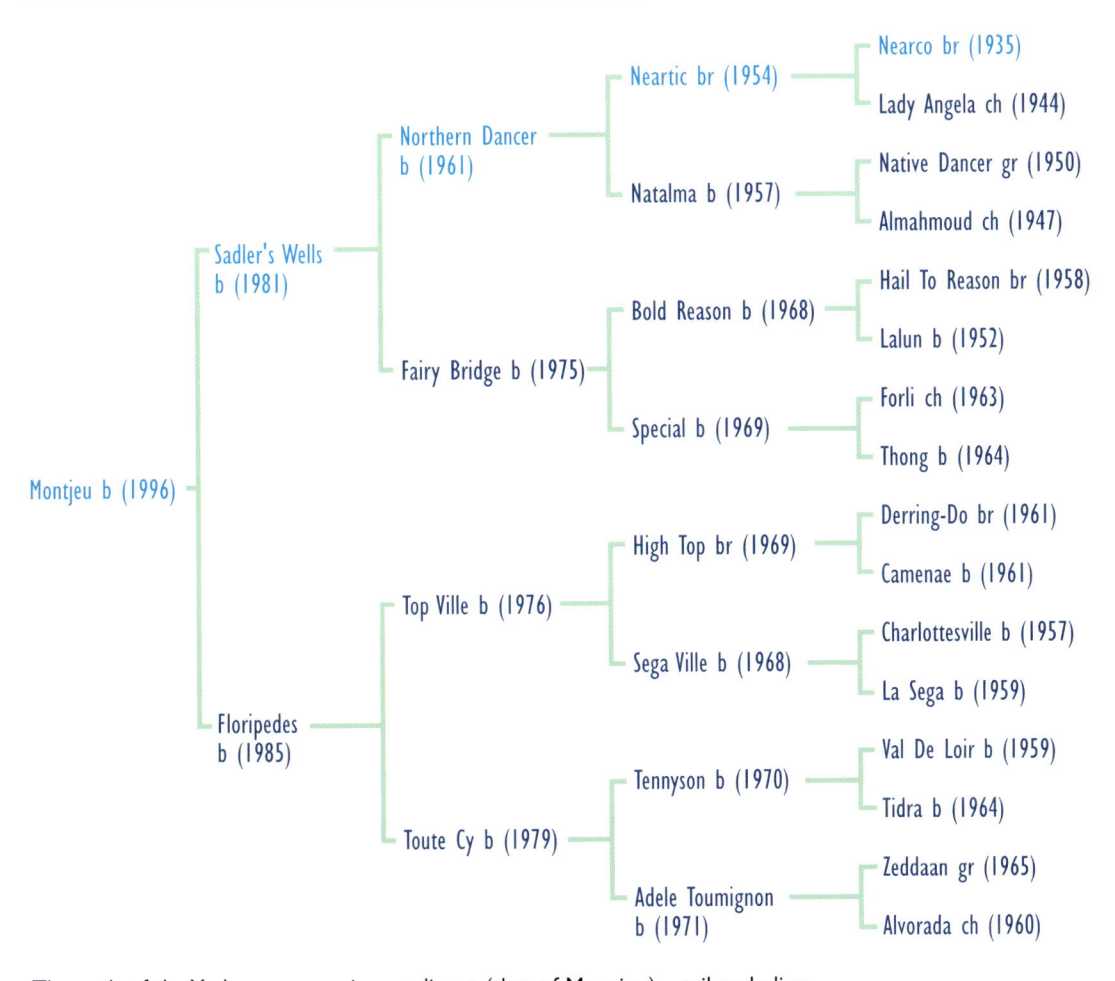

```
Montjeu b (1996)
├─ Sadler's Wells b (1981)
│  ├─ Northern Dancer b (1961)
│  │  ├─ Nearctic br (1954)
│  │  │  ├─ Nearco br (1935)
│  │  │  └─ Lady Angela ch (1944)
│  │  └─ Natalma b (1957)
│  │     ├─ Native Dancer gr (1950)
│  │     └─ Almahmoud ch (1947)
│  └─ Fairy Bridge b (1975)
│     ├─ Bold Reason b (1968)
│     │  ├─ Hail To Reason br (1958)
│     │  └─ Lalun b (1952)
│     └─ Special b (1969)
│        ├─ Forli ch (1963)
│        └─ Thong b (1964)
└─ Floripedes b (1985)
   ├─ Top Ville b (1976)
   │  ├─ High Top br (1969)
   │  │  ├─ Derring-Do br (1961)
   │  │  └─ Camenae b (1961)
   │  └─ Sega Ville b (1968)
   │     ├─ Charlottesville b (1957)
   │     └─ La Sega b (1959)
   └─ Toute Cy b (1979)
      ├─ Tennyson b (1970)
      │  ├─ Val De Loir b (1959)
      │  └─ Tidra b (1964)
      └─ Adele Toumignon b (1971)
         ├─ Zeddaan gr (1965)
         └─ Alvorada ch (1960)
```

The path of the Y chromosome in a pedigree (that of Montjeu) – tail-male line.

immediately comprehensible example. The first of the two diagrams overleaf illustrates the inheritance of haemophilia (basically, a tendency to prolonged bleeding from even minor injuries) in Queen Victoria's family. This is an X-linked disease which clearly reveals the unpredictable nature of X chromosome inheritance. Queen Victoria had a single copy of a mutation in one of the genes on the X chromosome that are involved in blood-clotting. The non-mutated copy of the gene ensured that the Queen did not herself have haemophilia. It was impossible to tell whether her daughters had inherited the good or the bad copy of the haemophilia gene until they had an affected son. It is often incorrectly stated that the X chromosome, like the mitochondrial DNA discussed in the previous chapter, follows the tail-female line. Reverting to the equine world for an example, the second accompany-

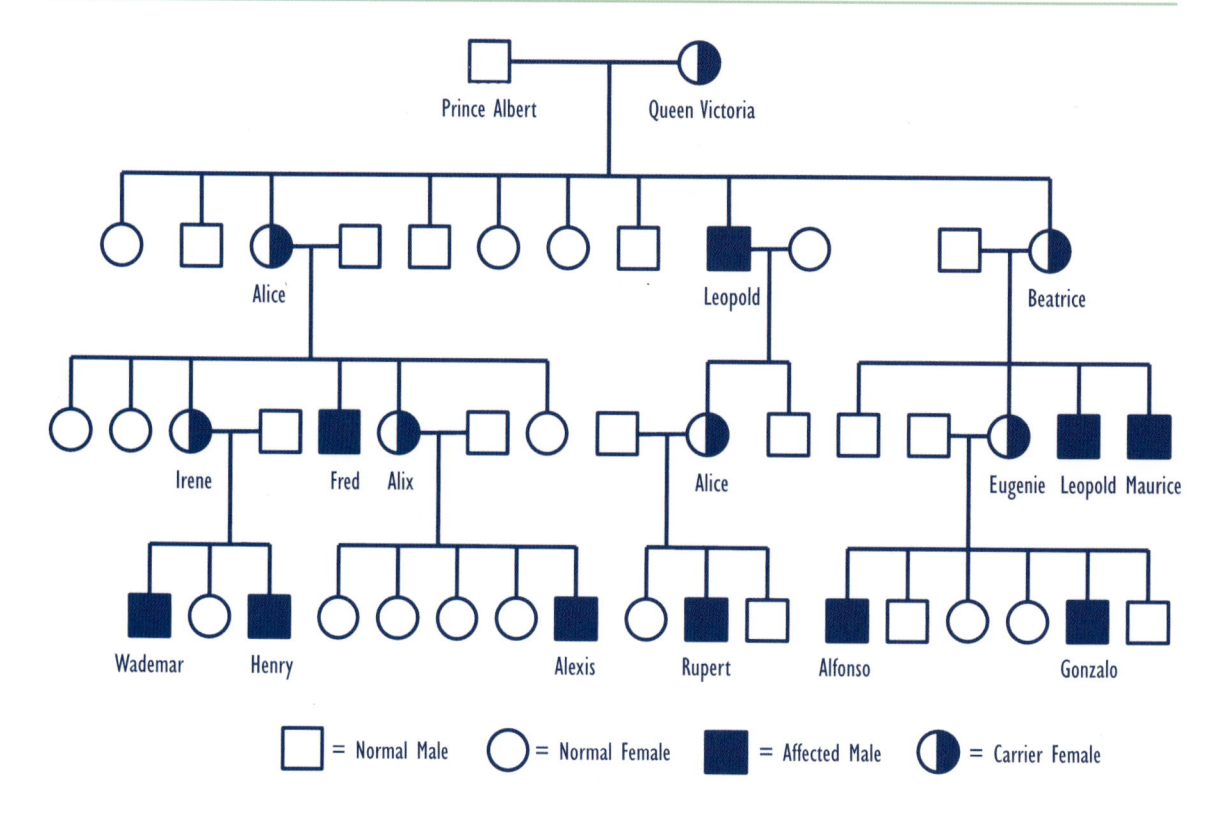

THOROUGHBRED BREEDING – PEDIGREE THEORIES AND THE SCIENCE OF GENETICS

The inheritance of haemophilia in Queen Victoria's family. It was not possible to know which of Queen Victoria's daughters were carriers of the haemophilia mutation until they produced affected sons.

ing diagram opposite illustrates that this is not the case and that the individual being examined could have received his X chromosome(s) from several ancestors in the pedigree. However, the recent discovery of genetic markers on the horse's X chromosome now makes it possible to distinguish between different Thoroughbred X chromosomes and to follow their inheritance through pedigrees in the future.

In the *X Factor* theory of large hearts, there appears to be a circular argument operating, in that the inheritance of a particular X chromosome is deduced by the presence of a high heart score, which it in turn encodes. The situation becomes even more complicated because the genes on the X chromosome have a unique feature in relation to the way in which they are expressed within cells. For genes not present on the X or Y sex chromosomes, each cell, regardless of whether it is present in a male or female, contains two copies. In contrast, for genes on the X chromosome, cells from males will contain single copies of the X chromosome genes, while those from females will have two copies of the X chromosome genes. The amount of protein produced from each gene in a cell is carefully controlled, and too much protein can be just as harmful as too little.

The familiar characteristics of Down's syndrome in man result from the presence of three copies of chromosome 21. The extra set of genes from the third copy of that chromosome leads to over-expression of these genes, with the resulting problems of mental retardation. It might be anticipated that when half the population (females) have two copies of a particular set of genes and the other half (males) have only one set, that it might result in biological problems similar to that seen in Down's syndrome. In fact, an

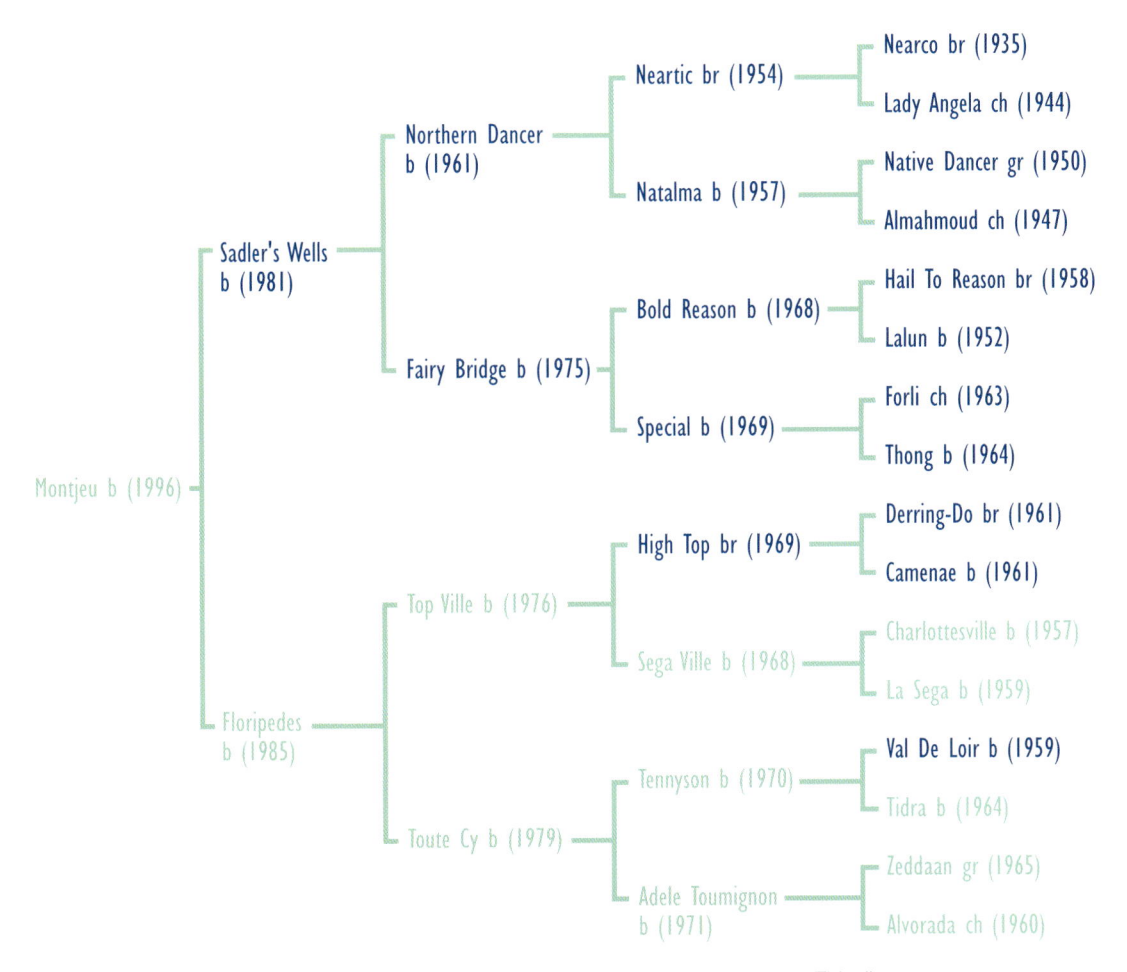

Montjeu b (1996)
├─ Sadler's Wells b (1981)
│ ├─ Northern Dancer b (1961)
│ │ ├─ Neartic br (1954)
│ │ │ ├─ Nearco br (1935)
│ │ │ └─ Lady Angela ch (1944)
│ │ └─ Natalma b (1957)
│ │   ├─ Native Dancer gr (1950)
│ │   └─ Almahmoud ch (1947)
│ └─ Fairy Bridge b (1975)
│   ├─ Bold Reason b (1968)
│   │ ├─ Hail To Reason br (1958)
│   │ └─ Lalun b (1952)
│   └─ Special b (1969)
│   ├─ Forli ch (1963)
│   └─ Thong b (1964)
└─ Floripedes b (1985)
   ├─ Top Ville b (1976)
   │ ├─ High Top br (1969)
   │ │ ├─ Derring-Do br (1961)
   │ │ └─ Camenae b (1961)
   │ └─ Sega Ville b (1968)
   │   ├─ Charlottesville b (1957)
   │   └─ La Sega b (1959)
   └─ Toute Cy b (1979)
      ├─ Tennyson b (1970)
      │ ├─ Val De Loir b (1959)
      │ └─ Tidra b (1964)
      └─ Adele Toumignon b (1971)
         ├─ Zeddaan gr (1965)
         └─ Alvorada ch (1960)

It is often incorrectly stated that the X chromosome follows the tail-female line. This diagram of Montjeu's pedigree illustrates that this is not the case and that the individual being examined could have received his/her X chromosome(s) from almost any of the ancestors in the pedigree shown coloured green.

elegant method has evolved to ensure that for most of the genes on the X chromosome there is an equivalent expression in males and females. Following fertilisation, initially both X chromosomes are expressed in female cells. However, once cell division has produced a female embryo with about 1,000 cells, one of the X chromosomes in each cell largely stops being expressed, a process called X-inactivation. From this stage on, a single X chromosome is expressed in female cells, just as happens in the male embryo from the beginning. One intriguing feature is that the choice of the X chromosome that is switched off in each of the cells is essentially random, so half of the cells express genes from one of the X chromosomes, while the remaining cells express genes from the other X.

TORTOISESHELL CATS

The consequence of this way of controlling gene dosage from the X chromosome in females is that mammalian females are genetic mosaics. The effect of this is clearly illustrated by the example of tortoiseshell cat in

Tortoiseshell cat – a genetic mosaic.

the accompanying photograph. The mutation producing red coat colour in cats is in a gene located on the X chromosome. Males that have the mutation have a solid red coat colour, as would females with the mutation on both copies of their X chromosomes. In female cats with a single copy of the mutation, the red gene is expressed in approximately half of their cells – those where the X chromosome with the red mutation is active – while in the other half of their cells the X chromosome with the mutation is inactivated and these cells will produce black hair. The patchwork pattern of red and black hairs is restricted to female cats, and is unique to an individual, reflecting the random nature of the X inactivation process.

Scientists originally thought that the expression of all genes on an X chromosome was shut down when that chromosome was inactivated, but recent results suggest that at least 15 per cent of X chromosome genes are expressed from both copies of the X chromosome.

From the above, it should be apparent that the expression of X chromosome genes is complicated and not necessarily consistent with Haun's theory which originally proposed that the large heart is coded for by an X-linked recessive gene. The possibility exists, but the facts as described above make it unlikely. The availability of genetic markers from the horse's X chromosome means that the large-heart *X Factor* hypothesis can now be tested, by examining the transmission of X chromosomes in pedigrees of Thoroughbreds that have had their heart scores estimated. It will be fascinating to see whether the inheritance of large hearts is associated with the Thoroughbred X chromosome, or whether, like most characteristics of the breed, the story is more complex.

CHAPTER 19

THE MUSCULOSKELETAL SYSTEM

Examples of physical frailty are nothing new in the Thoroughbred; even in the early days of the breed there were accounts of horses whose careers were compromised by inherited defects. However, what concerns many horsemen of our own era is a perceived increasing degree of unsoundness in the breed. It is an undoubted fact that today's runners average far fewer starts than their counterparts of even forty years ago, and while commercial factors play their part in that scenario, experienced trainers regularly complain that their charges cannot take the same amount of work as their predecessors.

The breed averages indicate that about one-third of all Thoroughbreds do not race, and the most significant reason for this high wastage rate is failure in the musculoskeletal system. The most common problems include both catastrophic and stress fractures, tendon injuries and damage to joints. On the other hand, one of the key features that identify the élite performer and separate him from his fellow is likely to be an efficient musculoskeletal system.

When inspecting youngstock with a view to purchase for racing, trainers and agents assess conformation to see whether the individual looks like a racehorse; conformation faults associated with particular stallions are recognised, indicating that a genetic component is involved and may be important. Conformation defects are liable to put undue stress on the musculoskeletal system, increasing the chance that a horse will not be able to stand the rigours of training and racing.

Many Thoroughbreds, particularly those destined for the sale-ring, undergo corrective surgical procedures early in their lives to correct conformation issues, but there is little published data to indicate whether such surgery, which takes place at an important time in skeletal development, improves or harms the long-term racing prospects of these individuals. What is known, of course, is that it frequently enhances their sale price.

The selection for speed throughout the history of the Thoroughbred has had its effect on muscle physiology, conformation and bone mineral density. This chapter examines what we know about these important components.

MUSCLE CHARACTERISTICS

One of the key physiological factors in Thoroughbred racing performance is the production of power by the muscles of the horse. The energy to provide this power can come from two sources, either aerobically using oxygen, or anaerobically using glycogen stored in the muscle fibres. The two different energy-generating processes are carried out by distinct muscle fibres, which are commonly known as slow-twitch and fast-twitch fibres. The slow-twitch fibres, also referred to as Type I, use oxygen transported to the muscle in the bloodstream. These fibres enable the muscle to keep contracting over a long period and are associated with endurance. The fibres themselves tend to be thinner than fast-twitch fibres, and muscle with a high percentage of Type I fibres tends to be slender. Human marathon runners have a very high proportion of these slow-twitch fibres, and are physically light and slender.

In contrast, the fast-twitch fibres, also called Type II, produce explosive power and speed in short time periods. These fibres tend to be more bulky, producing the heavy musculature common in human sprinters. The conformational differences between human sprinters and endurance athletes are replicated to some extent in the conformation of Thoroughbreds specialising in sprinting or middle-distance and staying races. The fast-twitch fibres are subdivided into Type IIa and Type IIb fibres: the Type IIb are the true fast-twitch fibres using glycogen exclusively, whereas the Type IIa fibres are intermediate and capable of using both glycogen and oxygen energy sources.

There are clear breed differences in the proportion of the different fibres present in an individual, which indicates some genetic control over muscle composition. For example, Quarter Horses have a high proportion of Type II fibres to enable them to run short distances quickly, while Arabs have a higher proportion of Type I fibres, which enables them to keep running over long distances. The Thoroughbred is intermediate between these two breeds, racing on the Flat between 5 furlongs and about 2 miles, distances much beyond 2 miles being quite rare. It is thought that the horse as a species originally evolved with a preponderance of fast-twitch fibres, as survival from attack by feline predators required only a short burst of high-speed running.

Thoroughbreds are all born with about 80 per cent fast-twitch fibres, though the proportions of Type IIa and Type IIb fibres are highly variable between individual horses, and are probably under genetic control. A greater proportion of Type IIb muscle fibres reflects sprinting ability. Most forms of training result in an increase in Type I and IIa fibres, producing greater stamina, often at the cost of speed. Thoroughbred sprinters do comparatively little exercise work, and it may be that this helps keep the proportion of fast-twitch fibres as high as possible.

The belief that genetic variation is involved in determining muscle type is supported by the fact that progeny will often closely mirror their parents in their optimum racing distance. There has been increasing emphasis on speed in the Thoroughbred, and in countries such as Australia, where winners over short distances are favoured by breeders as prospective stallions, those horses tend to produce top-class sprinters. Whether the increased muscle mass associated with speed places undue stress on the skeletal system which is not adapted for it, in turn leading to an increased risk of fracture, is not known.

Breeders have frequently tried to cross stayers with sprinters in the hope of generating an ideal middle-distance horse, but results have generally proved disappointing. Caro, a Group 1 performer from 1 to 1½ miles, whose parents were the pure sprinter Fortino and specialist stayer Chambord, stands out as a rare successful example of the ploy. The more usual failures may be explained by the breaking up of optimum combinations of gene variants, which enabled an individual to excel at one distance, with progeny ill-suited to any distance as the outcome.

Approximately 5 per cent of Thoroughbreds suffer from an inherited muscle condition traditionally called tying-up, which can disrupt their ability to perform. This disease, also known as recurrent exertional rhabdomyolysis, is characterised by muscle stiffness and cramping which can lead to muscle damage. It is most common in fillies with an excitable temperament and often results in lost training days.

Tying-up is one of the few genetic diseases thought to be inherited as a simple Mendelian trait in Thoroughbreds, and studies on a number of families in which the condition occurred concluded that the disease was inherited as a dominant trait, with variable expressivity. This means that not all individuals with the mutation have episodes of tying-up, possibly because an additional environmental factor, such as diet or exercise, is required to produce the condition. Alternatively, there may be additional gene variants, called minor modifiers, which need to be present for the disease to manifest itself. Several research groups are currently trying to locate the mutation responsible for tying-up. It would assist trainers in the management of their horses to know which of their horses were likely to suffer episodes of tying-up before they happened.

THE SKELETAL SYSTEM

Recent studies have found that, at any time, about one in a hundred horses in training has a fracture, and that over a period of a year, close to 10 per cent of horses in training will have a problem. The majority of these are stress fractures, which respond to rest, but the number of horses with injuries indicates that the Thoroughbred skeleton is a weak link in the physiological chain.

The forces on the forelegs when a Thoroughbred is racing at full speed are enormous, especially when one considers how fragile those legs look. Track surfaces are an important component of the stresses involved and increasing attention is paid to the condition of these surfaces, whether it is through the watering of turf tracks or the installation of artificial surfaces (Polytrack, Tapeta, ProRide etc.), with a view to reducing the number of breakdowns. Unfortunately, this is a complicated issue, as changes which reduce fractures in the forelimbs might increase soft tissue injuries in the hind legs.

There has long been intense debate about the racing of 2-year-old horses, whose skeletal development is not yet complete. Epidemiological studies found that the number of career injuries was actually reduced in horses who started racing at 2, compared to those who did not start their racing careers until they were 3. While this evidence has been used to support 2-year-old racing, it should be viewed with caution, as many of the horses who did not start racing until they were 3 had injuries that prevented them starting at 2, and so comprise a group who are 'less fit' than the group who did have a 2-year-old career.

Recent studies have found that conformation faults in the Thoroughbred have considerable evidence of heritability. In particular, back at the knee, offset knees, tied-in below the knee, weak hocks, and weak pasterns showed heritabilities ranging from 0.31–1.00. The same studies found evidence for horses with some of the conformation defects having less durability and worse performance.

Genetics is also involved in the variation seen in the normal size and shape of the skeleton. Just as height in humans is two-thirds genetic and one-third environmental, height at the withers has a similar genetic component in horses. Studies in pedigree dogs have found that the lengths of many bones vary in a co-ordinated fashion, and the same is expected in Thoroughbreds. This is no surprise when one considers that a small number of key growth factor genes are important in switching on other genes during development.

Studies in man indicate that several different genes have an effect on bone mineral density and on fracture rates, indicating that fracture is another complex trait. These 'fracture candidate genes' are being examined in the Thoroughbred and, if associations are found, veterinarians and trainers will be enabled to monitor and manage individuals with a greater susceptibility to fracture, hopefully increasing their success and improving their welfare. Several studies are also looking for the genes involved in osteochondrosis, a common developmental disease of joints characterised by the presence of fragments of articular cartilage.

TENDON ISSUES

The genetic basis of tendon problems is less clear, and such injuries are likely to have a strong environmental component. However, studies are underway to see if variation in the genes which produce the major components of equine tendon is associated with increased tendon issues.

The availability of powerful new molecular tools with which to study musculoskeletal defects should accelerate research and lead to useful diagnostic tests for a range of conditions becoming available over the next ten years.

CHAPTER 20
HERITABILITY OF ATHLETIC PERFORMANCE

Breeders have followed a number of different concepts in the development of the Thoroughbred. We can examine them now from the perspective of what happens at the genetic level, and describe the current genetic model of the difference between Thoroughbreds of widely differing athletic ability.

Several scientists have attempted to estimate the extent to which genetics influences Thoroughbred racing ability. In the early 1970s Professor Patrick Cunningham and colleagues in Ireland examined the inheritance of Thoroughbred performance in Britain by analysing the relationship between the *Timeform* ratings of about 800 3-year-old horses and those of their sires and dams. Although the results varied depending on the precise statistical methods used, they concluded that the best estimate of the genetic contribution to racing performance in the Thoroughbred is about 35 per cent. The remaining 65 per cent comprises non-genetic influences from environmental variables which include components such as nutrition, trainer and jockey, together with the age and sex of the horse. A subsequent study, also in the 1970s, looked at another group of more than 1,000 3-year-olds and obtained similar results, indicating that the estimate of about 35 per cent for the inheritance of racing performance was reasonably accurate for Thoroughbreds at that time.

The extent to which genetics contribute to a particular trait is called heritability, and values of heritability range from 0 to 1. When the heritability is 1, the trait is entirely under genetic control. For a Mendelian trait involving a single gene, like grey coat colour, there is a direct correlation between the presence of the grey gene mutation and grey coat colour. For traits with heritabilites approaching 0, there is little genetic contribution and environmental influences dominate.

Estimating the heritability of complex traits can be challenging, although some relatively simple methods exist. For example, Francis Galton (1822-1911), one of the pioneers in genetics, set out to examine the extent to which genetics controlled many human traits. He plotted a graph of the height of individuals against the mean height of their parents in order to estimate the heritability of adult human height. The slope of the best fit line on the graph (the regression coefficient) is a measure of heritability, the correlation between the trait in both parents and their offspring (see graph below). Galton found that approximately 57 per cent of an individual human's height is determined by the height of the parents, i.e. their genetic contribution. (It is worth noting that the greater the heritability of a trait, the better it will respond to selection for that trait.)

Interestingly, Galton also studied performance in horses and published his findings in the science periodical *Nature* in 1898. Examining the inheritance of prepotency in American trotting horses, he noted the uneven distribution of the pedigrees of exceptional performers and concluded that prepotency must be a highly heritable trait.

An analysis similar to Galton's method of assessing the heritability of

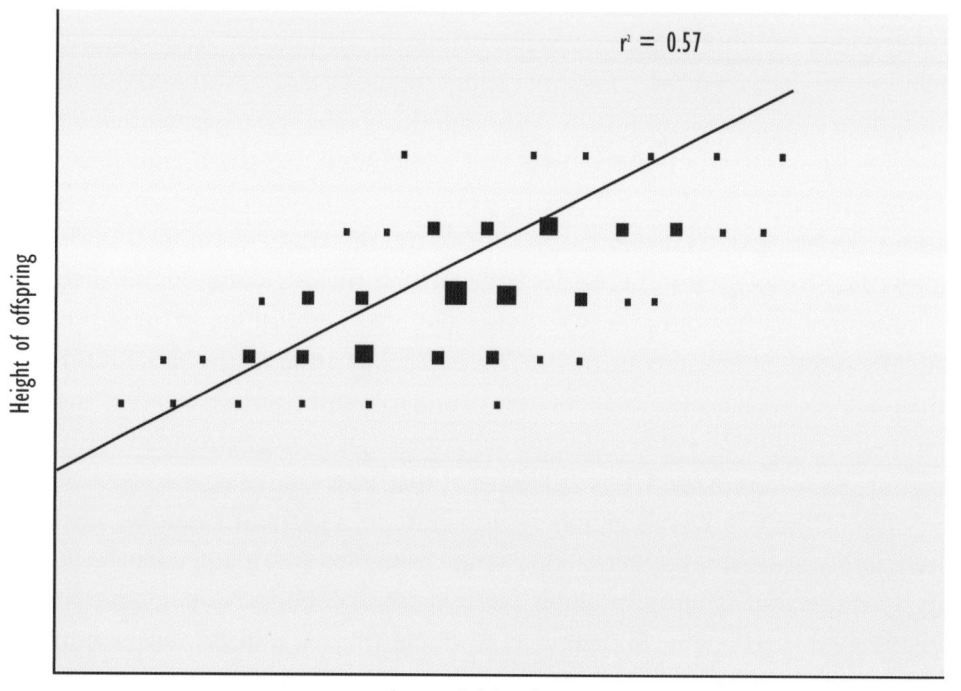

$r^2 = 0.57$

Height of offspring

Average height of parents

Galton's human height graph.

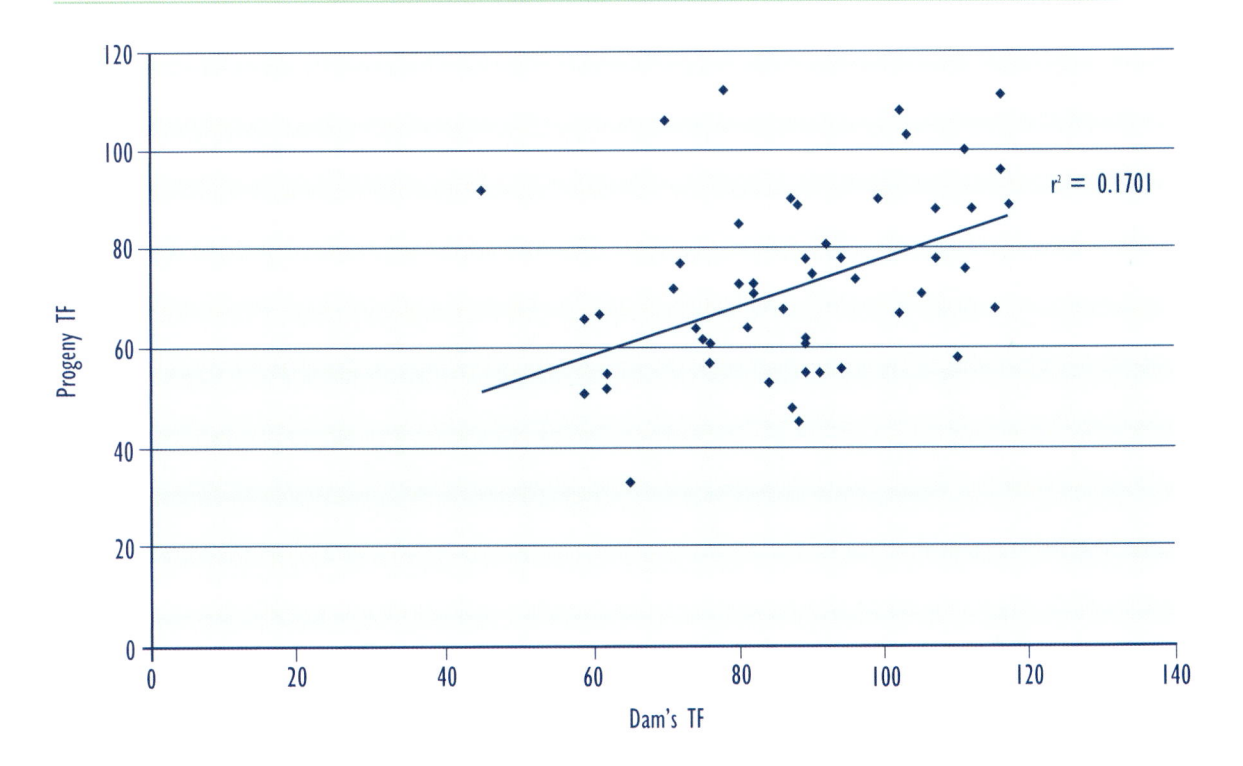

Heritability of racing performance in Thoroughbreds. Plotting the progeny's *Timeform* rating against that of its dam reveals the correlation between them. The R² value represents about half the heritability of the trait, that transmitted by the dam.

height in humans can be carried out for racing performance in Thoroughbreds. The performance ratings of the progeny of a particular sire can be plotted against the performance ratings of the dams, with appropriate adjustments made to the ratings according to the age and sex of the individual.

An accurate estimate of a Thoroughbred's racing ability is inevitably difficult to form. Race times are of limited use, as they can vary widely, depending on the tactical nature of races, and – in the United Kingdom especially – the very different topography of the many courses. Amounts of prize money earned may also prove a poor guide to racing merit, the estimates being easily skewed by a few races with very large purses. Several studies have used *Timeform* ratings or official handicap marks as good general indicators of athletic performance, and while they cannot be considered perfect, they are probably the best measures currently available.

When plotting a horse's ability against that of the dam, the slope of the line will estimate only half of the heritability value of performance, as only the genetic contribution from the dam is counted (see graph above.).

Assessment of the sire's genetic contribution is more difficult by this method, as most stallions fall into a narrow band of high ratings which they had to achieve to earn their opportunity at stud. It follows that estimates using regression on sire's ratings tend to have large standard deviations.

This simple analysis takes no account of the performance of other close relatives in the family, which would be included in more detailed estimates of heritability. The analysis is also complicated by horses who failed to achieve a rating. About one-third of a typical foal crop fails to reach the racecourse, often because of unsoundness or because they have no aptitude for racing. In other cases, well-bred fillies may be retired to stud either before racing or without having achieved a rating. The absence of these horses from the analysis introduces a bias into the heritability estimates.

It must also be stressed that heritability estimates are specific to the particular population studied. The values we have currently for the Thoroughbred come mainly from Britain and Ireland in the 1970s. Changes in the genetics of a population through selective breeding, together with alterations in environmental factors such as improved nutrition and new training methods, are likely to alter heritability estimates. We know that athletic performance is a complex trait involving many different body systems. Given that a wide range of physiological factors such as cardiac output, respiratory capacity, muscle type and the efficiency of energy production are important, we assume that a large number of genes contribute to the athletic ability of the Thoroughbred horse. What we do not know is how many genes are involved; in fact, the study of the genetics of athletic performance is in its infancy.

Some progress has been made in human sports genetics, however, and the 2006-7 human gene map for performance and health-related fitness phenotypes lists 239 genes associated with athletic ability in humans. Of these, 214 genes are on the autosomes, 7 on the X chromosome and 18 on the mitochondrial DNA. Although the population structure of humans and Thoroughbred horses is very different, it is reasonable to suppose that the physiological complexity of what governs performance will dictate that a similarly large number of genes will be involved in Thoroughbreds.

Two examples of human performance genes are informative. The first gene, called ACE, exists in two different forms in the human population, one of which is associated with a lower activity of the angiotensin-converting enzyme coded for by the gene. When studying a group of army recruits subjected to an intensive 10-week exercise programme, the individuals who were homozygous for the lower ACE activity form of the gene showed both an improvement in physical endurance performance and a greater change in several body measurements. These results indicated that their muscles had responded more to endurance exercise than individuals with the higher activity ACE gene. One component of the body changes observed during training which might account for some of the difference was an increase in growth of the left ventricle of the heart, which was significantly greater in the low ACE activity group. Interestingly, the same low activity form of ACE was found to be much more common in élite mountaineers than the frequency in the general public, again suggesting an association between this form of the gene and physical endurance.

Another human gene possibly affecting physical performance is the ACTN3 gene, which is exclusively expressed in Type II fast-twitch muscle fibres. Again, there are two common variants of this gene in humans, and one form produces no ACTN3 protein, as a mutation blocks its synthesis. Researchers found that the form of the gene producing the ACTN3 protein is linked to individuals engaged in power events like sprinting, while the gene variant that produces no ACTN3 was associated with endurance events. There appears to be an evolutionary trade-off between speed and endurance performance, which is all too familiar to Thoroughbred owners and breeders.

There are currently no published studies on whether variation in the ACE or ACTN3 genes exists in the Thoroughbred, or whether they have any effect on performance. The lead given by the researches in humans in this area will surely be followed by those engaged in the genetics of the Thoroughbred.

It is important to be clear about what is meant when we say that a gene is involved in a trait like performance. In one sense, nearly all of the ~20,000 genes of a horse are important, and so a mutation removing almost any gene could adversely affect a horse's racing ability. Here, however, we are interested in genes that have variants in the Thoroughbred population, where one form of the gene confers an athletic advantage to its holder, while the other form confers a relative disadvantage. The genetic merit of a horse can then be assessed in terms of the total number of 'good' gene variants that the individual inherited from sire and dam, and whether for each of the different genes the good forms were transmitted from both, one, or neither parent.

The importance of whether one copy or two of the desired form of the gene has been inherited will depend on whether the ability conferred by the beneficial form of the gene is expressed in a dominant, recessive or co-dominant manner. If the 'good' variant is dominant, the inheritance of a single copy will confer the maximum benefit, in much the same way that a single copy of the variant of the gene conferring grey coat colour confers greyness (see Chapter 15). Where the variant is recessive there will be no benefit unless the 'good' variant is inherited from both the sire and the dam. In the third case, for co-dominant alleles, the effect is additive, where possession of one copy of the 'good' variant confers an intermediate advantage, while possession of two copies confers the full advantage. We suspect that all three mechanisms are at work among the large number of performance genes contributing to racing ability in the Thoroughbred.

If we imagine a situation where 100 genes contribute to performance, not all the 'good' variants of these genes will have an equal effect. Rather than all of them contributing a 1 per cent improvement, one or two might be responsible for 10 per cent of the genetic variation, while other genes might produce less than 1 per cent difference.

On top of this, the 'good' form of each gene will exist at a different frequency in the Thoroughbred population. For some genes the 'good' form might be present in the majority of Thoroughbreds, while for other genes the 'good' variant might be rare. Taken together, a huge range of genetic ability should be present in the population. Bearing in mind that we believe genetics accounts for between a third and half of a horse's athletic ability, this wide range of genetic potential is nurtured in a world that is far from uniform. Complex interactions between the environment and the genetic composition of the individual animal exist, so that a foal with the genetic potential to be a top-class racehorse will very probably fail to produce good performances if raised, trained and ridden badly. On the other hand, an individual with a poorer combination of 'good' genes may produce form of a high order by reason of the excellent conditions in which he is raised and campaigned. For example, some trainers are particularly adept at handling sprinters, whereas others are more proficient with later-maturing Classic-distance horses. In the wrong hands, it is quite likely that a horse will not develop to his full genetic potential.

With this background, it is time to consider different Thoroughbred breeding strategies, and how they might operate in relation to performance genes.

CHAPTER 21

GENETIC DRIFT AND INBREEDING

The early chapters of this book described the foundation of the Thoroughbred, as it was understood by generations of horsemen who developed it as a distinct breed. As was explained, however, those origins were obscured by a lack of verifiable pedigree data, and some 300 years elapsed before molecular genetics, through the use of mitochondrial DNA, was able to shed light on the roots of the breed (see Chapter 17).

Those recent researches, which showed that several of the founding mares were themselves closely related – or, in some cases, possibly even the same individual – indicate that the genetic base for the Thoroughbred population is narrower than was imagined for centuries. Studies now ongoing, including the investigation of the genetic make-up of key Thoroughbreds through isolation of DNA from skeletons which have been preserved, also promise to provide exciting new information on the origins and development of the breed.

'What is a Thoroughbred?' From a genetic perspective, we might answer: 'An individual whose parents were both registered Thoroughbreds.' This answer can lead to a clearer picture of what a 'pure' breed is, and some of the genetic consequences that flow from establishing a stud book with a closed breeding population.

As related earlier in this work, all current Thoroughbreds can be traced back in their tail-male line to one of three founding stallions, and all descend from one of approximately seventy founding mares; but we should not read too much into these facts. A stallion may prove influential without establishing an enduring male line, and the Curwen Bay Barb was certainly one who made a significant impact. Similarly, a mare needs to produce daughters who produce daughters, and for that process to continue through the generations, but by delivering one colt who becomes influential at stud her contribution becomes valuable. Even so, most genetic variation in the Thoroughbred comes from a relatively small number of individuals, in terms of population genetics.

The *General Stud Book*, first published in 1791, was in eighteen volumes by 1897, when conditions for registration first rated a mention – and even then they were vague – but it had been a general principle, accepted by breeders over many years, that descent from horses previously registered was a requirement. The Thoroughbred has been essentially a closed breed for two centuries, and in that time development of the breed has been based on the genetic variation captured within the individuals included at the date of closure, together with variation derived from rare new mutations arising in the population.

The eighteenth and nineteenth centuries formed the key period for establishing the majority of domestic animal breeds (cattle, pigs, dogs and horses) that we have today. Many breeds, regardless of species, subsequently developed in similar ways as a consequence of some universal features of population genetics. In the early generations following the closure of a stud book to new 'bloodlines', the population size is small and much genetic variation is lost through a process called genetic drift.

The concept of genetic drift can be illustrated with an extreme hypothetical example. Imagine a founding individual who is heterozygous at every gene, i.e. has different variants for every gene. If this individual has a single offspring, through which it makes its contribution to the breed, half of the genetic variation in that individual is lost in one generation because it could pass on only one of its two variants.

Genetic bottlenecks restrict variation in small populations. As the breed establishes itself in the early generations, much of the initial genetic variation within it is lost, and over time other factors contribute to further loss of genetic variation, resulting in increased levels of inbreeding. One of these is the 'popular sire' effect.

The more popular males inevitably produce far more offspring than those who are less well supported, with the result that a proportion of the genetic variants present in less popular sires is lost by genetic drift. Selective breeding, using the best – or presumed best – stallions to produce better and more uniform individuals, can have its benefits, but they come at the cost of losing some variants that might be beneficial over the long term.

In order to adapt to changing demands, a population needs genetic variation. How many genetic variants for speed, which would be highly valued now, were lost in the early generations of the Thoroughbred breed, when a major requirement was the ability to race over long distances? The concentration on breeding for shorter distances in the late twentieth and early twenty-first century, and the neglect of stallions who might tend to impart stamina, have surely resulted in the loss of genetic variation.

Inbreeding refers to the presence of an ancestor at more than one position in a pedigree. Strictly, it requires the common ancestor to be present on both the dam and the sire's side of the pedigree. Inbreeding is remarkably common and indeed inevitable in Thoroughbred pedigrees, if traced through sufficient generations. For example, the five-generation pedigree of the noted stallion Montjeu contains no duplicated ancestors. However, at nine generations only about 60 per cent of the ancestors present are different individuals, with many featuring multiple times; for example, Montjeu has fifteen crosses of Phalaris.

What is true for Montjeu is typical for the Thoroughbred as a whole. It has been claimed that Phalaris, who was born in 1913, is in the pedigree of every current Thoroughbred, such that breeding any two individuals would duplicate him. Interestingly, when the number of different ancestors in nine generations, a measure of inbreeding, was compared among the top-rated ten 3-year-olds in 2006 and ten random poor performers with *Timeform* ratings of 50 or below in the same year, the figures proved remarkably similar. Thus inbreeding *per se*, does not generate either élite or poor performers. It is the precise genetic constitution generated in each case that matters.

European Thoroughbred breeders are increasingly concerned over the preponderance of certain bloodlines in European Thoroughbreds. Roughly a third of current Thoroughbreds are inbred to Northern Dancer within five generations, though again, this proportion does not vary much between élite and ordinary performers. The mere presence of a *name* in a pedigree, however, does not convey any information about which genetic variants have been passed on to their offspring. Two offspring of a sire have a 50:50 chance of sharing any specific genetic variant, and the independent segregation of chromosomes into sperm (see diagram on page 94) ensures that each offspring, with the exception of identical twins, is a unique genetic entity. If, for example, a sire was heterozygous for a dominant mutation contributing to athletic ability, half of his offspring would not receive the beneficial form of the gene from him, though they might receive a copy from their dam.

Many pedigree consultants, when planning matings, seek to double up on particular ancestors in the pedigree. Indeed, as seen above, Northern Dancer is often targeted for duplication in pedigrees. This was particularly noticeable in the first, and only, crop sired by Dubai Millennium. Owned by Sheikh Mohammed, and regarded by him as the best horse he had owned up to that time, the stallion had the opportunity to cover some of the best mares in the Thoroughbred population. Of note, roughly 60 per cent of the foals sired by Dubai Millennium were inbred to Northern Dancer within five generations, roughly double the proportion in the population as a whole and surely indicative of a deliberate strategy in the mating plans. The three highest-rated progeny of Dubai Millennium – Dubawi, Echo of Light and Belenus – were all inbred to Northern Dancer. However, other Dubai Millennium progeny inbred to Northern Dancer were not highly rated. It is the precise genetic information that is transmitted in each case that is important – something that cannot be deduced by examining a tabulated pedigree.

In addition to seeking to duplicate individuals close up in a pedigree, some pedigree advisers seek to place these duplications in matched positions in the top and bottom halves of the pedigree. It is hard to see the significance of this from a genetic point of view. In general, the effect of inheriting a good variant from any position in a pedigree is identical, such that whether they were inherited from a male or female ancestor in any particular position in the pedigree is irrelevant. One exception could be for the few genes that are genetically imprinted. This specific class of genes is discussed in the next chapter in relation to the maternal grandsire effect.

The presence of multiple crosses of the same individual in a pedigree is inevitable. The number of ancestors doubles as we move back each generation; two parents, four grandparents, eight great-grandparents, etc. Current-day Thoroughbreds are separated from the individuals who founded the breed by about thirty generations, so potentially they would have 2^{30} ancestors when the breed was founded. We know from the stud book records, however, that the breed was founded by a comparatively small number of individuals, probably less than a hundred. It is therefore impossible for a Thoroughbred to avoid having significant numbers of ancestors duplicated, sometimes a large number of times, in earlier generations of their pedigrees. For example, Eclipse occurs 117 times in the pedigree of St Simon, who, as noted in Chapter 15, himself features 164 times in the first twelve generations of recent French champion sire Linamix. The numbers are typical of the breed as a whole.

From a genetic perspective, inbreeding has several consequences. In the first instance, it increases the proportion of homozygous genes. Breeders who inbreed to famous ancestors are attempting to increase the proportion of 'good' forms of the performance genes in the foals they produce. The potential advantage to inbreeding is that it can increase the effect of beneficial recessive or co-dominant genes. But it also increases the risk of producing an individual with two copies of deleterious recessive mutations, where the famous ancestor had only a single copy.

The real chance of establishing homozygosity for unlinked genes depends on how far back in the pedigree the common ancestor occurs. The table on page 96 shows the number of chromosomes transmitted by an individual in each generation. In the sixth generation there are sixty-four ancestors. Horses have sixty-four individual chromosomes, so an ancestor in the sixth generation will *on average* contribute a single chromosome to the individual in question. (More accurately, they will on average contribute one sixty-fourth of the chromosomal genetic material transmitted. This is a consequence of the process of meiotic recombination, which shuffles an individual's paternal and maternal chromosomes during sperm or egg formation.)

Given the random nature of chromosome segregation, statistics predict that some ancestors in the sixth generation will have contributed no genetic material to the individual concerned. Even a duplicated ancestor in the fifth generation, who on average will contribute two chromosomes each time, is highly unlikely to pass on any specific chromosome (or region) such that it becomes homozygous five generations down the line. Accordingly, it is hard to understand the genetic logic of pedigree analysts who strongly attribute particular athletic performance characters to the duplication of an ancestor in the seventh, eighth, or ninth generation.

Ideally, inbreeding 'fixes' particular desirable traits, such that they then breed true in subsequent generations. For example, pedigree dog breeds were created by repeatedly selecting for particular physical traits. Dog breeders achieved fixation for the genes controlling the sizes, shapes and colours that characterise each breed by intense selective inbreeding for these traits. Genetic variation for such traits was largely eliminated from the breed, because the genes involved in breed characteristics are homozygous: individuals will breed true for those characteristics because there are no alternative forms of the gene in the population. Some variation in individual dogs will still exist because many of these traits do not have a heritability of 1, and so are subject to some environmental influence. Regions of the genome that did not contain genes for the selected breed characteristics retain genetic variation within the different dog breeds.

In the 300 years of selective breeding that has shaped the Thoroughbred horse, certain genetic variants have probably become fixed in a similar way. Indeed, if in the early days of the breed there had been a 'speed gene' – a variant in a performance gene that, by itself, conferred dramatically improved athletic ability – theory predicts that it would have rapidly become fixed in the population. The alternative poor-performing form of the gene would have been eliminated.

The scientific measure of inbreeding, called the inbreeding coefficient, provides a statistical measure of how inbred any individual is. It is frequently estimated by looking for common ancestors within five generations. Duplicated individuals occurring in generations further back are ignored, as they are considered to have only a relatively minor effect on the levels of homozygosity. Estimated inbreeding coefficients for modern Thoroughbreds are not high when compared to some other breeds of domestic animals, although they are among the highest among horse breeds. When we examine the DNA of Thoroughbreds using genetic markers that vary between individuals, usually between 40-50 per cent of those markers are homozygous. This is a high level of homozygosity compared to other horse breeds, or breeds in other domestic species.

One consequence of inbreeding can be a decrease in reproductive fitness. This is thought to be linked to the production of individuals with homozygous lethal recessive mutations, which result in non-viable foetuses. Such reduced reproductive success is called inbreeding depression.

There have been significant changes to the structure of the Thoroughbred breeding industry over the past three decades. They include increased production of foals, increased stallion book sizes, and the transportation of stallions across hemispheres to breed year-round. These changes have been accompanied by a decrease in the number of different stallions producing the Thoroughbred foal crop in Great Britain and Ireland. In 1996 a total of 1,006 stallions registered in Great Britain and Ireland produced foals, but ten years later that number had dropped by a third, to 653. Many of the 'missing' stallions would have been responsible for a small number of foals, but overall the decrease in stallion numbers reduces the effective population size of Thoroughbreds and decreases genetic variation within the breed. Over the long term, a decrease in effective population size will result in an increased rate of inbreeding.

It is difficult to establish whether there is any evidence of reproductive depression in the Thoroughbred. Several confounding factors complicate such an analysis. The use of progesterone hormone assays and ultrasound examination to identify ovulation in the mare and thus optimum times for stallion covering, together with the use of synthetic hormones to control the ovulation cycle, have both led to improved conception rates of 90 per cent per season, while the improved screening has reduced the average number of coverings by a stallion taken to get a mare pregnant to about one and a half. This, in turn, has facilitated the increase in stallion book sizes. However, despite the improved conception rates, there is significant foetal loss during pregnancy and only about 80 per cent of breeding mares foal successfully. While the conception rate has increased dramatically over the past twenty-five years, this increase, achieved through veterinary intervention, could be masking inbreeding problems.

Some foetal loss is undoubtedly caused by non-genetic factors, such as viral abortions and twisted placental cords. The role of inbreeding depression is currently unknown, though it is interesting that a number of commercial stallions have higher than normal early embryonic deaths, which might indicate a genetic problem. Regardless, the dramatic changes that have taken place in the Thoroughbred breeding industry recently require careful monitoring and statistical modelling to look out for early signs of genetic health problems.

CHAPTER 22
NICKS AND BROODMARE SIRES

An apparent affinity between certain individuals in the breeding population is commonly known as a nick. The term is generally applied to matings between a particular sire and the daughters of an unrelated stallion which produce a higher than expected proportion of good performers.

An early example of this phenomenon was the record of Herod mares mated with Eclipse in the 1770s, and there were later manifestations involving Bend Or and daughters of Macaroni in the 1880s and Phalaris with mares by Chaucer in the 1920s. In recent years a nick familiar to European breeders has been that between Sadler's Wells and mares by Darshaan or his sire Shirley Heights. These crosses have proved very successful, with, to the end of 2009, fourteen individual winners of European Pattern races produced from daughters of Shirley Heights mated with Sadler's Wells, including In The Wings and Alexandrova. Daughters of Darshaan, in their matings with Sadler's Wells, have produced eighteen individual Pattern winners, including High Chaparral, Islington and Milan.

The theory of nicks, though, is reminiscent of the Bruce Lowe theory on family numbers and success in Classic races. Similar questions to those that were directed to assessing Lowe's theory need to be asked to critically assess the veracity of the nick theory. In Lowe's case, the success of mare family lines was highly correlated to the proportion of individuals from those families in the Thoroughbred population. The success of certain family lines thus probably reflected their relative opportunities of winning Classic races, rather than some inherent, unique property of the family line. When looking at nicks, the questions to be considered include: what proportion of poor racehorses were produced by the nick, what proportion of top-quality winners were produced by the stallion with mares from other stallions, and what proportion of top-quality races were won by the

Sadler's Wells, fourteen times champion sire in Britain and Ireland between 1990 and 2004, has produced many good winners from matings with daughters of Shirley Heights, and that stallion's son, Daarshan. Sadler's Wells was also a pure-breeding bay, as is his son Montjeu.

produce of those mares when mated with other stallions? That last angle is frequently omitted from discussions of nicks, even those that take a statistical approach. It is obviously important, as superior dams will often produce top-class stakes-winners by a number of different stallions, allowing the supposed nick to be seen in its proper perspective. In this case, the mating of two superior individuals is doing what we expect it to do.

For example, the nick between Northern Dancer and Mr Prospector, which seemingly works both ways, is a mating between two of the strongest Thoroughbred breeding lines in the world. Given the high covering fees that both stallions stood for when they were alive, the female offspring produced by either are likely to be very well-bred individuals, that is, the progeny of top-quality dams. Is it surprising, then, that such crosses between individuals with a preponderance of 'good' copies of performance genes are frequently able to produce excellent racehorses?

Another criterion for assessing the reality of specific nicks is to look hard at how much data is actually available. For several years the American magazine *Blood-Horse* has produced an annual volume that provides an extensive analysis of stallions crossed with the daughters of other stallion lines, and identifies those crosses that have been most successful on the racecourse. The amount of data available for many young sires is insufficient to have statistical confidence in the suggested affinities.

Several different types of nick have been proposed, but the sire-broodmare sire nick is the only one where there is at least a close enough relationship between the individuals involved for certain gene combinations to be reproduced in a fair proportion of the offspring. Some of the other nicks that have been mooted, such as those involving key ancestors far back in the pedigree, seem implausible; the more distant the genetic relationships involved in the supposed nick, the more unlikely the presumed effect is to be real.

In addition, our expectations for the success levels of a nick need to be realistic. When two Throughbreds are mated, an enormous number of possible genetic combinations can be produced, owing to the independent segregation of chromosomes and the process of recombination in formation of sperm and egg. These same constraints apply to the individuals proposed to nick, so that any increase in number of top-quality offspring produced from nicks would be expected to be relatively modest.

The conclusion is that genuine nicks in Thoroughbred breeding are rare. In genetic terms though, it is possible to propose rational explanations for the phenomenon of nicking, especially those nicks involving close genetic relationships, such as the sire-broodmare sire nick. Given that nicks often involve crosses between two unrelated lines, one explanation is the possibility that the benefit derives from heterosis. Better known as hybrid vigour, this is the production of improved offspring resulting from an increased proportion of heterozygous, or varying, genes. Hybrid vigour is well documented in plant breeding, though less familiar in animal breeding. The extraordinary ability of the Thoroughbred to run distances ranging between 5 furlongs and 2+ miles (or 4 miles in the early days of the breed), may have resulted from the heterosis created by breeding imported Eastern horses with horses native to Great Britain.

In current breeding terms, the improvement attributed to nicks could result from reducing the number of negative recessive gene variants in the homozygous state. Given the molecular data on the extent of relatedness in modern Thoroughbreds, as indicated by the high level of homozygosity, even apparently unrelated lines probably share significant amounts of genetic material inherited from common ancestors further in the past. This makes it less likely that heterosis is the explanation for the success of nicks. If hybrid vigour were to account for high-class performance in a horse resulting from a nick, transmission of that quality to subsequent generations would be unlikely. An increase in homozygosity for the negative recessive genes, and thus poorer performance, would be the predictable outcome.

An alternative genetic explanation for nicking is that the daughters of some stallions are able to provide combinations of 'good' variants of genes that complement those of the stallion with whom the nick takes place.

Not all of the broodmare sire's daughters would receive the correct combinations of complementary genes; the shuffling of genetic material that takes place during sperm and egg production would ensure variations. However, those who did would have an increased chance of producing better offspring when mated to that stallion. In this case we might expect that the nick would often be reversible, with the daughters of the stallion also proving complementary with the broodmare sire.

Several of the better-supported nicks have been observed to work both ways round, which may indicate that there is some substance to those nicks. The strength of any nick resulting from a complementary influence of beneficial alleles will be affected by both the contribution those genes make to racing performance, and by the relative frequency of the 'good' alleles for those genes in the Thoroughbred population. Theoretically, the nick would be strongest when the genes involved made a large contribution to performance and the best alleles were relatively rare. If the genes involved had a minor effect on performance and the 'good' alleles were common in the Thoroughbred population, the genetic make-up resulting from the nick would not be very different from that generated by random matings.

Currently, nicking remains an interesting idea that could become verified as increasing amounts of molecular genetic information on Thoroughbreds are generated in the future.

Conventional genetic theory, dating back to Mendel, maintains that the gender of the parent from whom a gene variant is inherited has no effect on the action of that gene. For example, it is irrelevant whether a product of mating inherits the dominant grey coat colour mutation from sire or dam; the individual will be grey if the mutation is present. However, studies on mice in the mid-1980s in England demonstrated that for *some* genes, it did matter from which parent an individual inherited different forms of a gene. These genes were transmitted in a switched-off form from one sex, whilst the other sex passed on an active form of the gene.

This phenomenon is called genomic imprinting: genes *not expressed* when inherited from the father are called paternally imprinted, whilst genes *inactive* when inherited from the mother are called maternally imprinted genes.

While grey coat colour is clearly not an imprinted gene, consider what the patterns of inheritance would look like if the grey gene was paternally imprinted (see diagram opposite). In this case, mating a heterozygous grey stallion, i.e. with a single copy of the mutation producing grey coat colour, to mares without a copy of the grey mutation, would generate a population in which none of the offspring was grey. The grey mutation would be transmitted from the sire in an inactive form because it is paternally imprinted. None of the male offspring generated would produce grey individuals when subsequently mated to mares without the grey mutation, because, while half of them had the mutation, it would again be transmitted in an inactive form. In contrast, half of the female offspring of the grey stallion would have inherited an inactive, imprinted form of the mutation, which they would pass on to half of their offspring in an active form; these would be grey horses. Imprinting thus creates an unusual pattern of inheritance, with the trait skipping a generation.

This resembles the maternal grandsire effect, where an exceptional racehorse proves ineffective as a sire of racehorses, but in the next generation his daughters are found to be exceptional broodmares, producing male and female progeny of ability. The most famous example of the maternal grandsire effect concerns Secretariat, whose offspring, though better than average, were rarely top-class racehorses. A number of

NICKS AND BROODMARE SIRES

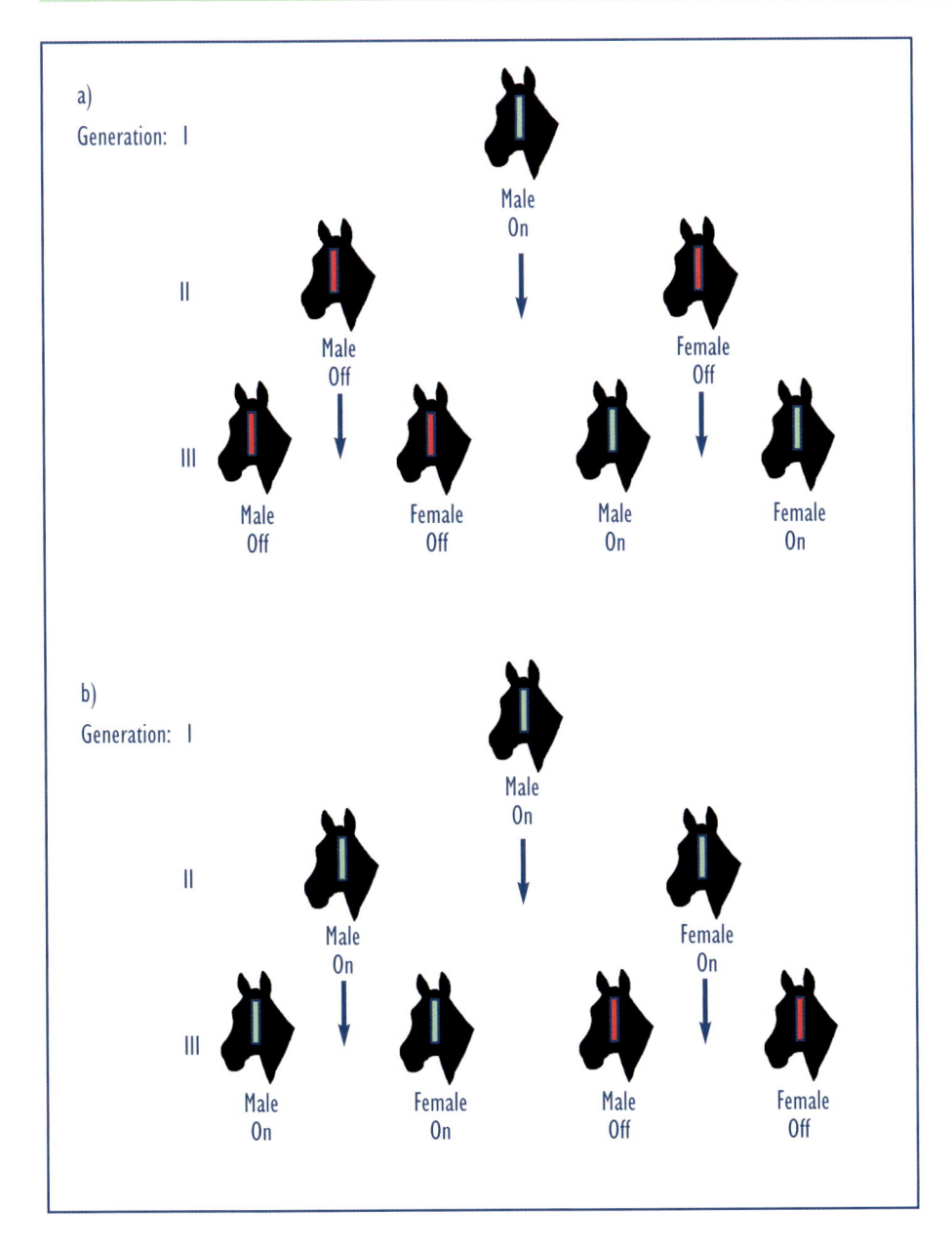

a)
Generation: I — Male On
II — Male Off, Female Off
III — Male Off, Female Off, Male On, Female On

b)
Generation: I — Male On
II — Male On, Female On
III — Male On, Female On, Male Off, Female Off

The effect of imprinting through generations (see text). Imprinting is the determination of the expression of a gene by its parental origin.

a) In paternal imprinting, the allele inherited from the sire is not expressed. His sons will also transmit the allele in an inactive form, while his daughters will pass it on in an active form.

b) In maternal imprinting, the allele inherited from the sire is expressed and will be transmitted in an active form by his sons. His daughters will transmit the allele in an inactive form to their offspring.

his sons obtained decent opportunities at stud, but turned out to be ordinary sires. In contrast, several of Secretariat's daughters became great broodmares, producing top-class runners and sires, such as A.P. Indy, Gone West and Storm Cat. Could it be that the genes that Secretariat inherited from his dam, Somethingroyal, in an active form, which he passed on to his offspring in a paternally imprinted, inactive form, have been reactivated in his daughters and are in part responsible for the production of exceptional offspring by some of these daughters? That may be the case, but there are other genetic explanations.

For instance, consider the fate of Secretariat's X chromosome. None of his sons received his X chromosome, because as males they must have inherited his Y. While all of his daughters inherited his X chromosome, expression of the genes contained in it is no simple matter; as related in Chapter 18, X inactivation would shut down the genes from one copy of the X in each cell. The inactivation of Secretariat's X chromosome in half of the cells could well dilute the beneficial effect of any performance mutations. They would, though, find their full expression again in the 50 per cent of sons of these females who inherited Secretariat's X chromosome.

However, in the case of both genomic imprinting and X chromosome genes, we would expected that these sons, albeit good racehorses, would not prove to be good sires. This is clearly not the case with Storm Cat, Gone West and A.P. Indy, who rank among the most successful stallions in the world.

Horsemen recognise that the maternal grandsire effect is not long-lasting and tends to become diluted within a few generations. Neither of the scientific explanations provided can easily account for this, or the success of Storm Cat, A.P. Indy and Gone West on the basis of a maternal grandsire effect. It is possble that, in many cases, the effect results from chance, where fortuitous gene combinations arise in a few of the broodmares' progeny and credit is then apportioned to the maternal grandsire.

CHAPTER 23
SELECTIVE BREEDING

The origins of pure breeds of domestic animals went hand in hand with attempts to improve the quality of those animals through selective breeding. Robert Bakewell (1725-1795) was one of the first people to make strenuous efforts at animal improvement by routinely mating specific individuals together. Previously, livestock of both sexes were kept together in the fields, breeding at random, resulting in progeny with essentially random characteristics. Bakewell separated males from females, and allowed only specific matings to take place. Furthermore, by inbreeding his livestock he fixed and exaggerated traits he felt to be desirable. Bakewell was also well aware of the importance and value of progeny testing. In contrast to most of his contemporaries, who closely guarded their better livestock, he leased out his young bulls and rams to his neighbours so that he could more quickly test their value as breeding animals.

The significance of progeny testing derives from the fact that superior stock express a combination of good genetics and good husbandry. By evaluating the progeny of several bulls and rams, Bakewell was able to distinguish those males which regularly passed on their superior qualities, which reflected their superior genetic merit. So, from an early point in the history of Thoroughbred breeding the concepts of 'breed the best to the best and hope for the best', together with the idea of carefully assessing the quality of the progeny when evaluating breeding stock, were recognised. Indeed, it could be argued that the breeding of racehorses has not evolved beyond this point.

It is clear from the history of domestic animal species, including the horse, that selective breeding works. For example, the enormous differences in body shapes, sizes and coat colours of different pedigree dog breeds reflects the ability of animal breeders to partition genetic variation into different closed breeding populations. In this way, genetic variation within a breed is largely removed for those genes controlling the breed characteristics, resulting in the production of a uniform 'type' with the required breed traits. This predictability of the results of matings between pure-bred animals is destroyed if two individuals of different breeds are mated together. Just think how hard it is to guess the breeds that mated to produce most mongrel dogs.

For farm species such as cattle, pigs and poultry, traditional selective breeding has led to massive increases in production efficiency, with the yields of milk, meat and eggs increased several times over their levels of a hundred years ago. Again, the message is clear: selective breeding works, and is a powerful tool. In these cases, the breeding goal for the farmer has been clear, and repeated selection and mating of the best-producing animals over several generations has steadily improved the yields he was seeking.

With the emergence of large animal breeding conglomerates, the amount of data collected and analysed to maintain steady increases in production levels through selective breeding is impressive. Interestingly, many farm animal production companies use modern molecular genetics to complement and improve their traditional selection methods. A new discipline called marker-assisted selection uses genetic markers linked to beneficial traits to identify animals with the best genetic profiles. Several pig production companies use twenty or more genetic markers, linked to a range of meat traits, to select their breeding stock. They have successfully speeded up the traditional selection process using modern genetic technology.

Some increases in production efficiencies have not been achieved without costs, such as increasing leg problems in fast-growing broiler chickens, increased disease susceptibility in cows producing large volumes of milk, or decreased fertility, which reduce the financial benefit derived. Genetic selection must be applied intelligently, and there are limits to what is possible.

Are the examples quoted above, concerning the development of pedigree dog breeds, or increased production in farm animals, really relevant to the selection and breeding of Thoroughbred horses? Many of the traits selected by these breeders are genetically complex, being controlled by multiple gene variants, each of which, on their own, has a relatively small effect. As such, the examples are analogous to what Thoroughbred breeders are trying to achieve when they seek to breed a top racehorse; the same underlying genetics apply in relation to athletic performance – also extraordinarily complicated, and determined by many different factors.

Selective breeding, with particular emphasis on the employment of the best male racehorses as stallions, has been the norm in the industry for some 250 years, and for much of that time breeders were wary of using horses with apparent constitutional defects. The 1867 Derby winner Hermit, notorious as a breaker of blood-vessels, was retired to stud at a fee of only 20 guineas, having been defeated in his last eleven races. He was 'on probation' in his first few years as a stallion, while breeders waited to see whether his progeny inherited his affliction; as it turned out, only a small minority were known to be affected, and Hermit was champion sire for seven consecutive seasons, while his fee rose to 500 guineas.

The 1886 Triple Crown winner Ormonde, widely regarded as the greatest racehorse of the nineteenth century, became a roarer before the end of his second season in training. His owner-breeder, the 1st Duke of Westminster, sold him to Argentina when he was 6 years old, reportedly because he did not want the horse to spread his unsoundness in the British breed. A likelier reason for the export of his unbeaten champion was that the Duke knew that an illness suffered in his first season at stud had left Ormonde sub-fertile, but the excuse given was generally credited at the time. Then, as now, removal of weak stock from the breeding population – culling, as it is known – was recognised as an important measure toward maintaining the health of the breed but, particularly since the last quarter of the twentieth century, the actions of many stallion owners and breeders have tended to reflect a desire for short-term financial benefits rather than concerns for the long-term preservation of soundness in the Thoroughbred.

As mentioned previously, perception of increasing fragility in the breed has been noted frequently in recent times, especially by experienced trainers, who complain that the modern horse cannot take as much work as those of previous generations. Numerous statistical studies in America have shown a marked reduction in the number of career starts by early twenty-first century runners, compared with those of only twenty or thirty years ago. Who can doubt that the Thoroughbred is becoming weaker, or be unaware of one of the principal reasons? Unsound horses with good racing records are routinely allotted places at stud, and by not removing a higher proportion of them from the breeding population, we are propagating unsoundness.

In a similar fashion, the proportion of mares conceiving twins has risen appreciably over the last twenty years, and one possible explanation for this is inadvertent selection. It is generally understood that mares carrying twins rarely foal successfully – a natural phenomenon ensuring that the genes responsible for the dual ovulation which causes twinning are kept at a low level in the population. However, the advent of ultrasound scanning for pregnant mares has enabled veterinary surgeons to identify mares carrying twins and 'squeeze' one of the conceptuses, thus allowing the mare to produce a single foal. The foals produced in this way are more likely to carry genes for twinning than other foals and the proportion of these genes in the population will rise. The unwanted result of an apparently beneficial veterinary procedure might be that more mares will become pregnant with twins and require more veterinary help.

The time taken to effect improvement in breeding and the extent to which it may be achieved is dependent on the amount of selection applied to the breeding population and the generation interval, which in Thoroughbreds is about ten years. In the present era, selection on the male side is intense, illustrated in Britain and Ireland by the fact that only 1.5 per cent of male Thoroughbreds registered with Weatherbys go on to stud. Of this select group, an even smaller number are successful at stud, i.e. by having a significant impact on the breed through the production of large numbers of offspring and the establishment of breeding lines.

In contrast, selection of females is weak, with about 50 per cent of all female Thoroughbreds registered with Weatherbys entering the breeding population. This high ratio of mares used for breeding has been encouraged by an extensive programme of races at home and keen demand for youngstock from abroad, natural incentives for many mare owners to breed for financial gain. However, in recent years there has been an over-supply, and the arrival of worldwide economic recession in the second half of 2008 has resulted in significant financial losses. Unsurprisingly, the products of low-grade mares, lacking in pedigree, performance and soundness, have suffered most in the marketplace.

The lack of selection on the distaff side in Thoroughbred breeding inevitably presents a major barrier to genetic improvement, and although the recession current at the time of writing will doubtless lead to many inferior females being withdrawn from the production line, their removal will make little difference; a technique which could bring advances has been developed and is available, but it has not been sanctioned by the Stud Book authorities who control the breeding of Thoroughbreds.

Embryo transfer – the implantation of embryos into surrogate mares – is a procedure which would enable better-quality mares to produce several offspring per year instead of the one decreed by Nature. In this way the number of foals born might be maintained while improving the overall quality of the breed, but current regulations do not even allow foals to be conceived by artificial insemination, so the introduction of embryo transfer is something for the distant future, if ever.

The current structure of the Thoroughbred breeding industry presents another barrier to genetic improvement through selective breeding. In the old days, when racing was dominated by wealthy owner-breeders, the breeding goal was to produce the best racehorse possible. The breeding goal of most Thoroughbred producers now is an animal who will generate a high price at the yearling sales. This leads to mating plans based on fashion, and, in defiance of logic, the most fashionable stallions are often the newest recruits to the ranks.

Although everyone is aware that the vast majority of stallions are destined to be relatively unsuccessful at stud, breeders routinely place their trust in unproven horses to the extent that some 40 per cent of most foal crops have sires whose progeny have not been tested on the racecourse. Given the large books of mares covered by many of these unproven stallions, some may have 500 foals before it becomes clear that they are failures. Many of the females produced find their way into the breeding population to disseminate unfavourable genetic combinations. While the production of commercial yearlings takes precedence over the goal of producing successful racehorses, the breeding industry will not develop Thoroughbreds of greater genetic strength.

The question of how much the breed has improved since its origins has been widely debated. A study led by Professor Patrick Cunningham, in Dublin, looked at winning times for three English Classic races – the Derby, the Oaks and the St Leger – and noted that although times had improved from the 1840s up to about 1910 they had since been relatively static. In contrast, the average performance of the whole population of Thoroughbreds had improved during the period 1952-1977. The finding that the Classic winning times had stagnated became known as 'Cunningham's paradox'. The widely read and interesting paper in *Scientific American* (1991) in which these ideas were presented concluded by questioning whether the Thoroughbred might have reached its physiological limits. In particular, the authors hypothesised that the factor limiting the improvement in winning times might be the clearance of lactic acid, levels of which rise dramatically in the blood during exercise.

However, many factors influence winning race times, and only some of them relate to the physiology of the horse. Several external factors are likely to have had a major effect on race times. For instance, almost all courses in England are now watered to provide good, safe going, something that was not done in the past. Firm ground is naturally conducive to fast times and some of the fastest were recorded on sun-baked turf in the pre-watering era. The direction and speed of the wind also have an obvious bearing on winning times, and, of course, races are never actually run against the clock. In addition, some scepticism about the accuracy of both race distances and times before the introduction of modern techniques may well be justified.

Despite these factors, which would seem to militate against fast times in the modern era, records are occasionally set. For example, in 2007 Finsceal Beo established a new mark for the 1000 Guineas over the Rowley Mile course at Newmarket, and in the same year Lucarno's electronically measured time for the Doncaster St Leger was the fastest on record, save for the races of 1926 and 1934, when a pressman's stopwatch was the probably less reliable timing device.

The faster times noted by the Cunningham study in the first decade of the twentieth century no doubt owed most to the revolution in riding style introduced from America, and the more recent improvements are also largely attributable to environmental factors, notably better nutrition, health and training. Given the huge number of combinations possible with the amount of variation present in the Thoroughbred, it seems unlikely that we have reached a genetic performance limit. Indeed, Professor Cunningham and a colleague found a steady improvement when they looked directly at genetic gain in the Thoroughbred at a population level.

No history of the Thoroughbred could fail to recognise the achievements of major owner-breeders whose successes in selective breeding brought them long periods of prominence on the Turf. Examples from the twentieth century in Europe would have to include such as Federico Tesio, the 17th Earl of Derby, and Marcel Boussac, and in our own day the Aga Khan and Khalid Abdullah stand out among their contemporaries. It is possible that none has consciously thought in terms of genetics in developing his stud, but part of the explanation for their success is readily supplied by genetics.

The best breeders painstakingly build up a high-quality broodmare band, and over time acquire extensive evidence of the success or failure of different mating strategies within the related families they have established. By culling the poor performers, the proportion of good gene variants in the remaining herd increases. The environmental variables are also reduced, with the majority of foals raised and fed in the same way. This increases the chance that differences between individuals are related to genetic merit rather than good husbandry, such that the selection of the best performers is more likely to identify those individuals capable of passing on their superior merit. These advantages inevitably take several generations of horses to build up, but they result in more consistent outcomes for the breeding operation.

It is important to understand the theoretical benefits that should result from selection. As recorded earlier, matings between the Derby winner and the Oaks winner, supposedly representing the pinnacle of selective breeding in England, have been tried on numerous occasions, and the results have often been judged to be disappointing, in that they rarely produce another top-class winner. Such crosses illustrate the important phenomenon known as regression to the mean (see graphs overleaf). In Chapter 16 the concept of epistasis was introduced; the interactions between alleles of different genes. Top, élite individuals are likely to possess three genetic components that contribute to their ability. The first is that they will have good copies of the important performance gene variants. Second, their genetic variants are optimised in relation to whether those gene variants act in a recessive or dominant manner. Third, the combinations of the different performance genes which interact are also ideal.

Whilst an élite individual will be more likely to pass on good genetic variants, it is unlikely that all the dominant/recessive combinations will be re-created in their offspring, and they are unlikely to be able to re-establish all the interacting gene combinations intact, with the consequence that their progeny will tend to have lower ability than they themselves did.

For example, if the Derby winner has a *Timeform* rating of 130 and the Oaks winner one of 123, both rank far above the average for their respective sexes. Their ability reflects the strength of the three genetic components described above. The average Timeform rating for 3-year-old colts is about 79 and that for 3-year-old fillies is about 72, so our notional Derby and Oaks winners are therefore rated about 51lb higher than the average for the breed. As detailed in Chapter 20, the heritability of

PARENTAL GENERATION

Number of individuals

Not used for breeding — M^A — Selected for breeding — M^B

Timeform rating

PROGENY GENERATION

Number of individuals — M^C

Timeform rating

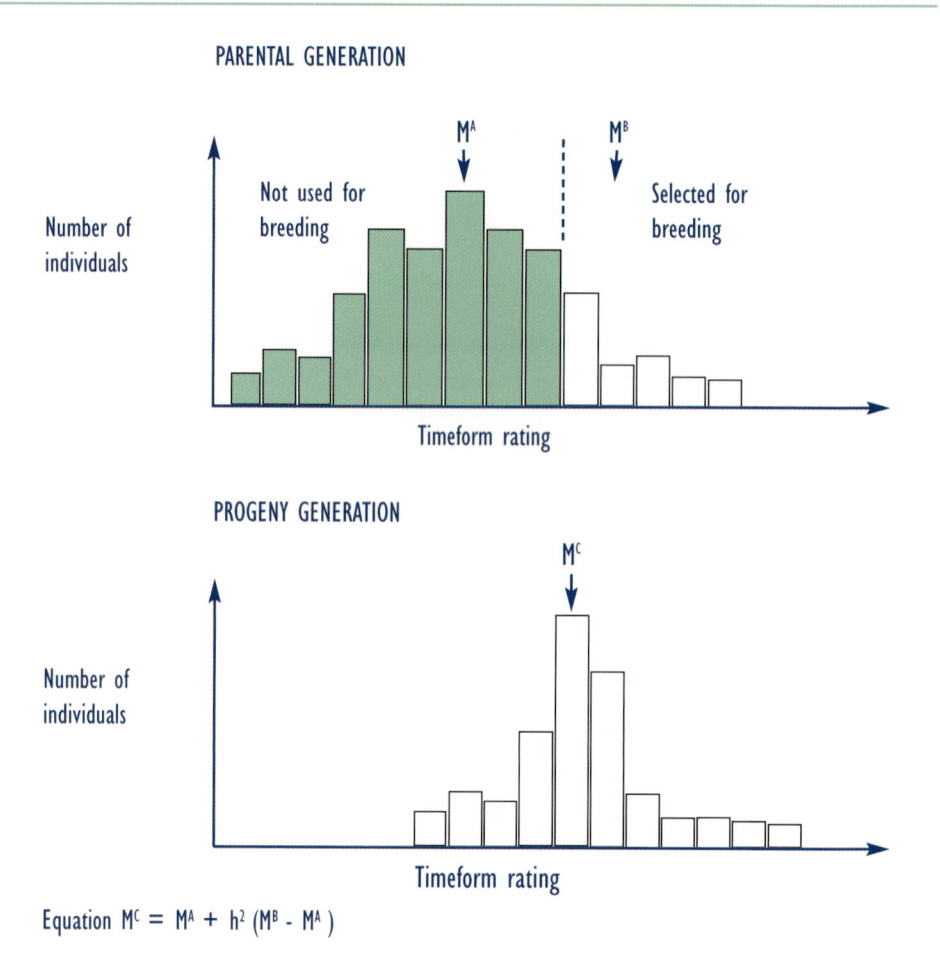

Equation $M^C = M^A + h^2 (M^B - M^A)$

Regression to the mean. The distribution of *Timeform* rating in the Thoroughbred population is approximately normal, with a mean of M^A. If selection for performance was used as a criterion for breeding and the individuals in green were not used, the mean *Timeform* rating of the breeding individuals would be M^B. When the distribution of the *Timeform* ratings for the offspring of the selected breeding stock is examined it has a mean *Timeform* rating of M^C, which is lower than M^B, but higher than the initial mean of the population, M^A. This is called regression to the mean. The extent of improvement obtained by different levels of selection can be predicted from the equation, where h^2 is the heritability of the trait under study.

performance is estimated at only about 35 per cent, so they will only pass on an average of 17-18lb advantage over the average for the breed. Accordingly, we would expect the average 3-year-old produced by our notional Derby and Oaks winners to be *Timeform*-rated around 97 if a colt, and 90 if a filly. This clearly represents an improvement over the existing breed average, but is not the mark of a top-class winner.

The *General Stud Book* shows many instances of matings involving the winners of the Derby and Oaks, and a number have produced good results, but only one Derby winner – Lammtarra in 1995 – has been bred that way. He was by Nijinsky, the 1970 Derby winner, out of Snow Bride, who was awarded the 1989 Oaks on the disqualification of Aliysa. The more common outcome of such unions, because of regression to the mean, is a product better than the breed average, but deemed a disappointment, given the quality of the parents.

The Thoroughbred has been selected to perform under different conditions in the course of its history. In the early days of the breed, races over long distances predominated, and the genetic make-up that rendered Eclipse unbeatable in his era, would be completely non-commercial today. There has been increasing specialisation, and the creation of distinct sub-populations in the breed, examples being sprinters and stayers, turf horses and dirt horses, soft ground horses and top-of-the-ground horses. Many stallions are regarded as being either sires of sprint horses or sires of distance horses. The introduction of Polytrack and other synthetic surfaces in the US has even been accompanied by advertisements for stallions claiming that their offspring are particularly successful on all-weather tracks. Whether such claims are valid or not, it is likely that the optimum physiology and conformation required to win races at the highest level is different for both race distances and surfaces. Over time, assuming that selection is being accurately applied, differences in the genetics of the Thoroughbreds racing at different distances and on different surfaces should become apparent. It will be fascinating to see if this has, in fact, happened as more and more genetic data becomes available for the breed.

CHAPTER 24

THE GENETIC HEALTH OF THE THOROUGHBRED AND THE FUTURE OF THE BREED

After 300 years of development, what is the current state of the Thoroughbred horse in terms of its genetic health?

On one hand, we have a breed in which there are very few inherited diseases with a simple Mendelian basis. In Chapter 19, the muscular condition, recurrent exertional rhabdomyolysis (tying-up), was mentioned and this is one of very few genetic conditions in Thoroughbreds thought to be caused by a mutation in a single gene. Even here, there is some doubt that the genetics of the disease is quite that simple; other genes may play a role in the expression of the disease. Could it be that selectively breeding for athleticism in the Thoroughbred for so many generations has effectively removed bad gene variants from the population?

We know that other horse breeds have diseases caused by mutations in a single gene, and the mutations responsible for many have already been identified. These diseases include hyperkalemic periodic paralysis (HYPP), glycogen branching enzyme deficiency (GBED), hereditary equine regional dermal asthenia (HERDA) and polysaccharide storage myopathy (PSSM) in Quarter Horses, severe combined immunodeficiency (SCID) in Arabs, and junctional epidermolysis bullosa (JEB) in Belgian Draught Horses. Genetic screening tests are available and in some cases are used by breeders for selective breeding of healthier horses, the aim being to breed from individuals who cannot produce an affected offspring.

SCID for example, is a recessive condition in which affected foals die within a few months of birth, as they lack a functional immune system with which to fight harmful bacteria and viruses. If the owner of a highly successful Arab stallion were to test and find that his horse was a carrier for the SCID mutation, it would not mean that breeders should stop using that animal. Instead, the mares should be SCID-tested before mating, and the stallion should cover only mares who tested clear of the mutation. About 8 per cent of Arab horses carry the SCID mutation, so that proportion of mares would be unsuitable for this stallion.

Remember that, for a simple recessive disease, mating two carriers together will give a one in four chance of producing an affected individual. If only mares who are tested clear are mated to the carrier stallion, the progeny will consist of half who are genetically clear of SCID and half who inherit the mutation and are carriers of the mutation. Over time, it is possible to reduce the frequency of the mutation in the population without causing economic disruption.

Of course, breeders might decide simply not to use a stallion with the SCID mutation, which would be a sensible course of action, if the frequency of the mutation in the population was very low, say around 1 per cent. Rigorously enforced, the disease would be eliminated in one generation. However, where the mutation is more common, one effect of not breeding to any carriers would be to reduce genetic variation in the breed for tens and possibly hundreds of genes present on the same chromosome as the mutation. In the case of a stallion who was an exceptional example of the breed and clearly had many beneficial genes, along with his one known harmful mutation, a decision not to use him at all might be counter-productive.

On average, each human being carries three recessive lethal mutations, so that the logic of not breeding from any carrier individuals, if applied to the human race, would quickly create serious problems for the survival of our species. In reality, management schemes to effect gradual reduction and, ultimately, elimination of recessive disease mutations can be easily established. They need not have much economic impact on the breeder unlucky enough to have a stallion or mare carrying the disease mutation and are beneficial to the long-term health of the breed.

Such efforts are facilitated by enlightened breed societies which educate, promote and help manage such eradication schemes. Several examples in pedigree dog breeds may be cited, one case involving breeders of Irish Setters in the UK, who have successfully removed a mutation causing another lethal immune system disorder, canine leukocyte adhesion deficiency (CLAD). The Kennel Club played an important role in helping to publicise and manage the scheme by co-ordinating the exchange of information between breeders.

The situation with dominant genetic diseases is different, as there are essentially no healthy carriers; a single copy of the mutation causes disease. In this case there are potential economic consequences of identifying dominant mutations in an expensive stallion. Fortunately though, dominant diseases are rare in most domesticated animal species because breeders can directly see the presence of the mutation by its effect, and have usually chosen not to breed from affected individuals.

In the list of equine inherited conditions given earlier, only one disease, HYPP, is inherited in a dominant manner and its presence in Quarter Horses has an interesting history. All affected Quarter Horses can be traced back to a single ancestor, called Impressive. The HYPP mutation is in a gene for a muscle protein and results in increased musculature in individuals with the defect. While the disease makes horses susceptible to episodes of muscle tremors and paralysis, the increased musculature proved very successful in the show ring, such that individuals with the mutation were highly prized. This led to the wide dissemination of the HYPP mutation through the popular sire effect, where stallions with the mutation were used more often at stud than those without it. Whether the HYPP mutation is a positive or a negative characteristic in Quarter Horses has been widely debated.

Does the absence of single gene diseases in Thoroughbreds mean that the breed is genetically healthy? As mentioned earlier, nearly a third of Thoroughbred foals born fail to make it to the racecourse (which remains the intended destination for the vast majority), suggesting that all is not well with the health of the breed. The high wastage rate indicates that the years of selective breeding in Thoroughbreds may not have been that successful. Selective breeding does work, but it can also have unexpected and unwanted outcomes, such as the leg problems common in fast-growing broiler chickens. The pressure to increase the speed of Thoroughbreds may have resulted in a breed with increased unsoundness as the body adapted to meet the selection goal of speed. A useful analogy in that context might be a Formula 1 racing car – a machine adapted to enable it to achieve maximum speed, but more prone to breakdown than an average road vehicle.

It is reported that Thoroughbreds today have lighter bone than in the past, which, though potentially enabling them to run faster, might also increase their risk of fracture. While catastrophic fractures on the racecourse occur only rarely, the incidence of stress fracture in the breed is high, with about 10 per cent of Thoroughbreds likely to have a problem in any one year. There is likely to be a complex genetic basis to an individual horse's risk of suffering a bone fracture. If genetic tests for mutations that increase these risks of bone problems become available in the future, their implementation will not be as straightforward as that described above for simple single gene diseases.

For complex conditions, most individuals in the population are likely to have some 'good' and some 'bad' gene variants, making it hard to devise mutation eradication schemes. In the shorter term, such tests could be of benefit in identifying individual horses at increased risk of fracture, enabling careful management of training and racing regimes to improve their career prospects. The identification of such mutations may have an economic effect on the Thoroughbred industry, but the mutations may be linked to speed and therefore of value, rather than their being a cause of diminished value.

There are several other conditions in the Thoroughbred that are thought to have an inherited component, though little is known about their heritability. These include defects such as parrot mouth, cryptorchidism, roaring, osteochondrosis (OCD) and wobbler syndrome. Anecdotal evidence is that these conditions are often familial, though more data needs to be collected before the extent to which genetics is involved can be accurately assessed.

THE FUTURE

While it is unwise to try to predict the future, it seems certain that the sequencing of the equine genome will accelerate our understanding of the genetics of the Thoroughbred. The genetic tools being developed will enable many of the ideas of breeders and their advisers to be scientifically tested and answered once and for all. The genetic shuffle that takes place every time a sperm or egg is produced will not change, though it may be possible to remove a few low cards from the deck!

As this book was nearing completion, Dr Emmeline Hill and her colleagues in Dublin published a paper showing that a mutation in the muscle myostatin gene was associated with optimum racing distance in Thoroughbreds. It was known that mutations in the myostatin gene in cattle yield greatly increased muscle mass; the results for Thoroughbreds suggest that the increased muscling visually associated by horsemen with sprinters is related, at least in part, to alterations in the myostatin gene. The finding of a simple relationship between a single gene and optimum running distance is also interesting as the prediction of distance capability by pedigree experts was one of their more reliable forecasts. It will be fascinating to see how the breeding and racing arms of the Thoroughbred industry react to the availability of DNA tests for aspects of athletic performance.

We will undoubtedly learn more about the origins and development of the Thoroughbred horse. Careful monitoring of the extent of inbreeding and its potential effect on fertility is needed as a result of the changes that have taken place in the breeding industry over the last thirty years or so. The new molecular tools under development will make this task much easier and more accurate.

It is likely that screening tests will be developed to enable more horses to reach their potential and race more often by identifying those at increased risk of breaking down, thus providing trainers and veterinary surgeons with information crucial to the correct management of their training and racing regimes.

Genetics is a vital part of what makes the Thoroughbred breed special, but it is only in combination with the skill and attention to detail of horsemen that the potential in each individual horse can be realised.

APPENDIX

HARDY-WEINBERG EQUATION

In a randomly mating population it is possible to estimate the frequencies of the gene variants (alleles) in the population using the Hardy-Weinberg equation.

This equation states that
$$p^2 + 2pq + q^2 = 1$$

where p^2 and q^2 are the frequencies of the two homozygous *genotype* classes (in this case *EE* and *ee*) and 2pq is the frequency of the heterozygous carrier genotype (*Ee*): p and q represent the frequencies of the *alleles E* and *e* respectively. To estimate the proportion of heterozygous bay horses (*Ee*) in Thoroughbreds the following calculation is made.

Twenty-five per cent of Thoroughbreds are chesnut and therefore homozygous (*ee*) for the recessive *e* allele. The value of q^2 in the Hardy-Weinberg equation is thus 0.25. The square root of 0.25 will give the value of q, which in this case equals 0.5. As $p + q = 1$, the frequency of the $p = 1 - 0.5$. The frequency of the two alleles in the Thoroughbred population is therefore 0.5 for both alleles. The predicted frequency of homozygous *EE* bay horses (p^2) is $0.5^2 = 0.25$, i.e. 25 per cent of the Thoroughbred population. The predicted frequency of heterozygote, *Ee*, horses is 2pq = 2 x 0.5 x 0.5 = 0.5. So, using the Hardy-Weinberg equation we were able to calculate that 50 per cent of the Thoroughbred population and 66 per cent of the bay individuals are *Ee* heterozygous bays.

The Hardy-Weinberg equation can be used to estimate allele and genotype frequencies for any gene variant. When deviations from Hardy-

Weinberg predictions are observed it can provide a useful insight into the process of genetic inheritance. It might be that the population is not mating at random, and that selection, conscious or unconscious, is being applied. Selection does not have to be directly on the trait studied, as distortion will be seen if the trait is closely linked to other genes which are under selection.

BIBLIOGRAPHY

Allison, William, *The British Thoroughbred Horse*, Grant Richards, London, 1901.

Becker, Friedrich, *The Breed of the Racehorse*, British Bloodstock Agency, London, 1936.

Bobinski, Kazimierz, *Family Tables of Racehorses*. J.A. Allen, London, 1953.

Bowie, M.S.J., *Progressive Thoroughbred Breeding*, published privately, England, 1979.

Bowling, A.T., *Horse Genetics*, CABI, Oxford, 1996.

Bowling, A.T. and Ruvinsky, A. (eds.), *The Genetics of the Horse*, CABI, Oxford, 2000.

Brown, C.F., *The Turf Expositor*, Sherwood, Gilbert & Piper, London, 1829.

Budiansky, Stephen, *The Nature of Horses*, Weidenfeld and Nicholson, London, 1997.

Copperthwaite, R.H., *The Turf, the Racehorse and Stud Farm*, Day & Son, London, 1865.

Craig, Dennis, *Breeding Racehorses from Cluster Mares*, J.A. Allen, London, 1964.

Darwin, Charles, *On the Origin of Species*, John Murray, London, 1859.

Estes, Joseph A., *The Estes Formula for Breeding Stakes Winners*, Russell Meerdink Co., Neenah (Wisconsin, USA), 1999.

Falconer, D.S., *Introduction to Quantitative Genetics*, Oliver & Boyd, Edinburgh, 1964.

Faversham, Rommy, and Rasmussen, Leon, *Inbreeding to Superior Females*, Australian Bloodhorse Review, Sydney, 1999.

Frentzel, J.P., *Family Tables of English Thoroughbred Stock*, Paul Parey, Berlin, 1889.

Gillham, Nicholas Wright, *A Life of Sir Francis Galton*, Oxford University Press, 2001.

Hampton, Harold, *The First Scientific Principles of Thoroughbred Breeding*, Scientific Breeding & Racing Publications, Auckland, 1954.

Hanckey-Smith, Nicholas, *Observations On Breeding For The Turf*, G. Whittaker, London, 1825.

Harper, Clive, *The Thoroughbred Breeders' Handbook*, Highflyer International, New York, 1997.
The Thoroughbred Broodmare Book, Matter of Record, Derby (Kansas, USA), 2003.

Haun, Marianna, *The X Factor*, Russell Meerdink Co., Neenah (Wisconsin, USA), 1997.

Henig, Robin Marantz, *A Monk and Two Peas*, Weidenfeld & Nicholson, London, 2000.

Hewitt, Abe, *Sire Lines*, Thoroughbred Owners & Breeders Association, Lexington, 1977.
The Great Breeders and Their Methods, Thoroughbred Publishers, Lexington, 1982.

Hislop, John, *Breeding for Racing*, Kingswood Press, London, 1992.

Keylock, Harry, *The Mating of Thoroughbred Horses*, Britsh Bloodstock Agency, London, 1942.

Lawrence, John, *The History and Delineation of the Horse*, Albion Press, London, 1809.

Lehndorff, G., *Horse Breeding Recollections*, Horace Cox, London, 1883.

Leicester, Sir Charles, *Bloodstock Breeding* (2nd edn.), J.A. Allen, London, 1983.

Lesh, Donald, *A Treatise on Thoroughbred Selection*, J.A. Allen, London, 1978.

Llewellyn, Sir Rhys, *Breeding to Race*, J.A. Allen, London, 1964.

Lochner, Dan H., *Modern Dosage Theory*, Equine Research, Grand Prairie (Texas, USA), 1992.

Lowe, Bruce, *Breeding Racehorses by the Figure System*, Horace Cox, London, 1895.

Mackay-Smith, Alexander, *Speed in the Thoroughbred*, Derrydale Press, New York, 2000.

McLean, Ken, *Genetic Heritage*, K. & C. McLean, Lexington, 1996.
Quest for a Classic Winner, K. & C. McLean, Lexington, 1996.
Designing Speed in the Racehorse, Russell Meerdink Co., Neenah (Wisconsin, USA), 2005.

Miller, Michael, *How to Breed a Racehorse*, Knapp, Drewett & Sons, London, 1939.

Mitchell, Frank (ed.), *Racehorse Breeding Theories*, Russell Meerdink Co., Neenah (Wisconsin, USA), 2004.

Morland, Thomas Hornby, *The Genealogy of the English Race Horse*, J. Barfield, London, 1810.

Morris, Tony, *Thoroughbred Stallions*, Crowood Press, Swindon, 1990.

Nicholas, F.W., *Introduction to Veterinary Genetics* (2nd edn.), Blackwell, Oxford, 2003.

Oettingen, Burchard von., *Horse Breeding in Theory and Practice*, Sampson Low, Marston & Co., London, 1909.

Osborne, Joseph, *The Horse Breeder's Handbook*, Edmund Seale, London, 1898.

Palmer, Joe, *Names in Pedigrees* (2nd edn.), Thoroughbred Owners & Breeders Association, Lexington, 1974.

Porter, Alan, *Patterns of Greatness*, Highflyer International, London, 1992.

Prior, Charles and Florence, *Stud-Book Lore*, Livesey, Shrewsbury, 1951.

Roman, Stevan A., *Dosage, Pedigree and Performance*, Russell Meerdink Co., Neenah (Wisconsin, USA), 2002.

Society for Promoting Horse Breeding in Poland, *Tabulated Pedigrees of Thoroughbred Horses*, Warsaw, 1931.

Sykes, Bryan, *The Seven Daughters of Eve*, Bantam Press, London, 2001.

Tesio, Federico, *Breeding the Racehorse*, J.A. Allen, London, 1958.

Upton, Roger, *Newmarket and Arabia*, Henry S. King & Co, London, 1873.

Varola, Franco, *Typology of the Racehorse*, J.A. Allen, London, 1974.
   The Functional Development Of The Thoroughbred, J.A. Allen, London, 1980.

Vuillier, J.J., *Les Croisements Rationnels Dans La Race Pure*, Legoupy, Paris, 1902.

Wall, John F., *Breeding Thoroughbreds*, Charles Scribner's Sons, New York, 1946.

Walsh, John H., *Manual of British Rural Sports*, G. Routledge & Co, London, 1856.

Wentworth, Lady, *Thoroughbred Racing Stock* (2nd edn.), George Allen & Unwin, London, 1960.

Willett, Peter, *An Introduction to the Thoroughbred*, Stanley Paul, London, 1966.
   The Thoroughbred, Weidenfeld & Nicholson, London, 1970.

Wright, Howard, *Bull, the Biography*, Portway Press, Halifax, 1995.

Youatt, William, *The Horse*, Baldwin & Cradock, London, 1831.

PERIODICALS

Blood-Horse

Bloodstock Breeders' Review

British Racehorse

General Stud Book

Nature

Racing Calendar

Sporting Gazette

Sporting Magazine

Sporting Times

Thoroughbred Times

Timeform

INDEX

Abdullah, Khalid 172
Abernant 107, 109
ACTN3 gene 151
Aga Khan 76–7, 172
agouti gene 118–19
Aimwell 106
Alcock's Arabian 19, 105–6, 110, 113–14
    alternative names 106
Alexandrova 160
Ali Bey 38
Aliysa 175
alleles
    definition 116
    estimation of population frequencies 181–2
Allison, William 68, 71, 74
Almanzor 24
American trotting horses 148
Ancaster, Duke 26
ancestors
    founding stallions 106, 153
    genetic contribution to descendants 95–7
    numbers in pedigrees 110–12, 156–7
angiotensin-converting enzyme (ACE) gene 150–1
Anne, Queen 17, 18
A.P. Indy 166

Arab horses
    genetic disease 176–7
    importation of 16–17
    muscle fibres 143–4
    speed 64
    white markings 122
Arcot Lass 53
artificial surfaces 145, 175
Asil 64
astrology 79
auction sales 51–2
Australia 68, 87, 88
autosomes 101
Average Earnings Index 81

Bab 110
Bakewell, Robert 36–7, 167
Bartlett's Childers 23
Basset hounds 72–3
Bateson, William 72–4
Bay Bolton 33–4
bay coat colour 115–18, 122, 123, 161
Bay Middleton 10, 76
'Beacon' 70
Becker, Friedrich 79–80
Belenus 156
Belga 107
Belgian Draught horses 176
Ben Battle 74

'Ben Beacon' 43
Bend Or 76, 160
Big Game 79
black coat colour 118–20
black type 84
Blacklock 58, 60, 61
Blandford 79
Blaze 22, 24
Blood-Horse 80–1, 125, 162
Bloodstock Breeders' Review 75, 80
Bloomsbury 53
Bobinski, Kazimierz 83–4
Bold Ruler 133
bone quality 146, 179
Bonecrusher 87
Boussac, Marcel 77, 172
breeding industry 51–2, 112, 158–9, 171
Brigadier Gerard 85
Bright's Roan 22
Brimmer 33
broodmare sires 163–6
broodmares, *see* mares
Brown, C.F. 50–1
Bucephalus 23
Bull, Phil 81–3, 85, 97
Bunsow, Robert 75
Bustler 23
Buzzard 58
Byerley Turk 17, 23, 37, 56, 106

Cade 36
canine leukocyte adhesion deficiency (CLAD) 178
Caro 107, 144
cats, tortoiseshell 140–1
Cavendish, William, Duke of Newcastle 12–14, 36
'Cecil' 54
Chaleureux 78
Chambord 144
Charles II 13–14, 15
Chaucer 160
chefs de race 77–8, 85–6
Cheny, John 19–25, 38
chesnut coat colour 38, 74, 115–18, 122
Chismon, William 71
chromosomes
    contribution down generations 96–7
    definition 101–2
    recombination 96, 113, 157
    segregation 93–5, 155, 157
Civil War 13
Classic races 45
    matings between winners 173, 175
    winning times 171, 172
coat colour 73–4, 115–23
    bay 115–18, 122, 123, 161
    black, white and roan 118–20
    chesnut 38, 74, 115–18, 122
    distribution in TBs 116
    grey 105–14, 116, 120
    official descriptions 115
    recording in *General Stud-Book* 62–3
    wild horses 105
Cobham Stud 68–9
Compton Barb (Sedley Arabian) 38
conception rates 159
Confederate Filly 22
conformation defects 142–3, 146
Coombe Arabian 38
Copperthwaite, R.H. 57, 63
Corlettt, John 61
corruption 52–4
Cossack 60
Crab 114
Craig, Dennis 84
Crick, Francis 100
Cromwell, Oliver 13, 18
Cunningham, Professor Patrick 147, 171–2
Curwen Bay Barb 106, 153
Curwen, Henry 24

Damascus Arabian 38
dappling 122, 123
D'arcy, James 15, 128
D'arcy, James (second) 36
D'arcy's White Turk 19
D'arcy's Yellow Turk 19
Darley Arabian 36, 37, 56, 106, 136
Darshaan 160
Darwin, Charles 65, 104
Davill's Woodcock Mare 129
de Vries, Hugo 73
Derby, 12th Earl 39, 50
Derby, 17th Earl 77, 172
Derby (Epsom classic) 52, 53, 99, 171, 173, 175
Devonshire Childers, *see* Flying Childers
Dink, David L. 89
Diomed 31
diseases, genetic 144–5, 176–9
distances, *see* racing distance
DNA (deoxyribonucleic acid) 100–4
    coding of genetic information 102
    discovery 100
    mitochondrial 102, 124, 126–7
Dodsworth 18, 19, 23

dog breeding 157–8, 167–8, 177–8
Dolabella 79
domestication of horses 105, 129
dominant genes 116, 119, 120, 178
dosage 76–8, 85–6
d'Osma, Prospero 11
Down's syndrome 139
Dubai Millennium 156
Dubawi 156

Eagle 40
Echo of Light 156
Eclipse 17, 41, 45, 56
    duplication in pedigrees 156–7
    heart size 132
    nicks 160
    pedigree 47–8
Edwards, James 9–10
eggs, formation 93–5, 96, 113, 157
embryo splitting 120–1
embryo transfer 171
embryonic death 159
environmental factors 93, 152, 173
epistasis 120, 173
Estes, Joe 80–1, 86, 88, 125
eumelanin 116
evolution 103, 104
exportation of horses 51
extension gene 119

falsification of pedigrees 53–4
families, Lowe's list 66–8, 80, 124–6, 160
farm animal breeding 92, 167, 168
Faversham, Rommy 86
Fawconer, Thomas 27
Felton, John 12
Figure System 69
Filho da Puta 41
Finsceal Beo 172
Flying Childers 22, 23, 36, 38, 41, 64
foetal loss 159

Fortino 144
Foudroyer 113
founding stallions 106, 153
fox, silver 105
fractures 145, 146, 179
Franches-Montagnes 121
Frentzel, J.P. 66

Galloway 10–11
Galopin 61, 76
Galtee More 95
Galton, Francis 65, 72–3, 77, 148–9
gametes, formation 93–5, 96, 113, 155, 157
GBED, *see* glycogen branching enzyme deficiency
Geary, Alfred 60
gene–environment interactions 152
General Stud Book 10
    Arab horses 17–18
    Classic winner matings 175
    coat colour recording 62–3
    Introduction 30–1, 65
    origins 19, 29–34
    pedigree anomalies 128, 130
    registration conditions 154
genes 102–4
    conserved 103
    structure 102–3
genetic drift 154–5
genetic markers 112–13, 114, 158, 168
genetic mosaics 140–1
'genetic sibling' 87
genetic variation 104, 153–5
genetics
    awareness in horsemen 91–3
    definition of terms 100–4
    principles 93–7
genome
    defined 100
    sequencing 100–1, 103, 179

genomic imprinting 156, 164, 165
Ginistrelli, Edoardo 78
Gladiateur 60
glycogen branching enzyme deficiency (GBED) 176
Godolphin Arabian 24–5, 35–6, 37–8, 39, 43, 45, 56, 106, 136
Godolphin, Earl of 25, 26
going 145, 175
Gone West 166
Goos, Hermann 66, 71
grey coat colour 105–14, 116, 120
    development in foal 106
    genetic mapping 112–13
    imprinting 164, 165
    inheritance patterns 107, 108
    pedigree origins 105–12
    selection of true breeding 114
greyhounds 133

haemoglobin 131
haemophilia 137–8
Halbronn, Chéri 71
half-siblings 95–6
Hampton, Harold 86–7
Haphazard 40
Hardy-Weinberg equation 115, 116, 181–2
Haun, Marianna 134–40
Hautboy 33, 48
Hawley, Sir Joseph 60
heart rate 131
heart size 131–4
    assessment 133–4
    gene control 135, 138–9
Heber, Reginald 25–7, 37
height, heritability of 146, 148
Henry VIII 11
hereditary equine regional dermal asthenia (HERDA) 176
heritability 147
    complex traits 148–9

Mendelian traits 147
Hermit 76, 169
Herod 41, 43, 45, 56, 160
heterosis 162–3
heterozygosity 107, 114
High Chaparral 160
Highflyer 43–4
Hill, Dr Emmeline 127–9, 179–80
Hislop, John 85
homozygosity 107, 116, 157, 163
    grey coat colour 107, 114
    levels in Thoroughbreds 158
horse breeding, early history 10–14
human genome project 92, 97, 100, 103
humans
    genetic disease 137–8
    heritability of height 148
    inbreeding 50
    mitochondrial DNA studies 127
    performance genes 150–1
Hurst, Charles Chamberlain 73–4, 75
hybrid vigour (heterosis) 162–3
Hyperion 118
hyperkalaemic periodic paralysis (HYPP) 176, 178

Iambic 64
importation of horses 16–17, 37–8
imprinting, genomic 156, 164, 165
In the Wings 160
inbreeding 38–9, 46, 50, 65, 155–9
    coefficients 158
    definition 155
    European Thoroughbreds 155–7
    genetic consequences 157–8
introns 102
Irish Setters 116, 177–8
Ironside, Gilbert 35–6
Islington 160

James I 11, 12–13

Javelin 44
jennets 11
Jigg of Jiggs 38–9
Jockey Club, The 32
jump racing 134
junctional epidermolysis bullosa (JEB) 176

Keylock, Harry 83
King Fergus 44
King Tom 63
KIT gene 120, 121

Lammtarra 175
Lawrence, John 39
Linamix 107–12, 125, 157
line-breeding 88
lines of inheritance 57–8, 83–9
    female 66–8, 80, 83–4, 86, 124–6, 160
    male 48, 56–8, 64–5
Lister Turk 17, 19, 48
Llewellyn, Sir Rhys 84, 85
Lonhro 118
Lowe, Bruce 65–8, 70, 124
    mare family lines 66–8, 80, 83–4, 124–6, 160
Lucarno 172
Lunadix 107–8

Macaroni 160
Maccabeus 52
McLean, Ken 88
Makeless 33
male potency 38, 40–1
malpractice 52–4
'Mankato' 74
mares 124–30
    importance of 100
    Lowe's families 66–8, 80, 124–6, 160
    mitochondrial DNA 127–30

nicks 160–4
    'royal' 11, 15–16
    selection for breeding 170, 173
    sires of 163–6
marker-assisted selection 114, 168
market breeding 51–2, 171
Markham Arabian 12
Markham, Gervase 12
Marshall (Selaby) Turk 19, 23
Marske 48
Master Robert 109
Matchem 36, 41, 43, 45
maternal grandsire effect 164, 166
MC1R gene 116
mediaeval times 10–11
melanocytes 116, 122
Melbourne 63, 76
Mendel, Gregor 51, 61, 72, 164
Mendez 107, 109
Mercury 44
Milan 160
Millais, Sir Everett 72–3
Minoru 79
Mitchell, Frank 88
mitochondria 102, 126
mitochondrial DNA 102, 124, 126–30
Mohammed bin Rashid Al Maktoum, Sheikh 156
molecular biological tools 114, 168, 180
Mona 109
Mont Blanc 119
Montjeu 137, 155
Moonah Barb mare 18
Morland, Thomas Hornby 39–41, 48, 56
mouse genome 103
Mulatto 53
Mumtaz Mahal 110
muscle myostatin gene 180
muscles 143–5

fibre types 143–4, 151
oxygen supply 131–2
tying-up 144–5
mutations 104
    causing diseases 176–8
    chesnut coat colour 116
    grey coat colour 106–7, 120
    white coat colour 119

Nasrullah 89
natural selection theory 104
New Zealand 68, 86–7
Newcastle, Duke of, *see* Cavendish, William, Duke of Newcastle
Newmarket
    Beacon Course 45
    establishment as sporting venue 12–14
Newminster 62–3, 76
nicks 89, 160–4
Nijinsky 175
Northern Dancer 155–6
Nowell, Alexander 51
nucleotides 100

Oaks winners 173, 175
Oglethorp Arabian 33
Oglethorpe, Sutton 16
Old Hautboy 33
Old Merlin 33
'Old Testament' plan 48
origins of Thoroughbreds 153–4
Orlando 52
Ormonde 169
Osborne, Joseph 70–2
Owen Tudor 87
owner-breeders, success of 172–3
oxygen transport 131–2, 134

Paris House 112–13
Partner 43
pedigree analysts 91, 156

pedigrees
  anomalies 128, 130
  duplication of ancestors 110–12, 156–7
  early recording 19–20, 22–4
  sales catalogues 84
Peel, Jonathan 52
performance, see racing performance
Persimmon 95
Petong 112
Phalaris 155, 160
Phar Lap 132–3
pheomelanin 116
physiology, heart volume 131–4
Pick, William 28, 33
pigments, coat 116
Pincher, Chapman 93
Place, Rowland 18
Place's White Turk 18–19
Poland 83–4
polysaccharide storage myopathy (PSSM) 176
Pond, John 25, 51
'popular sire' effect 154
population structure 110–11
Pretty Polly 85
Prince Rudolph 69
Prior, Charles 19
prize money earned 149
production of Thoroughbreds, expansion of 112
PSSM, see polysaccharide storage myopathy

Quarter Horses 143, 176, 178
Queen of Trumps 60

race times 149, 171–2
racing, for breeding 49–50
Racing Calendar 27, 29–30, 37
racing distance
  early horse racing 45
  optimum 144, 180
racing performance
  environmental factors in 152
  genes controlling 150–1
  and heart size 132
  improvement in Thoroughbreds 171–2
  measures of 149–50
  scientific studies 93
racing results, first compilation 19–20
Rasmussen, Leon 86
Ratan 60
ratings, see *Timeform* ratings
recessive genes 116, 177
recombination 96, 113, 157
regression to the mean 173–4
Regulus 24
reproductive fitness 158–9
Reynolds, Frank 68
rhabdomyolysis, recurrent exertional 144–5, 176
Ridsdale, Robert 53
roan coat colour 119–20
Robertson, James Bell 74–5, 79–80
Rolfe, Robert Allen 72
Roman, Steven 76, 78, 85
Royal Charger 87
'royal mares' 11, 15–16
Royal Society 73
Running Rein 52

Sadler's Wells 160, 161
Sainfoin 88
St Bel, Charles Vial de 132
St Simon 61, 76, 112, 156
Saward, Patrick 43
SCID, see severe combined immunodeficiency
screening tests 180
Secretariat 133, 164, 166
Sedbury stud 15–16
Sedley Arabian (Compton Barb) 38
segregation 93–5, 155, 157
  grey coat colour 107, 108
selective breeding 154, 167
  barriers to genetic improvement 168–71
  disease eradication 176–8
  livestock 92, 167, 168
  pedigree dogs 157–8, 167–8
  specialisation 175
  use of Classic winners 173, 175
severe combined immunodeficiency (SCID) 176–7
sex chromosomes 101–2, 135
sex determination 135
Shirley Heights 160
Shorthouse, Dr Joseph Henry 59–61, 65
siblings, genes shared by 95–6
Sierra 88
Signorina 78
Signorinetta 78
sires, see stallions
skeletal system 145–6
Smith, Nicholas Hanckey 45–8
Snap 41
Snow Bride 175
Social Gulf 107, 109
Somethingroyal 166
soundness 169–70, 178–9
South Africa 87
Spain 11
Spanker 38
specialisation in breeding 175
sperm formation 93–5, 96, 113, 155, 157
Spilletta 48
Sporting Chronicle 74
Sporting Gazette 59
Sporting Kalendar 25
Sporting Magazine 31–3, 35, 44
Sporting Times 59–61
'spotting' genes 121

sprinting ability 144, 180
sry gene 135
Staaden, Ross 88
stallions
   advertisements 21–2, 24
   broodmare nicks 160–4
   broodmare sires 163–6
   duplication in pedigrees 155–7
   founding 106, 153
   genes passed on to offspring 155
   influential 89
   numbers 158–9
   potency 38, 40–1
   selection of 170
   unproven 171
statistical data 89
staying ability 144
Storm Cat 166
Stradling (Lister) Turk 18, 19, 48
stress fractures 145, 179
Sun Chariot 79
surgery, corrective 142–3
Sykes, Brian 127

tail-female lines 66–8, 80, 83–4, 86, 124–6, 160
tail-male lines 56–8, 64–5, 136, 137, 153
Tattersall, Richard 32, 51–2
Teazle, Sir Peter 44, 50
telegony 54, 57, 59, 68
tendon problems 146
Tesio, Federico 77, 78–9, 99, 172
The Tetrarch 109–12
Thormanby 63
Thoroughbred Times 89
Timeform 82
Timeform ratings
   and heart score 134
     heritability 147, 149–50, 173–4
Tocal Stud 68

Tongue, Cornelius 54–5
tortoiseshell cats 140–1
Towers, William Sidney 29–31, 42, 48, 65, 72
track surfaces 145
training 152
trait mapping 112–13
traits, 'fixing' 157–8
Trakehnen stud 66
Tramp 53
The Turf Register 33, 34
Tuting, William 27
Twilight 101
twins
   frequency of 169–70
   white markings 120–1
2-year old racing 145
tying-up 144–5, 176

Underley Stud 51–2
United States 68
unsoundness 169, 178–9
Upton, Roger 62–3, 64
Userhat, Tomb of 105

Variation 52
Varola, Franco 76–8
Vedette 63
Victoria, Queen 137–8
Villiers, George, Duke of Buckingham 11–12
Voltigeur 63
Vuillier, Jean-Joseph 76, 85

Walker, Benjamin 27
Walker, William Hall 71, 79
Walsh, John Henry 56–8, 62
wastage rates 142, 150, 178
Watson, James 100
Waxy 41, 57–8
Weatherby, Charles 51
Weatherby, James 27, 29, 32

Weatherby, James (younger) 29–30, 42
Weldon, Raphael 72–4
Wellesley Grey Arabian 38
Wentworth, Lady 19, 38, 105
Whirligig 22
white horses 119
White Man 79
white markings 120–3
White Turk 23
Willett, Peter 85, 97
William, Duke of Cumberland 43
William III 16
Wilson's Chesnut Arabian 38
Windham 23
Windhound 63
Winning Colors 120
Winning Post 74
Wormwood 23
Wright, Howard 97

X chromosome 101–2, 122, 134–40, 166
   gene content 135
   inactivation 140, 141, 166
   tracing origins 136–8
X factor theory 134–40
X-linked disease 137–8

Y chromosome 101–2, 135, 136
yearling sales 171
Youatt, William 47–9
youngstock
   conformation defects 142–3
   wastage 142, 150, 178